OUTLANDERS

Hidden narratives from social workers of colour
(from Black & Other Global Majority Communities)

Compiled & edited by
Wayne Reid & Siobhan Maclean

Published by
Kirwin Maclean Associates
4 Mesnes Green, Lichfield
Staffordshire
WS14 9AB

enquiries@kirwinmaclean.com
www.kirwinmaclean.com
01543 417800

First published in 2021
Kirwin Maclean Associates
4 Mesnes Green,
Lichfield Staffordshire
WS14 9AB

Creative direction by R.Jaffer-Clarke
Graphic design by Tora Kelly
Printed and bound in Great Britain by 4edge, Essex

ISBN - 9781912130566 (Book)
ISBN - 9781912130559 (Ebook)

A catalogue record for this book will be available from The British Library.

Just because I carry it all so well, it doesn't mean it's not heavy.

- Unknown Author

This anthology is a joint enterprise between Kirwin Maclean Associates and BASW England

PASSION LED US HERE

Contents

Preface

Essays

Poetry

Stories

Reflections

About the Editors

- *Wayne Reid*

Wayne Reid is a Professional Officer, Social Worker and Anti-Racism Visionary at the British Association of Social Workers (BASW) and lives in Sheffield. Wayne qualified as a Social Worker in 2010, but the entirety of his frontline social care experience spans over 20 years. He has worked for private fostering agencies; the Probation Service; a youth offending team; a community mental health service; a child protection service and with care leavers. Wayne's diverse role at BASW England involves supporting national groups on: mental health, criminal justice, professional development and students and newly qualified social workers (NQSW's). Wayne's work with students and NQSW's and social work practitioners is extensive. This has involved guest lecturing, facilitating training; leading national campaigns and organising national conferences.

Wayne's career reflects his dedication to supporting vulnerable members of society and working with diverse professionals from across all sectors to improve service delivery. Wayne's diverse career has enabled him to understand the dynamic contextual factors that affect the planning, implementation and review of effective Social Work services and the direct impact this has on service-users and professionals. Wayne's experiential knowledge and skills include: supporting/supervising service-users and staff; working with professionals and stakeholders from various professional backgrounds; building/maintaining collaborative/reciprocal networks; evaluating complex outcomes and implementing new strategies.

As a Black male Social Worker, Wayne understands some of the challenges that some service-users and practitioners from minoritised groups can face. From his experience, Wayne believes academic and 'life education' are essential to improve an individual's quality of life and life chances. He adds: "Social Work is a vital international vocation that: coordinates support for the most vulnerable people in society; assesses and manages risk; addresses problematic behaviours and relationships; champions equality and social justice; optimises service-users' strengths, promotes human decency and creates meaningful opportunities for social mobility".

Twitter
@wayne_reid79
@BASW_UK
#CrushingStereotypesDaily

- Siobhan Maclean

Siobhan Maclean has been a social worker for 30 years and a practice educator for 27 years. Siobhan works independently providing training and consultancy services to social work employers and Universities. She has a particular passion for supporting students and practitioners in the areas of theory and practice and reflective practice. Since the impact of COVID-19 Siobhan has enjoyed working with a group of social work students to develop regular online webinars for social workers. The group that came together to develop these sessions called themselves Social Work Student Connect.

In 1999 Siobhan set up Kirwin Maclean Associates as an independent social work publisher based on the values and ethics of our profession. Siobhan saw many social work textbooks being published by large corporations which didn't necessarily reflect the values and ethics of the profession. She set up Kirwin Maclean (combining her birth name with a married name) in order to develop a publisher which reflected the profession, working towards social work ethics in the development, printing, marketing and distribution of books and resources. She now works with her husband Simon Bates in managing the flourishing publishing business. Siobhan and Simon work to ensure that the publisher gives back to the profession, so the profits generated from the publications go either to charity or to the development of further resources for the profession.

In 2013 Siobhan had a stroke. This impacted on her work and her understanding of social work in many ways, as experiencing services often does. Since that time, she has not been a direct case holder, although she still supports other social workers in discussing their work directly. She also still works as an offsite practice educator.

Siobhan was privileged to hold the position of Honorary Secretary of the International Federation of Social Workers (European Region) for a number of years, although after the stroke, limits on her ability to travel impacted on her international work. The growth of virtual working has meant that she has been able to start some international work again and she is currently co-directing a project looking at the transition from student to practitioner with Omar Mohamed, one of the authors in this anthology. Siobhan is committed to ensuring that there is a platform for the voices of people with varied experiences of social work and spends time supporting social workers and people with lived experience to write for publication.

The initial idea for this publication came from Siobhan, but as a white woman she recognised the need to work with colleagues to bring this to life. She is immensely grateful that Wayne Reid agreed to take on the role of co-editor.

Twitter @SiobhanMaclean
Facebook Siobhan Maclean and Siobhan Maclean Social Work Resources
Website www.siobhanmaclean.co.uk

PREFACE

Power and Purity

- *Wayne Reid*

I write these words with a mixture of anticipation, trepidation and excitement...

The book you are holding was originally an idea conceived by my collaborator, Siobhan Maclean. In late 2018, Siobhan and I met at a social work event where we both had exhibition stands. We chatted and Siobhan expressed her wish to produce a book that amplified the experiences and narratives of Social Worker's from Black and ethnic minority backgrounds (especially people of colour).

Initially, I was just keen to contribute to this book. In my over-enthusiastic stupor, I found I'd sent my submission to Siobhan within a few days of our chat. After several months of me badgering Siobhan, she explained that as an independent Social Worker, she was finding it impossible to devote much time to the project. Siobhan mentioned she wanted to find an Editor and I offered to utilise my networks to identify someone. This coincided with the COVID-19 pandemic, the brutal murder of George Floyd and the global resurgence of the Black Lives Matter movement. Also, my work on anti-racism in Social Work (as part of my role at BASW) quickly accelerated. You can see examples of this work in the miscellaneous section of this anthology. Due to my passion for reinvigorating anti-racism in Social Work, I offered to undertake the Editorial role and thankfully Siobhan accepted.

My vision for this anthology is to replicate the format and vibrancy of *The Good Immigrant* (Shukla, 2016) and *IC3: New Black Writing in Britain* (Newland and Sesay, 2000). Both books I've read and loved. Also, I drew some inspiration from the much-revered *Black Perspectives in Social Work* (Ahmad, 1990). Although, this body of work specifically encapsulates the perspectives of Social Workers of colour in England. These narratives vividly illuminate the personal and professional lived experiences of Social Workers who are discriminated against based on the colour of their skin. I'm honoured to be involved with a publication of this calibre and distinction. Each contribution is priceless. Eternal thanks to all of the contributors.

So, why the book title *Outlanders*? Well, for me it represents a question people of colour are frequently accosted with: "Where are you *really* from?" A question we are often asked with little compassion or cognition that England might actually be where we were born. It seems that for some, we can only ever be outlanders.

I need to highlight that throughout this anthology we interchangeably refer to 'Black and Other Global Majority Communities', 'people of colour', 'Black and Ethnic Minority' groups and BAME. This is reflective of the complexity and subjectivity of language related to ethnicity and race. We acknowledge there is no universally acceptable definitions and terminology, but this must not hold us back from promoting racial equality. We regard 'Black' here as an inclusive and legal definition, which includes people who share lived experiences of the effects of institutional and structural racism.

In this anthology, you will read compelling essays on anti-racism, social work education, suicide and language. You will read reflections on career ambitions, cultural divisions and self-identity that will evoke rumination. You will read stories that will open a window your heart, that will transport you to the other side of paradise and teleport you into the future. You will read poignant poetry on microaggressions, silence and racial abuse.

The power and purity in each submission should not be underestimated. Each author entrusts you with their perspectives of their lived personal and/or professional experiences. The reality of their individual truths cannot be denied.

Having read each submission (as part of the editing process), I found the unique creations of each author were profound and conveyed deep-rooted heartfelt narratives that should be understood by all (inside and outside of social work). From the rebellion espoused in '*Are you sure you're in the right place?*' to the near-futurism of '*Into the future*' to the vivid vibes projected in the '*The other side of paradise*', this anthology will induce mixed emotions in readers which is necessary for positive change.

This anthology enables you to drape yourself with a patchwork of fabrics that is rich with cultural diversity. This rich patchwork also spotlights a dimension of social work professionalism that is often dismissed, discredited and overlooked by the dominance of white supremacy within the social work profession and society more broadly.

I'd like to finish by thanking you, the reader, for investing your time and hard-earned money in this book. I sincerely hope your interest is rewarded with lifelong edutainment and an opportunity to healthily challenge your worldview. If your passion for anti-racism is emboldened – either as a person with lived experience or as a proactive ally – then more power to you!

Ultimately, my desire is for this anthology to be considered a valuable resource to educate, empower and equip Social Workers from all backgrounds in policy, practice and education for decades to come.

'One world, one race... the human race!'

Narratives: The golden thread of social work?

- Siobhan Maclean

As a white child growing up in and around an area of Manchester which reflected racial and cultural diversity, I became aware of my white privilege early in life, although that wasn't a phrase that I used at the time. When I started my social work training 35 years ago, I was shocked by the whiteness of the University both in terms of the practical environment, the social work cohort and the curriculum. I remember minimal questioning of structures and institutional racism even as we explored the impact of the Brixton 'riots' on society. We did little on anti-racist practice and I remember the energy of the student's union, the relationships that I made and the music and club scene at the time teaching me more about race and privilege than anything I covered on my course. Towards the end of my training, anti-racism gained momentum within social work training and I recall being challenged by different perspectives early in my career. I read 'Black Perspectives in Social Work' by Bandana Ahmad, now considered a classic text, which was published weeks after I qualified. I have a particularly clear memory of reading 'The Black Student's Voice: Report of a Black students' conference' (Burgess, Crosskill and La Rose-Jones 1992) when I was training to be a practice teacher (as we were called at the time) and what I learnt from this has stayed with me in the many years since. This background has influenced my strong commitment to learning from a collection of individual narratives.

Over the last few years, I have found myself looking for the narratives of students and social workers which might influence a renewed urgency about anti-racism in social work, but I couldn't find them. I had an idea of developing a collection of narratives which I first mentioned to Wayne Reid at an event in 2018. Wayne was really keen and sent me something almost straight away, but I didn't have much more than Wayne's piece and an idea. Wayne's recollection is that I was struggling to devote the time needed, on reflection I wonder if I felt out of my depth. As a white woman, what could I do? So, I asked Wayne to take the lead editorial role and the vision began to take shape. Watching events unfolding in 2020 and the murder of George Floyd, I was reminded of my white privilege, the danger of white silence and the urgency of this anthology. Working with Wayne to bring this together has been a joy. Everyone can find something in the contents of this anthology. Every time I have picked it up, I have found something different has spoken to me.

In our editorial roles, we have changed extraordinarily little. These narratives belong to the people who submitted them, and we have tried to take good care of them. My friend and colleague, Prospera Tedam (who has contributed to the anthology) said recently that it is painful to revisit the trauma of racism and being asked to speak and write about this every day. It must be incredibly traumatic. I held that in mind when we contacted people about their submissions, and we have made very few changes to the original submissions. There are differences in the language used and as Wayne explains in his preface, the terms 'Black and Other Global Majority Communities', 'people of colour', 'Black and Ethnic Minority' groups and BAME are used interchangeably because we use the language that the authors themselves use.

Wayne describes this collection as a rich patchwork of fabrics. In thinking about the golden thread that might weave these fabrics together I have pulled out a few of the themes that stand out to me in reading this collection. Whilst the people contributing their pieces didn't know who else was contributing and what they would contribute, there are many 'golden threads' in this anthology.

Many of the pieces draw on quotations from Martin Luther King Jnr and this shows to me the importance of role models. I have been left asking myself where are the role models for social workers of colour? The essay by Diana Katoto and Omar Mohamed illustrates the way that students are looking for role models. If you can't see yourself reflected in the profession, what does that mean for your confidence and sense of belonging? A recurring word in the anthology is invisible. The invisibilisation of social workers of colour in our profession is nothing short of scandalous. When we say that we are committed to equality and diversity, how is that reflected in what (and who) is visible in the profession? As some of the narratives included in the anthology show, the impact of COVID-19 and new ways of physically distanced working could leave people even less visible. People like Shabnam Ahmed, who shares how she has 'found her brave' and set up a YouTube channel are beginning to ensure there is visibility. I hope that this anthology will go some way to providing role models for the future. Certainly, I think Wayne Reid is a role model to many and the final section of this anthology demonstrates the range of work that Wayne is undertaking to demand a renewed commitment to anti-racism in the profession.

Alongside invisibility, a core theme of the anthology is silence. Syra Shakir's poem highlights the 'Forced Silence' and Anneta Pinto-Young asks 'Can I Speak?' while Colleen Simon shares 'The things I couldn't say'. In fact, silence was a core theme in the actual process of compiling the narratives. A couple of people initially submitted their contributions anonymously (indeed one person used the pen name 'Silenced'). Having spoken to these authors as the book came together, they decided that they would like to include their names. I am glad that they feel that they do not need to be silenced in the anthology but am equally sad that silence is a core theme in both the process and the product of what we have done. Ironically though it is impossible to read this book in silence. I have gasped, shouted, cried and at times even laughed as I have read the contents over and over. I implore you, as a reader, do not continue the silence in social work. Silence kills!

Sometimes people talk about a book giving people a voice. This book does not do that. All of the authors in this collection have, and already had, a voice. It is their voice. It is not for anyone else to give. This book though does provide a much-needed platform for a collection of voices. Ellah Kandi in 'Determined by Fortitude to Overcome' shares her experiences of belonging to a choir. I hope this book provides a choir for the individual voices brought together that will 'break the silence' (Syra Shakir). The music created by that choir is at times disturbing and challenging but it is always powerful when voices sing in unison.

Where people are neither seen nor heard, is it any wonder that trust becomes a key issue? Trust, or the lack of it, is certainly a recurring theme in the submissions. In her reflection, Irine Mano tells us that she "had to trust the medical professionals helping me" and yet both Jean Dillon and Eddie Dube tell us, in the essays section, that there is a mistrust of health services. Eddie Dube goes on to powerfully explain that an 'us and them' mentality "thrives on mistrust." Even in the stories section trust sits as a core theme, particularly in Asmaat Khan's dynamic and disturbing story. Trust is a key aspect of relationships, so an exploration of this theme and what we can do to rebuild trust and connections must be a question for every reader.

Wayne suggested that dedications or shout outs from each author could be included in this anthology. If I am honest, this isn't something I would have thought of. I have written a number of things and have rarely done a dedication, but I have even found that reading these has been uplifting and enlightening. The number of authors who have referred to their practice educators has reinforced my commitment to my practice educator role. The dedications have demonstrated to me that practice educators can (and do) make a real difference not just while a student is on placement, but also through a social worker's career.

In compiling the submissions into sections, I have found myself uncertain about what would be best where and things have moved around a few times! What makes an essay and what makes a reflection may not always be clear, but what is clear is that there are key messages which weave together the submissions whatever category they are in. Jennifer Simpson's essay on 'the language of deficit' really speaks to me as a practice educator, but the links between that essay, the poem 'Tainted dream' (S Abraham) and Cosmas Maruta's reflection 'the comment' are so clear. The power of language!

We left the call for submissions very fluid and open in an attempt not to limit voices. I was particularly surprised by the number of poems we received. I have never thought of myself as a poetry fan. Having endured 'poetry appreciation' lessons at school, I can't say I have ever appreciated it! However, the poems section has had a profound impact on me emotionally. I notice that in his preface Wayne states that mixed emotions are 'necessary for positive change'. As part of the compiling and editing process, I have needed to read this collection many times and it has taken me on an emotional rollercoaster. A few times I have laughed at some of the humour used, I have often cried but most of all I have been angry. I kept on asking myself why? Why are social workers, spaces, systems and structures treating people this way? Of course, 'why?' is always a key question in social work. Contemporary leadership approaches call on leaders, managers and organisations to 'start with why' and 'find your why' (Sinek 2009). In my view good social work should have 'why?' not just at the start but also at the heart. Maybe, in fact, 'why?' is the golden thread of these narratives.

Through my social work career, I have used the very basic What? Why? How? framework (Maclean, Finch and Tedam 2018). This anthology helps to explore:

- What is racism?
- Why is it happening?
- How can it be challenged?

As a white social worker, I recognise that I need to ask myself:

- What is my role in this?
- Why am I doing this?
- How can I change?

I am incredibly proud of this anthology and what it brings to social work. The initial vision that I had has taken me on a powerful and enjoyable learning journey and I am humbled to have been involved in bringing these narratives together. We have priced the book to make it as accessible as possible to everyone and all the profits will go to the Social Worker's Benevolent Trust (Wayne's choice) so it will give to the profession in the future in many ways.

The SHARE model (Maclean, Finch and Tedam 2018) illustrates that we are influenced by Seeing, Hearing, Action, Reading and Evaluation. I have referred to the connecting threads in this anthology around seeing and hearing. Eddie Dube's essay tells us that what was different about George Floyd was that we 'saw him'. I hope that what is shared in this anthology means that not only might readers see things differently, but that each of us will take action because of what the voices we have heard and the narratives we have read. The thread I referred to in relation to the power of language provides us with a clear shared action plan.

As we were doing the final proofs of the collection, a dear friend and colleague died as a result of COVID-19. I have been working with Paul Yusuf McCormack for many years. Yusuf was a great ally to our profession, despite the fact that at the start of his life he was robbed of his birth name and cultural identity by the care system. Yusuf was a giant of a man, the very role model that I have talked about in this preface. Isaac Newton famously said, "If I have seen a little further it is by standing on the shoulders of giants". This collection of narratives illustrates the past, present and future and we stand on the shoulders of the giants who have contributed. On my part this book is dedicated to Yusuf who called on us not to 'make a difference' but rather to 'BE the difference'.

What can we do to BE the difference? I will leave the answer to one of the authors in this collection. In the poem 'the flames of racism' Narinder Sidhu, says:

"Love is always the way, just ask those who have felt it."

References

Burgess, R. Crosskill, D. and La Rose-Jones, L. (1992) The Black Student's Voice: Report of a Black students' conference. (London) CCETSW.

Maclean, S., Finch, J. and Tedam, P. (2018) SHARE: A New Model for Social Work. (Lichfield) Kirwin Maclean Associates.

Sinek, S. (2009) Start with Why: How Great Leaders Inspire Everyone to Take Action. (London) Penguin.

- Maris Stratulis

I am proud and honoured on behalf of BASW England to support the partnership development and collaboration of all contributors to this book and for the hard work, passion and dedication of the Editors, Wayne Reid and Siobhan Maclean, in making this anthology come to fruition.

Racism denies history, heritage, identity, self-definition and voice. Racism murders and kills. The impact of the brutal death of George Floyd (and the resurgence of the global Black Lives Matter movement) not only highlights overt racism, but the daily interconnected microaggressions that Black and Ethnic Minority people experience on a daily basis, including verbal, behavioural and environmental social injustices - both intentional and unintentional, overt and covert.

The voices within this anthology are rich in diversity, strong, moving, poignant and powerful – as allies we must listen, learn and take action to collectively challenge all forms of racism. Contributors have shared their personal history, experiences and wisdom with honesty and courage. As allies read this anthology - discuss it, promote it, share it within your professional and personal life and amplify the experiences and narratives of Social Worker's from Black and Ethnic Minority backgrounds.

This is an important resource for social work students, social workers, educators, policy makers, colleagues, family members, friends, allies, children and young people. Challenge and be challenged to influence, shape and change social work now and in the future.

Maris Stratulis
BASW England National Director

ESSAYS

What do universities think intelligence looks like?

- Dr. Prospera Tedam

Ask any Black academic in the United Kingdom and I am certain they will have the visible or invisible scars of racism to show for their time in the academy. I applaud any UK Higher Education Institution (HEI) that takes equality and diversity seriously and has clear, robust, and straightforward process for formalising grievances of racism. I say this because although all HEI's will have policies, it is rare to find that these policies are user friendly. In a sense, they can feel like a deliberate ploy to frustrate or discourage formal grievances from being made.

In this piece, I examine one of my many experiences of racism and reflect on the title of this paper adapted from Edo-Lodge (2017) – *what do universities think intelligence looks like?*

During my career in higher education in England I have on occasion been brought to tears by racist behaviour. I have talked about some of these experiences in public and I have written about others in my scholarly work. Here, I recount one incident that left me pained, bruised, and questioning whether I belonged in this space of academia.

I arrived at work one morning at my University and was speaking on my phone outside the building where my office was located. It was around 9:00am and as I was on the phone, a White man comes out interrupts me and says, 'you're late'. I look up at him momentarily and continue speaking, thinking he probably was not talking to me. He leaves then returns a second time shouting 'I will not tell you again, you're late and if you continue on your phone, you won't be allowed to take the exam'. I came off the phone briefly, and asked 'what exam'? At which point he calmed down slightly and said, 'the midwifery resit exam'.

With pain in my soul, I ended my call and said 'why do you think I am coming for an exam? I am a Senior Lecturer in Social Work and my office is in this building. He responded, 'I'm sorry but I thought you were coming to take this exam and we are missing one candidate so I thought it might be you'. He attempted to hurry away, and I went in pursuit to the room where this exam was taking place. There, I saw a room full of Black women taking the said exam. I asked the man his name and told him I would be making a formal complaint to the university Examination Unit.

In the interaction described above, overt, and institutional racism is being played out. There are a few questions here for readers to reflect upon:

What sort of training had this exam invigilator received to support him with his role?

What messages had he internalised over the years about Black students' intellectual and academic abilities?

How is it ok to walk up to someone and address them in a racist and sexist manner from a position of privilege?

I share these stories not to create despair but rather to offer hope and some ideas about ways in which we might respond to similar incidents in the future. I also present them as a counter narrative to what may have been told by someone else.

My silence will not protect me

I did not stay silent. As Audre Lorde once asked; 'who wins if we don't speak'? Not us.' I emailed the Exams Unit and when I received no response, I went to see them in person. There I met a member of the team who apologised but seemed unsure of what to do next. I sought out the Course Team whose exam it was and notified the module leader about what had occurred. Finally, I sent an email to the Dean of my Faculty copying both the Exam Unit and the Midwifery Course Team expressing my dissatisfaction not only at the way I had been treated but also about how it came to be that all the students re-taking that exam were Black women when the midwifery profession and student composition was largely white. I put it to them that racism was at play and they needed to seriously address institutional forms of racism. I took the opportunity to educate them about the disproportionate numbers of Black students failing social work at that time. Following on from this, I was nominated by the Dean of my Faculty to join the University Equality and Diversity Committee where I remained active until I left that employment.

Although I have highlighted here how I responded to an incident of racism, there have been many racist battles that I have felt unable to take on usually because I was exhausted or frustrated by the obstacles towards resolution. The ones that I have pursued resulted in positive outcomes. It will be tiring, it will be frustrating and it may cause you more trauma than you anticipated, however it is important for me that as Black African woman, I speak up and speak out regardless of whether the label of 'angry Black woman' will be assigned to me. Staying silent was not an option then and still not an option today. How am I supposed to honestly teach social work students about anti-oppressive practice and the importance of advocacy, activism, and challenging discrimination in all its forms without reflecting on my own experiences of experiencing and challenging racism? I generally have no problem identifying and calling out racism however I understand and appreciate that for some students and practitioners, this may not be an option they feel is always available to them. Months later and when I was able, I joked with colleagues that in hindsight, I should have obliged, gone in and taken a seat and once the questions were given to me, I would write a letter of complaint to whoever would be marking the resit exam!

As a social work educator and trainer, my philosophy is one where I strive to create an inclusive learning environment for all, where each student or participant is respected and listened to. I have always aimed, through my research to recognise the diverse pathways through which race may influence experiences and outcomes for social workers, service users and students. I acknowledge that the experience I have just described needs to be viewed with an intersectional lens because had I been a man, this racist incident is unlikely to have occurred for the reason that the students taking the resit were all women.

Clearly, there needs to be an urgent shift in the way 'intelligence' in UK Universities is understood, otherwise the disproportionality in graduate outcomes in terms of progression and attainment for Black students will remain and possibly worsen. Black Lives Matter in all spaces and at all levels. Racial positioning of Black academics in the UK has resulted in disproportionately poorer experiences for this group. University leaders must examine their structures, policies and procedures to ensure that perpetrators of racism are appropriately dealt with and Black staff supported.

References

Eddo-Lodge, R. (2017) Why I'm no longer talking to white people about race. New York. Bloomsbury.

Lorde, A. (1984) Sister Outsider. Essays and Speeches. New York: Crossing Press.

Are you sure you're in the right place?

- Zoe Thomas

I write this piece as an act of rebellion. This piece is a one woman protest and should be read as a display of activism. At the moment, this approach feels like the only tool available to me to demonstrate my utter disgust and embarrassment at being part of the way of life that is social work. Let's face it, social work means much more than the job title. Yes, we all embark upon our own unique journeys towards social work and thereafter. But essentially, we are here with the common goal for social justice. Aren't we? But social justice for who? In this piece I will share a bit of the personal to contextualise my professional experience as a social worker. These experiences manifest into felt reality. It hurts. It wounds. And, it is real. Therefore, I speak unapologetically.

I qualified as a social worker in 2007. Since then I have worked as a social worker for local authority child protection teams. Along the way I did some work in social work higher education but always alongside my practice role. A few years ago, I began a part time fee waiver social work PhD. More recently, with a commitment to finishing my PhD I made the difficult decision to leave my beloved advanced practitioner social work job and after being interviewed by three white academics, I too 'became' an academic; a social work academic....or so I thought.

I describe myself as a working class black woman with multiple ethnic identities. Racism didn't feature in my practice role as a social worker as much as one might think. A few sly looks here and patronising statements there. A lazy racist stereotype here and a bit of casual 'banter' racism there. Of course that was from the other professionals, including my social work colleagues. The ACTUAL racism, the racism that is visible and expected, and met with horror and disapproval, REAL racism, the racism of 'service users', well, it just wasn't so prevalent. Other than being called a nigger or a black bastard by people who were in seriously desperate situations, where they were seriously and desperately clinging onto any scrap of power they could find, other than that, racism just wasn't really something I felt when I was knocking on doors. After all, racism is not about the personal prejudice and discrimination of powerless individuals. Racism is hidden away and disguised. It's not about a few bad apples. The whole tree is rotten. Racism is about unstoppable collective power, unquestioned entitled authority and privilege at the expense of others. So in contrast to my social work practice job, when I 'became' a social work academic, I entered a sterile world of emotional disconnect, privileged disinterest, white denial, the protection of fragile white feelings with a dose of insincere apologetic smiles of apathy and a few sympathetic nods. Let's get this out in the open. In academia, being white is normal. That means that my black face and my black experience is a visible mark of difference. It's not normal to be a black academic. Social work academia is no different. We talk about it at length, how terrible it is. It's often some sort of agenda item or on a list. On very special occasions, like Black History Month being black in academia is desperately celebrated as a commendable exception and achievement. Being black in academia is shrouded by the constant affirmations of white academia; what it really means to be an academic rather than a novelty exception. When being a black academic is not the flavour of the month, I'm regularly hurried along out of corridors and lecture theatres by white lecturers who can't even see that I too am trying to set up to deliver a lecture. I have been shuffled out of buildings with students during fire drills. I have been looked at and questioned with utter contempt by a white academic because they thought I didn't belong in the room, '...are you sure you're in the right place...this is for academics?'

As I walk down the academic corridors, through the public spaces on campus and sit in very important intellectual meetings I have been subjected to the invasion of a white hand in my black hair. A white hand, with the unquestioned privilege and feeling of entitlement to inflict an act of silent terrorism on my black hair, to lay a powerful white hand on my black body; my unprotected black body that can't fight back. Can you imagine if I did? The appearance of my black body is constantly and overtly under public scrutiny. My body shape, my body size, what clothes I'm wearing, how old I look, what my hair is like.... This has happened in formal public forums such as rooms filled with prospective social work students coming for admissions interviews. It happens in social work lectures full of social work students and in meetings with academic colleagues. In these white spaces I am reduced to being a body. I am reduced to being a black body, exhibited for scrutiny and publicly judged. Humiliated. During my time as a social work academic the exposure and spectacle of my blackness has been so much greater than my experience as a social worker, my practice specialisms, the relationships I have with students, neither my teaching nor my scholarly activity are as important as the fact of my blackness.

Soon after I started in the social work department at the university, of course I was interrogated by a few of my new academic colleagues. Naturally everyone wanted to know who the new person was. One such interrogation involved, of course, my own confession. As usual, social workers are compelled to share parts of their struggle and I was no different. And so, during the interrogation I laid out some of my experiences as a working class black woman and how this has shaped my politics, social work practice and teaching. Whilst clutching imaginary pearls in horror, my white academic colleague told me of their shock and disbelief. As if it were a compliment I was told 'but I just think of you as middle class'. As if I had such audacity to actually think of myself as a black working class *academic*. As if by occupying the white space of social work academia somehow the stains of race and class are washed away. As if I would want them to be. It went on! As I casually talked about being followed around shops by store detectives and having to regularly negotiate unwanted police attention my colleague was well and truly clinging on to those imaginary pearls. With visible discomfort and now I'm sure wishing the pearls would transform into some sort of extremely comfortable, soundproof protective booth my colleague managed to tell me how terrible it is that this *still* exists. Now it was my turn. I was fresh off the boat from social work practice so had not yet acclimatised to the shores of social work academia. As I fumbled around frantically clutching my imaginary chunky African beads I was horrified that a social worker was actually shocked that my black life was affected by racism.

I have an ongoing battle trying to prove myself and justify my appointment as a social work academic. After all, we know that in teaching and learning evaluations black women academics are much more harshly treated than white men. I pondered this when I first realised, after some time, that a colleague had somehow turned me into her receptionist. I don't know how or when it happened but, suddenly, I had become the receptionist for my colleague. It was weeks before I realised. When I did realise, I noticed that my colleague was coming into my office to ask me how many students had been knocking, did I take a message, next time would I mind taking a message, can I pass on this and that message. Until I realised that it was being made clear to me that my place was servitude I had actually just been going along with it. I hadn't even noticed I was living in servitude. I was so busy getting on with my work that I hadn't noticed my worth was being constructed before my very eyes. It was so skillfully and naturally executed. It felt normal. After I did realise, I resigned with immediate effect.

As a PhD researcher in the final stages I enthusiastically and passionately planned to use my position as an academic to gain as much relevant experience as possible. I expressed a real keen interest in becoming involved with social work PhD supervision. However I was told that at the university to sit on a PhD supervisory team I would need to have completed my PhD first. Although disappointed it did seem an achievable aspiration. Within a matter of days it had come to my attention that a white colleague in the team, with less relevant experience than me, who did not have a PhD and was not on a PhD research programme had just been appointed to sit on a social work PhD supervisory team. Since then I have actually been invited to sit on a PhD supervisory team from within a different division. A division that isn't social work, the one who rejected my black enthusiasm and completely blocked and refused to support my black appetite for development and progress.

More recently, following the Tory win in the general election of December 2019 I was in discussions with a white colleague about how scary it feels as a black person in Britain. We talked, partly in jest, partly in fear about wanting to leave but where would we go. My white colleague told me that I am alright because I have family in Jamaica so I could go there. I'm not Jamaican. I have no family in Jamaica. I have no connections what so ever with Jamaica. This is lazy and sloppy racism. I was speechless. It reminded me of the 1980s where we were all half caste and coloured, and we needed to go back to where we came from; Jamaica.

Working in social work academia still feels like an honour and a privilege to me. It thrills and excites me. I love social work and I love teaching, learning and research. But having these experiences feels hostile. It is shameful and humiliating. Social work academia should be radical, responsive, adaptable and transformative. For me, the social work academy has a duty and responsibility to set a precedent. It should be one of scholarly protest and activism where academics are enthused to shift and collide with power, privilege and marginalisation rather than to be slumped in passive disconnect. Disconnect from social work practice, real life practice and the felt realities and lived experiences of people who live in the real world.

As a profession we should be leading the way, setting an example of challenging the hegemony of white privilege that prevents anyone else from holding positions of power and influence. It is an illustrative reality that in writing this piece I had to question whether to write anonymously for fear of damaging my career and repercussion. However, more recently and with more secure foundations I have decided to pursue a solution with this story. I do this as a call to action to my university in the light of its pledge to become an anti-racist institution.

Racism exists because of white privilege and I can't breathe because of it.

The narratives shared in this book belong to the individual authors. They do not represent the views and opinions of the authors' employers and they may have been experienced in contexts and settings different to their current employers.

Anti-racist Social Work and the Present Moment

- *Gurnam Singh*

Introduction

Social Work has a long history of engaging with questions of 'race' and ethnicity. In the post-war period, up to the later 70's, the framing of questions of 'race' was in terms of 'the immigrant problem' and 'cultural pathology' and the practice response was centred on rescuing black[1] people from dysfunctional and dangerous individuals, families, communities. However, anti-racist social movements emerging in the late 70's and early 80's began to expose and challenge Social Work and other sectors for what was deemed to be endemic and institutionalised racism. Though there has been considerable development since, empirically in the transformation of a profession that was almost entirely white and middle class to one that is very diverse, the issue of institutional and direct racism in social work is still very much alive.

The murder of George Floyd on May 25, 2020 by Minneapolis Police, coupled with the global COVID-19 pandemic and the disproportionate impact it has on black communities and indigenous people across the world, has given new impetus to ongoing demands for eradicating institutional racism and a rebirthing of Anti-racist Social Work (ARSW), which, as I have argued elsewhere, had become significantly marginalized under neoliberalism and

1 The term 'Black' is used in a generic political sense to refer to all those groups who have in one way or another been racialised in the context of European colonialism and imperialism.

managerialism (Singh, 2014). The toppling of slave trader Edward Colston's statue in Bristol seemed to turbocharge the debate about Britain's racist historic legacy and the demands for decolonization and racial justice. Of course, the movement for racial justice encapsulated by the #BlackLivesMatter (BLM) is much older and the current moment must be understood in the context of a series of major Government initiated reports over the past 25 years that consistently highlight ongoing structural racism in UK state institutions and processes (for more details see House of Commons/House of Lords, 2020).

Historical context

Conversations on how centuries-old western colonialism continue to impact and construct communities racialised as 'non-white' has seen a significant amplification in recent times. Historically, problems associated with racialised communities have tended to be explained away through racialised tropes linked with biological, moral, cultural and social pathology. The dominant narratives painted a picture of non-white people, (black people, brown people, global majority people, or people of colour), as being inherently and genetically predisposed to morbidity, mortality, educational failure, criminality and so on.

The post-war period, characterized by movements for decolonization on one hand and the establishment of welfare states and principles of universal human rights on the other, represented a period of hope. Not only did this moment offer an opportunity for European colonial states to divert from their imperial past, but specifically in terms of Social Work, it led to the emergence of a profession with an international focus and a common set of values and ethics built on ideas relating to human liberation, social justice and human rights (IFSW, 2014). And over the past 50 years, Social Work has become important site of struggle and contestation between the interests of the state and those groups made vulnerable by all manner of inequalities.

Although in different parts of the world, Social Work has its own unique features, there are common challenges and themes, such as: issues of how best to protect and safeguard children and vulnerable adults; of assessing and meeting the needs of a diverse population; of making sense of human needs and functioning and the question of responding appropriately to culturally diverse practices, beliefs and norms (Singh and Cowden, 2013). New approaches emerged in response to the needs of providing services for diverse populations. These ranged from politicised radical anti-racist and black nationalist approaches, through to active critiques of Social Work education and training and consensual models associated with ideas such as 'multi-culturalism', 'ethnic sensitivity' and 'cultural competence' (Singh, 2014).

Alongside approaches that focused specifically on the needs of minorities, we saw also the development of more general models of practice, such as 'anti-oppressive', 'anti-discriminatory', 'post-modern', 'radical' and 'transformative social work'. These approaches sought to address questions of multiple oppressions and intersectionality of 'race', gender, class, sexuality, disability, age and religion. Though these approaches were supposedly designed to counteract the tendency towards promoting the idea of a 'hierarchy' of oppressions, one consequence was that, in many instances, racism and the particular experiences, histories and struggles of oppressed and colonized people became lost in the desire to develop practice models beneficial to all equal opportunity target groups – including those who enjoyed considerable class, racial and/or gender advantage. Additionally, the role of Black Social Workers and the sacrifices they made and the battles they fought, and won, began to disappear from the collective memory, as the present generation of Social Work students seem quite oblivious to this important legacy. That is, until very recent times and the emergence of the BLM movement and the awareness gained - through social media in particular.

Development of ARSW and related models.

In the current period which, particularly due to the impact of the COVID-19 epidemic on BAME communities and the rise of the BLM movement and BLM-related politics, Social Work is experiencing a renewed interest in anti-racism (Singh and Masocha, 2020; Reid, 2020). The forms that a (post) COVID-19 era anti-racism might take are yet to be determined. However, as noted earlier, ARSW is not new and has over the past 40 years or so developed into comprehensive framework for navigating the complex manifestations of power and oppression in social working with all clients. So, what are the key characteristics of ARSW and can it be generalised as just 'good professional social work'?

When people seek to question ideas like 'anti-racism', 'anti-sexism', 'anti-oppressive practice' etc., there tends to be two broad thrusts to their argument - each of which reveals a deeper ideological positioning. There are what I call the 'agnostics'. These are people who have a very positive sense of their own moral standing. They have been brought up to be 'good' and to 'do good' and for them anti-racist discourse seems to be both unnecessary and diversionary. This position can be summed up in the assertion that '*I treat all people alike and I don't see their difference, just their humanity*'.

On the surface, such statements seem very noble, but on closer examination it betrays deep levels of complacency about the human condition. And at its worst, as the moral philosopher Hanna Arendt shows in her work, this refusal to see beyond one's own self-determined moral universe can result in what she characterised as a *banality of evil* (Arendt, 1968). This is a kind of collusion with oppression, whilst retaining a sense of moral integrity. The key observation she makes is that by not thinking critically about issue of oppression, one becomes confined to a very limited sphere from which to make judgement, and this results in what she terms is a state of '*thoughtlessness*'. Thoughtlessness, Arendt describes, is a failure of conscience that sustains oppressive ideology. She goes onto argue that the only remedy for such catastrophic failures of conscience is cultivation of everyday thoughtfulness, or what Husband (1995) terms the '*morally active practitioner*'.

So, what are the key elements of anti-racist social work (ARSW)?

1. Historical understanding.

Though historical and theoretical insights without action will not and cannot eradicate racism, a failure to learn the lessons of history will mean that we can never escape the vortex of racism and that we will be engulfed by it. Historical understanding of the relationship between politics, economics and ideology allows us to unlock the mechanisms of white dominance and black subjugation. Also, an emphasis on anti-racism provides us with a sense of the journeys that we have travelled, as well as offering insights into the material and psychological impacts that racist ideas have on all of us, as educators, students, practitioners and service users.

2. Critique welfare professionalism.

ARSW seeks to recognise the historical emergence of Social Work within the post war period, which can more broadly can be characterised as late modernity, late imperialism and post-colonialism and the emergence of modern industrialised welfare state. Here we are talking of the period that has resulted in a major dislocation of peoples – not just within countries, but also globally. Also, the radical transformation, and in many cases destruction, of the environments in which people have lived for centuries. It is also a period where the science of Eugenics was prominent.

3. Centering human dignity.

We all would claim to treat the people we work with as 'human beings'. Though it seems like a straightforward proposition, actually defining being human lies at the core of anti-racist practice. The question not only: "what is a human being?", but also "what are the conditions in which basic human rights, to freedom, dignity, life etc. may be compromised or denied altogether"? Dark times, such as those associated with genocidal regimes of the past or today, as we all see the devastating impact of COVID-19 on the most vulnerable sections of society, represent a serious threat to the conditions of being human. That is because our capacity to sustain the fragile human condition is completely dependent on the possibility of sharing a sense of human worth.

And when the contract we have with each other begins to break down, we enter a slippery slope towards what Arendt terms '*dispensability*' or '*superfluousness of life*'. For Arendt '*superfluous*' people are not only the oppressed or unjustly treated – they are made expendable (Hayden, 2014). Reflecting on the way that governments across the developed global north have been responding to refugee flows from the global south and east, or the UK governments response (or lack thereof) to the needs of vulnerable old people in care homes during the first few months of COVID-19, or the rationing of care and austerity policies that have had a devastating impact on the most vulnerable since 2008 - one can definitely detect a logic of 'expendability' at the root of many of these policies.

4. Developing alternative 'non-western' models.

In critiquing the dominant 'White western' models of social work developed since its inception, which often masquerade as 'good practice', 'evidence-based practice', 'common sense', 'rational social work' or simply 'professional judgement', ARSW seeks out methods of working that value lived experience and the knowledge/wisdom of people. The recently published '*Routledge Handbook of Postcolonial Social Work*' (Kleibl et al. 2019) is an extremely prescient example of the importance of developing alternative models of decolonised practice through engaging with grassroots struggles and communities in co-creating solutions.

If we look at the arena of child protection, one of the more successful innovations was the introduction of family group conferences in child protection, which originated from New Zealand and were used to allow Social Work practitioners to work with and not against Māori values and culture. Amongst other features, key aspects of this approach are based on the beliefs that families have the ability to make rational and sound decisions about: their future, the future of their children; the right environment and the correct information. Fundamentally, it is believed families instinctively know what is best for the children. (See Crow and Marsh 1998 for a comprehensive account of this approach).

Another area that anti-racist challenges have led to the development of new approaches, is the field of mental health - and in particular the development of crisis resolution/home treatment teams, that were pioneered by Professor Sashi Sashidharan in Birmingham in the 1990's. This approach is based on the belief that hospitalisation is nearly always detrimental for people who have a severe mental illness, such as schizophrenia, manic depressive disorders, or severe depressive disorders and that they should be treated at home or in the community (Sashidharan and Smyth, 1992). This approach is particularly relevant given the abundance of evidence that experiencing racism can be very stressful and have a negative effect on overall health and mental health. Also, we know that black people in particular are 4 times more likely than white people to be detained under the Mental Health Act. (Vige, 2019).

Whether it is child protection work, or acute mental health, all the research supports the case for community and family-based intervention. This approach presents its own challenges, especially where cultural traditions may vary within different communities, but the important point here is not to make judgements looking through a white European lens, but on universal principles that are actually held in all communities, though perhaps understood differently. It is the capacity to navigate between universal principles and diversity of approaches that underpin Social Work and anti-racism. In this regard, I find the African concept of 'ubuntu' very informative. Summarised in the phrase "I am because you are' ubuntu embraces the idea that humans cannot exist in isolation. Our humanity, and indeed our existence, is built on the need to belong to community, to connect and to care for each other. This philosophy requires a conscious shift in how we think about ourselves and others, especially in a world where the values of individualism have become so normalised. Ubuntu also challenges our sense of identity and being and sovereignty. In Ubuntu the 'I' and we are interchangeable. As Eze suggests, 'The 'I am' is not a rigid subject, but a dynamic self-constitution dependent on this otherness creation of relation and distance' (2010 p191).

Conclusion

The struggle against racism in Social Work is not new and there is a well-established literature base now on the emergence of anti-racist and anti-oppressive Social Work. However, neoliberal appropriation of Social Work since the 1980's has led to a beleaguered profession that appears to be strong on rhetoric, but weak on addressing structural racism. Whilst Social Work has made progress, this does not mean that everything is fine, and in some senses one can see history repeating itself - another generation of black Social Workers and students being compelled to engage in struggle for their voices to be heard. On a more positive note, we now have a solid body of literature on racism and ARSW, and a greater black presence within the profession, so perhaps the struggle for racial justice in Social Work will be easier to realise.

Increasing awareness of ongoing legacies of colonialism, primarily as a consequence of social movements, and the power of social media, has drawn attention to the ongoing brutality and oppression of Black, Brown and indigenous people the world over. Racism amounts to the reduction of complexity, where complex human beings are reduced to singular entities in order to create illicit explanatory shortcuts that pave the way for domination and exploitation of differences. In my final analysis, perhaps the question is not how can Social Work professionals can be anti-racist, but what are the consequences for those professionals and organisations that are incapable of this?

References

Arendt, H. (1968) Eichmann in Jerusalem: A Report on the Banality of Evil. Revised edition. London, Penguin.

Eze, M. O. (2010) Intellectual History in Contemporary South Africa. New York, Palgrave MacMillan.

Crow, G., & Marsh, P. (1998). Family group conferences in child welfare. Blackwell Science.

Fanon, F. (1967) Towards an African Revolution. Political Essays. New York, Grove.

Hayden, P. (Ed.) (2014) Hannah Arendt: key concepts. London, Routledge.

House of Commons/House of Lords (2020) Joint Committee on Human Rights Black people, racism and human rights. Eleventh Report of Session 2019–21. Available at: https://committees.parliament.uk/publications/3376/documents/32359/default/

Husband, C. (1995). The morally active practitioner and the ethics of anti-racist social work. *Ethical issues in social work*, 84-103.

Kleibl, T., Lutz, R., Noyoo, N., Bunk, B., Dittmann, A., &Seepamore, B. (Eds.) (2019). The Routledge Handbook of Postcolonial Social Work. Routledge.

IFSW, I. (2014) Global definition of Social Work. Retrieved Oct 2020. Available at: https://www.ifsw.org/what-is-social-work/global-definition-of-social-work/

Reid, W. (2020) How to promote an anti-racist culture in Social Work. Community Care, July 17 2020. Available at: https://www.communitycare.co.uk/2020/07/17/promote-anti-racist-culture-social-work/

Singh, G. and Masocha, S. (Eds) (2020) Anti-racist Social Work: International Perspectives. London, Palgrave Macmillan.

Singh, G. (2014). Rethinking Anti-racist Social Work in a neoliberal age. In: Lavalette, M. &Penketh, L. (eds.) Race, racism and Social Work: Contemporary issues and debates. Bristol: Policy Press.

Singh, G. and Cowden, S. (2013) Is Cultural Sensitivity Always a Good Thing? Arguments for a Universalist Social Work, In M. Carey and L. Green eds. Practical Social Work Ethics: Complex Dilemmas within Applied Social Care. London, Ashgate.

Sashidharan, S., & Smyth, M. (1992). West Birmingham Home Treatment Service: Evaluation of Home Treatment in Ladywood. Unpublished.

World Economic Forum (2020) How racism spread around the world alongside COVID-19 5th June 2020. Available at: https://www.weforum.org/agenda/2020/06/just-like-COVID-19-racism-is-spreading-around-the-world/

Vige, M. (2019) Race and Mental Health – Tipping the Scale. Blog, 19 June 2019. Mind UK, https://www.mind.org.uk/about-us/our-policy-work/mental-health-act-review/independent-review-of-the-mental-health-act-faqs/mental-health-act-blog-series/race-and-mental-health-tipping-the-scale/

How models are used to cure racism & other curious tales

- Jas Sangha

If theories explain why something is happening, then models show you what the phenomenon looks like. What is gravity? Why do parents abuse their children? Why are people racist? It may all be explained through theories - and a model will show you what the concept looks like. A model leads onto solutions for implementation, for policies and for the betterment of society. In this society - in social work, we have used and discarded plenty of models to deal with racism. These models are proposed to cure racism, right? Some are better than others - but all are eventually crushed, and reduced to a size zero as you will see...

Once, when I was 11, I prayed to God to end the incessant racism I faced. I didn't know how else to stop all that discrimination - apart from turning white!? Turning my colour, my culture, my religion, my accent and food completely white. This was for sure the only way to stop the incessant racist abuse that I faced in school as a British Indian boy, day after day after day after day.

These were the eighties days of speed, of Culture Club, Specials, two tones with Jam mods and girls on film. These red wedge days were marked out by colourful models of ethnically sensitive practice, and Marxist perspectives on race. Hats off to the fact that these approaches began to respect different people's cultures, ethnicities and geographies. Not only that, but being ethnically sensitive meant that you were acknowledging the strengths of

BAME communities - and a Marxist perspective started an intersection between class and race which was then forgotten and lost.

Which of these models do you think helped me out and stopped the abuse, and kept me safe and sound and brown? Do you really want to hurt me? Well perhaps in the eighties, only that pragmatic model of multiculturalism had any real legs. Here we had an approach where we recognised and accepted that we live in a culturally diverse society - and we had a vision to strive for a peaceful co-existence, as long as we could eliminate a teeny-weeny bit of inequality and fear that hung around. It did not quite work out that way, I'm afraid. Ethnically sensitive practices were too weak, and Marxism fell out of favour with new labour. But multiculturalism – well I do not know why we fell apart, that's a model that was looking good in curing racism... I'd like to take it home - but it faded out! The fears of the National Front, British National Party and Combat 19 and other racists marched on, I guess.

Was it any different for my dad, migrating from the Punjab? We turn back to the 50s and 60s, and those narrow-minded concepts of integration and assimilation are at the fore... With my dad living in rented houses with a dozen other Indians, and working in cotton mills, and drinking at weekends, and cooking daal... was he any happier? Was he adapting to an English way, acculturalisation, assimilation - and seeing his own culture disappear? No. In those days he firmly believed in principles of segregation and separation. He was Indian through and through. Not English, an Indian with a British passport, a Punjabi, a Jat Sikh, a worker, a husband, a father.

Segregation. Stick to your own kind - that's how he had race relations and relationships with race. That is how he survived. Remaining in your own Indian bubble, speaking

Punjabi with Punjabi friends in Punjabi Sikh temples with Punjabi chapattis, and Scottish whisky to wash it all down with. Later, in his retirement, I saw flashes of integration and acceptance of some acceptable aspects of the dominant white culture, but never of being assimilated. He made firm friends with our white neighbours, fully accepted my English wife, ate fish and chips on a Friday - washed down now with Russian vodka. But he never let on that he could speak English or that he loved his allotment that must have felt ironically like being back in the farms and fields of the Punjab.

Turn and turn again and trying to navigate white spaces at polytechnics and universities. These campuses were so different from schools. Gone was the blatant name calling and direct forms of racial hatred and discrimination. Now it was acceptance with subtle, covert, indirect, untouchable and unnameable forms of rejection - and little, tiny aggressions.

These were the 90s, and I was a model student doing the social work course at a new university still seen as a polytechnic. Didn't we have a nice time? Wasn't it such a fine time? To be someone must be a wonderful thing.

Yes, I was the model social work student caught within the model CCETSW Paper 30, and the dominance of anti-racist social work in the curriculum to address issues of race and racism. This anti-racist model and political and social movement that aimed to identify, oppose and eradicate racism in all its forms. Perhaps this one was the one? The special one? The cure to racism? I was 'black' back then. Not BME, BAME, Indian, British, Black and Ethnic Minority, Asian, Southern Asian or Other – but Black. Not in colour but politically, where all minorities were grouped together through a shared experience of racism - and united to fight it.

I was the token role model that had to talk about my experiences of race and racism in lectures. But you can take it too far. I remember being asked to join the Indian society and rejecting what I thought was prejudiced in itself?! I knew where I had come from but no idea where I was going. Ok then, perhaps those models of anti-oppressive practice, and anti-discriminatory practice which also became dominant in social work held the answers I sought in the 1990s? Anti-oppressive practice focused on understanding and questioning oppressive structures that are the root causes of racism, whereas anti-discriminatory practice used various means to directly fight and eliminate a range of discrimination in society. Not sure that worked out. These polytechnics no longer exist, neither do I in those discourses, but anti-racist social work is still around. Maybe anti-racism holds the key to cure racism?

One final turn, and I find myself as a social work lecturer in the new century. This time I am interviewing for prospective lecturers and find myself saddened by the lack of understanding of the struggles previously faced by Black and Ethnic Minority communities. Social work students do not know half of these models, and new lecturers know even less. Successive governments objecting to out-of-control political correctness have got rid of all the shaded areas. In these brand-new, model, glass fronted universities, anti-racism is side-lined - and marginalised.

Actually, the whole trio of anti-racist, anti-discriminatory and anti-oppressive are now drowned out by the new models on the catwalk, making an equilateral triangle of diversity, inclusion and equality. Neoliberalism may have increased the pay and living conditions of social workers, but we have truly forgotten the struggles and the fight for equality and an end to need and racism. Even when admitting to the existence of institutional racism and the need for something new, successive Governments head back to the start and to assimilation models of diversity.

Bland competencies or are they standards or capabilities march towards a generic colour-blind approach of diversity, that celebrates everyone's needs and cultures and differences in a happy-clappy sort of way. A place where of course no problems exist, and if they do then we do not discuss them or talk about them. I will keep going and going and going until you can't breathe and you can't catch your breath and I'm on your neck and there is no break in this sentence and you forget where it started.

In this colourful diverse world, everyone lives in harmony and are united by their - differences - if you know what I mean?! Let's celebrate our differences and ignore our oppressions and oppressors. People are inclusive, and ensure you are not left out in the cold when discussing what pubs to go to, and how lovely your kids are, and looking forward to Christmas. We are all equal now and have the same 50-inch TV and the same access to resources and capital, don't we all? We can forget that racism even exists, now we are distracted, isn't that a cure of sorts?

One final turn, then I promise then I'll stop. Now that we have a watered-down generic understanding of race and racism through equality, diversity and inclusion - what are we left with? I have a whole future in academia and these institutions must change. I'll start by getting staff to stop calling me a 'coloured' – a term a bit outdated now. Maybe I'll turn towards posher models of post colonialism, or decolonisation, or sashay along with critical race theory, critical race theory in education or intersectionality; maybe I should get trendy with colourism?

These models shimmy down the catwalk, but all trip up one by one. Whichever way you turn, these models do not work for me and maybe the next generation of social workers have turned away from these too, because their world is so different and vast and open. I see my children oblivious to all these epistemological turns about theories and models, but they see something in the corner of their eye... a new model of anti-racism perhaps? A new multicultural perspective maybe... or something completely new...

Where now? Social work and social work education in the slipstream of the *Black Lives Matter* movement

- Robin Sen

George Floyd's murder had a powerful impact on me, as it did many. Why this death became the tipping point for such a powerful garnering of support for the *Black Lives Matter* campaigns is hard to pin down. As a social worker and social work educator from a minoritised ethnic and sexual orientation, the aftermath of George Floyd's death brought to the fore fears that I had harboured for some time about the progress being made on racial justice. When I came out in the late 1990s I did not think I would see such legal and social strides on issues relating to sexual orientation in the subsequent twenty years. But nor did I think that in 2020 we would have recently witnessed the Windrush scandal, the election of a UK Prime Minister who had engaged in overtly racist discourse on multiple occasions or the election of a US President who deliberately stoked racial tensions. George Floyd's murder crystallised a nagging fear that we might be going around in circles in respect of achieving racial justice.

The issues raised by the *Black Lives Matter* campaigns are manifold - varied - and there are complexities and tensions within some of them. In this piece, I focus on social work education and practice in England, given that is where I have been primarily based professionally over the last decade. Social work education was at the fore of incorporating Anti-Discriminatory Practice and Anti-Oppressive Practice (ADP/AOP) from the 1990s onawards, giving anti-racism a central place in the initial curriculum for the original Diploma in Social Work. This made the profession a target for right-wing critics, who saw this as evidence of the profession's effete liberal left-wing predilections. The right-wing commentator Melanie Phillips provided just one example. Judiciously choosing her moment, Phillips responded to the public outcry in 2008 over the horrific killing of Peter Connelly by seeking to link it to the profession's commitments to ADP/AOP:

Social work is plagued by low-calibre recruits, whose training is more akin to indoctrination in political correctness, working in a culture which intimidates any dissent and turns morality and common sense inside out. (The Daily Mail, November 16, 2008)

Subsequently, in 2014, the DfE commissioned Sir Martin Narey to undertake a review of social work education in England. While this employed less acerbic discourse it contained a substantially similar critique of social work education curricula, arguing they covered too much material on ethics, ADP/AOP, sociology and social policy. Narey advocated for the separation of child and family social work from the rest of the profession, suggesting a child and family social work qualifying curriculum should be focused more narrowly on knowledge of child protection and child development. Michael Gove, the acting Secretary of State for Education, welcomed Narey's report by claiming that: "...in too many universities and in many social work texts, social work training can be dominated by an emphasis on inequality, empowerment and anti-oppressive practice."

Gove was also responsible for the removal of adoption agencies' legal duty to give "due consideration" to a child's "religious persuasion, racial origin and cultural and linguistic background" when placing a child for adoption in England. This move was in response to the finding that *some* groups of Black and Asian children were facing significantly greater levels of adoption delay and lower adoption rates than white children. The detail of these differences and the likely reasons for them are nuanced, as respected exploration of the topic has illustrated. It is worth emphasising that the previous law did not mandate that children had to be placed with adopters of the same ethnicity. Instead, quite reasonably, it required that due consideration be given to a number of key factors, relating to a child's identity, when an adoptive placement was being selected for them. For Gove, however, the argument that 'politically correct' social workers were harming ethnic minority's children's interests through ideological rigidity was too tempting to resist, even if it required distorting a complex picture for the sake of scoring political points: "Edicts which say children have to be adopted by families with the same ethnic background and prevent other families adopting them because they don't fit left-wing prescriptions," he emotively wrote in 2011, "are denying children the love they need."

Given such a context, it would be surprising if ADP/AOP had not played a less prominent role within social work over the last decade. Education and service providers knew there was governmental encouragement of social work as a purely technical-rational activity. It was notable, then, that on July 9th, 2020 Isabelle Trowler (Chief Social Worker for Children & Families), appeared to signal a shift away from this position. In a tweet, Trowler announced she had written to the Chief Executive of Social Work England (the regulator of social work in England from 2019), to seek "assurance that the regulator ensures anti-discriminatory practice is integral to the evidenced learning outcomes achieved, through SW qualifying programmes." Trowler was the Chief Social Worker in 2014 when the Narey report was published and had made no public comment regarding its criticisms of the focus on AOP/ADP within social work curricula at that time. Nor had she voiced any public opposition to the Government's decision to remove the duty to consider children's religion, ethnicity, cultural and linguistic background when placing them for adoption. While the Chief Social Worker's most recent statement is therefore welcome as an indicator of renewed commitment to the importance of AOP/ADP in qualifying social work curricula, the conspicuous absence of any acknowledgement of her own tacit support for the previous marginalisation of it is also problematic.

It is important to acknowledge that some of previous focus on ADP/AOP in social work curricula had weaknesses. The focus originated from a sound starting place - the desire to recognise and challenge the discrimination and oppression different groups face in society. However, this sometimes manifested itself as an approach which was more concerned about confronting discriminatory language rather than seeking to grapple with the complex underlying structural factors underpinning it. Language is of course important – it enables and constrains its referents, and its pejorative use can both offend and demean. But if ADP/AOP is restricted to challenging language while participating in practices which reinforce the social inequalities that allow racism to flourish, then it is bound to be ineffective. For example, if a child and family social worker uses the relative power of their role to admonish a white family for using racist language about ethnic minority families, but does nothing more than this, their actions are unlikely to start challenging the underlying causes of racism from which everyday racist discourse stems. I am not here suggesting that social workers should not challenge discriminatory discourse which they encounter; I am highlighting its limitations when undertaken purely in isolation.

In this regard, it is notable that several of the, largely

excellent, mainstream social work texts on ADP/AOP make little or no mention of social class as the basis of discrimination and oppression. This is a real gap, as the majority of families receiving social work intervention are poor working-class families - whose difficulties, while not entirely reducible to poverty, are heavily influenced by it. For some ethnic minority individuals and families – for example those families subject to No Recourse to Public Funds or unaccompanied asylum-seeking young people subject to discriminatory age-assessment – their poverty and loss of social rights are direct consequences of racist state policies and practices. To challenge these, social workers must both utilise the powers the state provides them with to garner available support for such individuals and families at the micro-level while, at the same time, challenging state policies which systemically discriminate against ethnic minority families and reproduce racist attitudes. Social workers will have different ways of advocating for such wider systemic change: some will use public platforms as part of overt campaigns for policy and political change; others will work through their trade unions or other professional organisations; and others still will engage in 'everyday activism' by engaging in and articulating micro-practices in a way that moves beyond isolated acts of resistance into action for organisational, community or social change. Whichever route social workers take, to be effective in challenging racism, they must find ways of linking individual expressions of resistance to racist discourse to wider movements for change which can address racism's underlying causes.

Another issue of current focus relates to the representation of Black, Asian and other ethnic minority colleagues within the social work profession, particularly within senior positions. Taking account of where social work is placed in this regard is well overdue, but it is important to question assumptions that addressing the representation of ethnic minority social workers within the workplace will automatically address issues of institutionally racist practices in social work. The current data is limited, but those for the children's social work workforce in England are presented below in ***Table 1***.

Table 1

	White %	"Mixed"[3] %	Asian %	Black %	Other %
As % of general population[1]	85.4	2.3	7.8	3.5	1.0
Senior manager[2]	88.7	2.1	3.8	4.7	0.6
Middle manager	85	1.9	4.4	7.5	1.2
First line manager	82.7	2.9	4.6	9.0	0.9
Senior practitioner	78.4	3.6	5.8	11.1	1.1
Case holder	75.6	3.7	5.5	14.3	1.0
Qualified without cases	78.3	3.8	6.6	10.4	0.9

1 Adapted from 2011 population census for England and Wales, adjusted to give figures for England only.

2 Figures of workforce from Children's Social Work Workforce 2018-19, provided via the DfE. These have been adjusted to exclude recorded unknowns in the returns.

3 The category descriptor "Mixed" is used in the source data and therefore mirrored here even though it is not my preferred terminology, hence the use of quotation marks.

The data in *Table 1* suggests that, compared to their numbers in the general population in England, white people are in fact under-represented in most statutory child and family social work positions in England, albeit less so as the positions become more senior. They are also slightly over-represented at senior management level and are notably the only ethnic group where their representation consistently increases with each level of professional seniority. Black social workers are over-represented at all levels of children's statutory social work, including senior management level, but the level of over-representation decreases progressively as the level of seniority increases. Dual heritage social workers (labelled "Mixed" above) are over-represented at less senior levels, but slightly under-represented at more senior levels. Asian social workers are under-represented at all levels, but their under-representation increases with the level of seniority. Those of "other" ethnicity are both under-represented and over-represented at different levels of seniority, but as with most other ethnic minority groups, they are most under-represented at the senior management level.

This snapshot provides only an initial overview, which is constrained by the current data available on this issue in the censuses from which it is drawn. It does suggest there is need for further exploration of these issues, which should include any barriers to the promotion of ethnic minority social workers within children's statutory social work. Long-term disparities in the representativeness of the social work workforce are important to explore, because if these are underpinned by institutional barriers to the advancement of any ethnic group then it is likely to be indicative of underlying systemic factors, directly or indirectly. Equally, it should be recognised that simply replacing some senior white managers with more ethnic minority managers is not an effective anti-racist strategy on its own.

Firstly, such a policy implicitly places responsibility on mangers from ethnic minority backgrounds for addressing institutionally racist practices - rather than seeing this as a shared responsibility. Secondly, it largely misconstrues the problem. White men or white women are not the barrier to better anti-racist social work practice, "white-men-in-suitism" is. By this, I mean a colonialist type attitude amongst some policy makers, policy advisors, civil servants and senior managers, which suggests they have all the answers to addressing all the problems within the profession. These attitudes permeate into practice and result in the imposition of statutory, policy and practice changes on individuals, families and frontline practitioners. At best such imposition is accompanied by tokenistic consultation with those affected, more often manipulation or a fundamental lack of any engagement is characteristic. Ethnic minority senior managers who replicate these managerial practices will be no more responsive to the needs and perspectives of individuals and families receiving social work services than the managers who preceded them, nor will they be any more genuinely consultative of frontline staff.

Comparing local authority social work teams or reflecting on the same local authority social work team under different management regimes, it is readily apparent that there are large-scale differences in working cultures. The single biggest variable influencing them is the extent to which senior managers succeed – despite the multiple constraints on them – in instilling more collegiate ways of working with people receiving their organisation's services and with frontline staff. Senior managers who succeed in this goal help create teams which are starkly more pleasant places to work and which are sites of social work practice where practitioners earnestly try to engage with the perspectives of individuals and families with whom they are working, rather than imposing professionally driven plans on them. Such teams are also far less likely to engage in institutionally racist practices as a result. Attempts to instil more participative cultures of practice at the local authority level are currently hampered by the operation of the Department of Education itself, key parts of which are wedded to a top-down, command and control model. The imposition of Statutory Instrument 445, which withdrew over 60 safeguards for children in care in England during the first pandemic lockdown without consultation, is a stark illustration of such a model. This model must end if statutory social work practice is to become more anti-racist. Adjusting the ethnic composition of senior social work management teams without doing these hard yards of opening up social work's decision-making structures to more participative ones is like shifting the deckchairs on the Titanic in the hope of altering the ship's course.

Social workers cannot change the world by themselves, but the resurgence of the *Black Lives Matter* movement has reminded us that overt commitments to progressive social change are an intrinsic part of being a good social worker. We need to harness the momentum this has given the profession to shift practice and the institutional arrangements of social work practice. In responding to the questions that the Black Lives Matter movement poses, the social work profession should find a clearer, stronger voice with which to articulate concerns about racism as well as commitments to challenging it. The articulation of these concerns and commitments needs to be coupled with a commitment to challenging the structural inequalities, disempowerment and disenfranchisement which underlie a good many of the expressions of everyday racism which are enacted and received.

Dr. Robin Sen,
Lecturer in Social Work, University of Dundee
Honorary Research Fellow, University of Sheffield.

With thanks to:
Dr. Calum Webb for help in preparing the statistics presented in *Table 1*.

The language of deficit

- Dr Jennifer Simpson

"Take no one's word for anything, including mine – but trust your experience. Know whence you came. If you know whence you came, there is really no limit to where you can go". (*James Baldwin, 1963*)

The work of Moule (2009) points to the prevalence of unconscious bias in every human being - and shows that it is rooted in stereotypes and prejudices that are not only deeply held, but also unrecognised. Furthermore, through the extensive research undertaken by Steele (2010), we are aware of the negative impact stereotypes have on academic performance - a common and all too real predicament of Black students. Combined, the work of Moule (2009) and Steele (2010) make clear that the disadvantages experienced by Black students, in terms of higher education - more widely (and this is inclusive of social work programmes), is a product of latent social beliefs and actions that, on a daily basis, promote disadvantage.

The effect of this continual disadvantage upon Black students is that they undertake their studies in an environment where the presence of stereotyping effectively reduces their self-belief and promise. It could be said that often what is forgotten is that all students, including those who are Black, come to us with their dreams. They come to us with their hopes and ambitions, and what they are likely to inadvertently experience is icy cold water poured over them by a language of deficit. Words such as: "you do not have", "you are not able", "you are not capable of", "you need to understand", "the problem you have is" and "the student has an attitude problem". In other words, the student is met with a vocabulary of deficiency.

Once a seed of deficit is sown it will grow and grow, and ultimately overshadow the capability of the individual student. Using the analogy of a tree, the Black student is a young sapling with all the potential to grow and produce wonderful fruit. Yet the sapling is placed in an environment that is not optimal in terms of growth - it might be located where the soil is too acidic or alkaline. If by chance any fruit does grow, it is the fruit of deficit ready to be picked and used to reinforce the words of deficit spoken over them. This ultimately leads to an educational experience where heads are not held high, a sense of achievement likely to be limited and the student is confined to just getting by.

If Black students are to experience something altogether different, we can no longer speak to them using the language of deficit. Instead, let us speak to them using a language of excellence. Let us mentor our Black students for excellence rather than deficit. If you look from the viewpoint of deficit, you will find deficits. If you look from the viewpoint of excellence, you will find excellence. Excellence begins with expectations of students doing incredibly well, that they have the motivation and determination to see the fulfilment of their dream. It means that they are met with words such as 'Yes, you can'. They are nurtured in an environment that is 'stereotype safe' and they are surrounded and embedded in a setting that is rich with opportunities that speak to their needs, aspirations and motivations. An environment that speaks to personal fulfilment, openness, diversity and academic challenge.

As a Black academic, I wish to engage in a language of possibility, a language of excellence, a language of achievement. There is a need to enable Black students to launch from a platform of excellence. If you expect more from your students, you will get more. If you speak in a language of deficit, you will see academic performance that mirrors your expectations.

So how might change be achieved? By firstly recognising that the problem is not with the Black student. Rather the problem is with the academic institution that speaks over him or her in a language of deficit - which then infects all those that work with the student. The environment of disadvantage has fostered a remedial support system that is individualised and focused on what needs to change in the student, with minimal attention being given to wider structural issues of stereotyping and attainment.

Let us promote excellence by encouraging and supporting our Black students to obtain those skills and abilities that enable them to problem-solve and aspire to academic excellence. Excellence is a journey and a path that needs to be mapped out with individual students, to enable them to see what they want to be and how they are going to get there, as well as what part they need to play in realising their ambitions.

In reality, this notion of excellence will speak to some students - but not all of them. That said, if those of us within social work education are committed to, and function from, a place of excellence, there will be students who will rise to this and this will exceed our expectations of them. These students will take on the world and show what can be achieved if they are nurtured and supported in an environment of excellence.

Social work educators have within their grasp the ability to be change makers. For this to happen the language spoken over Black students must change from that of deficit to excellence. There must also be the removal of systems, cultures and processes within higher education establishments that support deficit. This in turn will result in a reformation that is founded upon a language and vocabulary of excellence, which will ultimately provide the room and opportunity for Black students to rise to the expectation of excellence.

As things stand, if students were to be asked about their dreams, they would probably echo what was said by Martin Luther King Jr:

"And so even though we face the difficulties of today and tomorrow, I still have a dream" (Martin Luther King Jr, 1963).

DISCLAIMER: Opinions and information expressed do not relate to the official business of Nottingham Trent University. This narrative shall be understood as neither given nor endorsed by the University.

Exploring anti-racism in social work education

- Diana Katoto and Omar Mohamed

We went into social work because of its core values and ethics of social justice. Throughout the years, we have either experienced racial abuse or witnessed others go through it. The increasing statistics showcasing the injustices people are currently facing, pushed us towards social work. Here was a profession that promoted the importance of social change, social justice, equality, and human rights. We were walking into social work with the goal and passion to help provide people with the tools needed to fight these injustices. What we were not aware of was how invisible we would feel once in the world of social work.

The inaction for ethnic minority social work students, practitioners, and service-users to feel seen, heard and wanted is shocking for a profession with core commitments to inclusion, equality, and diversity. One way to bridge the gap of silence and to enable ethnic minority students, practitioners, and service-users to be heard is to promote anti-racism in social work and embed anti-racism in the entire social work curriculum.

Anti-racism is described by Professor Robert J. Patterson as an "active and conscious effort to work against multidimensional aspects of racism". It is about having the understanding that racism can be both conscious and unconscious: that it can happen on an individual level, but also at an institutional level too. This is important for social work education because it allows us to look inwards and outwards. It also challenges personal and professional values and enables us to take action on prejudices, stereotypes and biases.

Does the social work education system prepare students to effectively work with service-users from all walks of life? It can be argued that there is still a long way to go to get there. The first area to look at is the decolonisation of social work education. What are we being taught and from who? A large amount of social work knowledge is still based on Eurocentric, Western values, which have their advantages. However, this fails to be informed by wider social, political, cultural economic, and environmental ideas, which hinders the applicability of knowledge given and used. In order for social work students from ethnic minority backgrounds to feel visible, seen, and heard we need to start to diversify and decolonise what is being taught on social work qualifying programmes.

Why are the likes of Professor Claudia Bernard, Dr Suryia Nayak, Jahnine Davis, Zoe Thomas, Dr Prospera Tedam, Dr Gurnam Singh and others not integral to our social work education? Additionally, this highlights the voices of ethnic minority professionals is not highly regarded compared to their white counterparts. This is showcased in their marginalisation in teaching materials, references used in PowerPoint slides, academic papers and journals.

Not only does this affect students and professionals, but the impact of the lack of knowledge of this area is detrimental to ethnic minority service-users. It is damaging that there is a long list of serious case reviews and negative experiences of ethnic minority service-users receiving poor social work services due to a lack of commitment from the social work profession in being anti-racist.

Anti-racism in social work needs to start from early on in the training and development of social work students. There is simply not enough attention paid to racism, and anti-racism specifically in social work education. A one-hour lecture on discrimination that ticks the box for 'anti-oppressive values' does not effectively equip social work students with the complex and important impacts that racism has on both the people we work with and the workforce.

We need to address the elephant in the room: why are majority of social work academics white? This lack of representation and diversity in social work academics that teach on social work courses, effectively means the teaching materials are delivered through a whitewashed lens. Why is it, that when a University has a lecturer from an ethnic minority community, then and only then is anti-racism embedded in teaching?

This lack of diversity and representation in social work academics has a significant impact on student's feelings of acceptance and inclusion. If we do not see academics that look like us, it makes us feel unwanted, invisible, excluded, disempowered, and most importantly like outsiders (and outlanders). This skewed representation and diversity simply does not reflect society, the workforce or the people we will work with (in some areas). The stifled opportunities for anti-racist social work teaching (as a result of these factors) are critical in judging whether social work can truly call itself an anti-racist profession that promotes social justice and tackles inequalities.

Whilst anti-racism in social work should be embedded within the entire social work curriculum, we must also recognise what anti-racist social work does not do. Anti-racist social work has an essential focus on the unique experiences of ethnic minority people. This allows for an exploration of systemic and institutional structures that oppress and disempower ethnic minority groups based on their race, as well as individual experiences of racism from colleagues, peers, and service-users. Therefore, anti-racism is a critical movement to identify and challenge these experiences and amplify the importance of taking action to combat these, in order to reduce and remove the experiences of racism, on individual, personal and structural levels.

However, anti-racism does not take a person-centred approach in seeing people as complex people with multi-layered and multidimensional experiences of oppression, power, disadvantage, and privilege. With a focus on the experiences of racism, which is essential, this fails to acknowledge the intersectional experiences of people and their multiple oppressions. For example, a black person may experience racism as a form of oppression, and a woman may experience sexism as a form of oppression: therefore, a black woman experiences a multi-layered form of oppression with both racism and sexism combined, which consequently increases the negative impacts that these forms of oppression have on black women.

Similarly, people also experience a complex relationship between power, privilege, disadvantage, and oppression. For example, an Asian cisgender male may experience racism, however an Asian transgender male will experience an added layer of oppression through transphobia. Therefore, an Asian cisgender male has power and privilege by not experiencing transphobia, whereas an Asian transgender male will have a multi-layered experience of oppression. However, an Asian male will not hold this same power and privilege over a White British male, who will not experience racism, or transphobia.

This becomes more complex and difficult to conceptualise when we compare an Asian, cisgender, male, with a White British, transgender, male. This is because both of these people will experience both power and privilege, but also disadvantage and oppression, depending on different contexts. Does anti-racism address these complex experiences of oppression and power in different contexts?

Anti-racism can achieve a complete dismantling of racist structures and racism for ethnic minorities; however, a black woman will still experience sexism, and an Asian transgender male will still experience transphobia.

Social work should be striving to be more person-centred through seeing people with an understanding of complex, multiple identities and intersectional experiences of power, oppression, privilege, and disadvantage, which is ever-changing in a variety of contexts and due to a variety of factors.

Overall, anti-racist social work provides an essential, crucial, and important role in improving the experiences of ethnic minority social workers, service-users and students. This importance must be equal in social work education, and social work students must receive teaching and learning opportunities from a social work curriculum that integrates anti-racism. However, we must also begin to explore the importance of person-centred, holistic and intersectional approaches in social work when it comes to oppression. Unfortunately, 'anti-oppressive social work' has many limitations and the way this is used in practice and in education has little value in exploring the complex experiences of power, oppression, privilege, and disadvantage.

We hope to continue these conversations and strengthen our drive to re-imagine anti-oppressive social work through an intersectional lens that understands, explores and amplifies the importance of multi-dimensional and multi-layered experiences of power, oppression, privilege and disadvantage through key social work values of social justice, equality, and human rights.

Black male suicide, a ticking 'time bomb': personal reflections and considerations for suicide awareness and prevention

- Dr Jean Dillon

My Personal Story

I'm of African-Caribbean/Mixed Heritage. I have worked as a Mental Health Act Manager and Social Work Lecturer for over 20 years.

My beautiful son, Brett, took his own life in 2019. It came as a total shock to me. He had accepted help with the issues he was grappling with and was due to start a great new job. On the surface things seemed to be getting better for him. He said he was 'fine' when I spoke to him the night before his death.

How did this happen? I know about these things, don't I? Surely, I would have seen the signs? Can we ever really know how bad a person is feeling? *These are the heart-breaking paradoxes associated with suicide.*

Statistics

- The suicide rate for men in England and Wales in 2019 was the highest for two decades (ONS, 2020).
- There is a paucity of data on rates of suicide by ethnicity. The ONS are "limited to what is recorded on the death certificate and information provided by the Coroner, and this does not include ethnicity" (ONS, 2020).
- Black men are disproportionally more likely to be diagnosed with a serious mental illness (Care Quality Commission, 2010; MHF, (No date); Mind (No date).

- In the context of the COVID-19 Pandemic, "as of the end of June, one in ten people in the UK reported having had suicidal thoughts or feelings in the past two weeks, and in certain disadvantaged groups there are even higher proportions of people with suicidal thoughts and feelings" (MHF, 2020).

Black male suicide is a Ticking time-bomb: key contributory factors

- **Notions of masculinity and negative stereotypes.** 'The strong black man' and phrases like 'man-up'. Such notions may go back to slavery when black men were forced for survival purposes to suppress their sorrow and rage = ***mortification of the self and the soul.*** Negative stereotyping may also include a focus on outward appearances by mental health professionals, resulting in a failure to recognise when black men are at acute risk of suicide. For example, when my son presented at Accident & Emergency he was observed by the Health Care Professional who saw him, who stated in his report to the Coroner, that Brett was '*smartly dressed*'.
- **The impact of microaggressions linked to racism.** As a result of the BLM social movement, there is a greater recognition among White people of the internalised pain, associated microaggressions, and trauma linked to racism. For black men this typically starts in early childhood (The Swann Report, 1985) and can be triggered across the life course by stressful life events/ vulnerability factors such as relationship problems, substance misuse, work pressures, and more recently, worries linked to the COVID-19 pandemic.
- **Stigma and mistrust of mental health services** can result in black men's denial of self, a sense of shame, being guarded, distancing and deflecting behaviour

towards others when they express concern, and a reluctance to seek or access support. Manifestly, the potential for ***a dangerous withdrawal into self*** (Dillon, 1999; Mind no date).

Recommendations

- Data on the rates of suicide by ethnicity to be collated by the NHS and the Coroner's Office and included in national statistics.
- The development of 'culturally competent' risk assessment tools and interventions. These should be underpinned by a recognition that black men may present differently when at acute risk of suicide.
- Continued awareness-raising of black male mental health to help minimise stigma among different communities, to build trust in health care services/ professionals and to encourage access to mental health services.
- Suicide awareness initiatives such as: the One Life Lost is Enough (OLLIE) Foundation, a suicide awareness/ prevention charity. *The Brett Movement* is an initiative set up in honour of my son in 2019; it focusses on barber shops and gyms with the aim of looking out for signs of mental distress among black men, encouraging them to talk and signposting them to relevant services and support.
- More informal support initiatives for black men e.g. the Tuesday Club which my son attended involves black men meeting informally on a weekly basis, cooking Caribbean food together and, essentially, talking and sharing how they are feeling.

References

Dillon, J. (1999) *St. Albans African Caribbean Group Under Tens Survey*, The St Albans and District Early Years Development and Childcare Partnership.

Mental Health Foundation (2020) Coronavirus: *The divergence of mental health experiences during the pandemic: https://www.mentalhealth.org.uk/coronavirus/divergence-mental-health-experiences-during-pandemic*

Mental Health Foundation (no date) *Black, Asian and Minority Ethnic (BAME) communities: https://www.mentalhealth.org.uk/a-to-z/b/black-asian-and-minority-ethnic-bame-communities*

Mind (no date) *Working with young Black men: https://www.mind.org.uk/about-us/our-policy-work/equality-and-human-rights/young-black-men/*

National Mental Health Development Unit (2010) *Count Me In: 2010 Results of the 2010 national census of inpatients and patients on supervised community treatment in mental health and learning disability services in England and Wales*, London: Care Quality Care Commission.

Office for National Statistics (2020) *Registered deaths in England and Wales from suicide analysed by sex, age, area: https://www.ons.gov.uk/peoplepopulationandcommunity/birthsdeathsandmarriages/deaths/bulletins/suicidesintheunitedkingdom/2019registrations#:~:text=1.-,Main%20points,back%20to%20the*

The Swann Report (1985) *Education for All: Report of the Committee of Enquiry into the Education of Children from Ethnic Minority Groups*, London: Her Majesty's Stationery Office.

Power, trust and race

- Eddie Dube

Throughout my career as a social worker, I have worked in situations where trust is weak or entirely absent. This could be due to negative past experiences at the hands of social services such as perceived over-intrusion, a negative representation of social services in the media or historic abuse of power by the powerful.

Mistrust can also be rooted in history, such as the prejudices and injustices experienced by people of colour.

History matters – it is part of the bigger picture that shapes who we are. My lecturer used to remind us to always look at that bigger picture and avoid focusing solely on our own individual perspective - which can make us see only what we want to see and reinforce what we already believe.

History matters – it's part of the bigger picture that shapes who we are

It is that bigger picture that I want us to look at to help us understand what happened in 2020: the COVID-19 pandemic and the murder of George Floyd by police in America.

A Public Health England report found that Black, Asian and other minority ethnic people (BAME – a term I dislike for the way it stereotypes a hugely varied group of people) have been disproportionally affected by COVID-19, with death rates higher among people from those communities than any other ethnic group. The report pointed out that "...racism and discrimination suffered by Britain`s Black, Asian and minority ethnic people contributed to higher death rates from COVID-19 in those communities".

The Guardian reported that: "...racism and discrimination experienced by BAME key workers is a root cause affecting health and exposure to risk. For BAME communities, lack of trust of NHS services resulted in reluctance to seek care". Why is there a lack of trust in NHS services by people from these communities, when quite a large percentage of them work for the NHS in frontline roles? Is the report alluding to racial discrimination by the NHS, either in the form of institutional or organisational racism?

What is racism, anyway? For black people, it traces back to the slave trade, which justified its cruelties with a mixture of pseudo-science and negative stereotypes. The dehumanisation suffered by black people during the slave trade is part of our shared history and has unavoidably shaped our modern world.

But something being normal does not make it healthy, or right, nor does it mean we have to accept it

It might be unnoticeable to some, but it is there, passed down through generations like a family heirloom, or like a statue on a street - which we do not really notice or question because it's always been there. It feels normal to us that it is there.

But something being normal does not make it healthy, or right, nor does it mean we have to accept it. One of the most striking features of our shared history of racial discrimination was how *normal* it was. Almost everyone thought this way and black people were expected to accept it. These social norms have always been shaped by those who have power and want to keep it – it was the case during the slave trade, it was the case after our emancipation and is still the case now.

What made George Floyd different was that we saw him

Recent news reveals that the slave trade is still alive and well and is closer to home than we all care to admit. Many of us are unknowingly wearing clothes or using technology that are the end products of a supply chain which relies on exploitation and/or child labour.

Modern-day slavery surrounds us, and its victims live invisibly among us – serving our food, picking our crops and working in factories. From the outside, these people seem to have normal jobs, but behind closed doors they are exploited for personal gain, forced into debt and in some cases threatened with violence. The old slaveowner mentality never went away, it just evolved.

What made George Floyd different was that we ***saw*** him. The death of a man, captured on video in real time, at the mercy of someone who should be a protector, was a massive wake up call for us all. The murder of George Floyd refocused the spotlight on the power of the police. Why are black people so over-represented in the justice system, prisons, stop and search, not to mention COVID-19 deaths and unemployment?

The numbers might have something to do with the way black people have been portrayed: as animals, uncontrollable, criminally minded and dangerous.

As long as we are defined by our race and ethnicity, inequality and injustice will continue

Because of this, more black people are handcuffed by the police in the very first instance. The negative portrayal of black people has fractured our society, creating an 'us and them' mentality which thrives on mistrust.

What can we do about all of this? Laws and legislation which make discrimination illegal will take us part of the way, but it will depend on political willingness to apply them. Dr Martin Luther King Jr said: "*The law cannot change the heart but can restrain the heartless.*" So, we need more than just the law – we need systems that promote social justice and humanity. We need to start challenging ideas which keep us in bondage. As long as we are defined by our race and ethnicity, inequality and injustice will continue.

A new social contract is needed to build trust between black people, the state and its systems. State institutions need to start building trusting relationships that eradicate systematic segregation and discrimination - and this needs to happen quickly.

The Ethical Framework for Health and Social Care is a good tool that can be used to rebuild trust across the system. It can be used by the police force, health services, employers and even policy makers. The framework looks at the big picture, which makes it particularly relevant to the current climate - not just in light of COVID-19.

Responding to COVID-19: the ethical framework for adult social care (Department of Health and Social Care)

1. Respect

Recognise that every person and their human rights, personal choices, safety and dignity matters.

2. Reasonableness

Ensure that decisions are rational, fair, practical, and grounded in appropriate processes, available evidence and a clear justification.

3. Minimising Harm

Strive to reduce the amount of physical, psychological, social and economic harm that the outbreak might cause to individuals and communities. In turn, ensure that individual organisations and society as a whole cope with and recover from it to their best ability.

4. Inclusiveness

Ensure that people are given a fair opportunity to understand situations, be included in decisions that affect them, and offer their views and challenge. In turn, decisions and actions should aim to minimise inequalities as much as possible.

5. Accountability

Hold people, and ourselves, to account for how and which decisions are made. In turn, this requires being transparent about why decisions are made and who is responsible for making and communicating them.

6. Flexibility

Be responsive, able, and willing to adapt when faced with changed or new circumstances. It is vital that this principle is applied to the health and care workforce and wider sector, to facilitate agile and collaborative working.

7. Proportionality

Provide support that is proportional to needs and abilities of people, communities and staff, and the benefits and risks that are identified through decision making processes.

8. Community

Commit to get through the outbreak together by supporting one another and strengthening our communities to the best of our ability.

For further advice and guidance on this framework, visit:

https://www.gov.uk/government/publications/COVID-19-ethical-framework-for-adult-social-care/responding-to-COVID-19-the-ethical-framework-for-adult-social-care.

Post-colonialism

- Wayne Reid

My Jamaican grandfather Ernest came to England as an economic migrant (via several other countries) in the late 1950's, as part of the Windrush generation. A generation that was enticed to fill workforce shortages and promised the "streets were paved with gold". Ernest and my grandmother (Gertrude) had 8 children (including my mother). Ernest worked for the local bus service. He began a relationship with a white woman who worked in the canteen and surprisingly left the family home to be with her. Gertrude became terminally ill and died. My mother and her siblings, who were young adolescents at the time, had brief spells in care and then fended for themselves as very young adults in the 1970's. This trauma understandably destabilised them individually and collectively – which disadvantaged their early lives immeasurably in a multitude of ways.

Race and class were the major elements of my childhood. We lived on predominantly White council estate in Sheffield. My parents are private people. My father is as an upholsterer and my mother makes curtains. At the time, they worked long hours - but we were skint. Growing up, we had an anti-social next-door-neighbour who was overtly racist - there were a few altercations – but nothing too serious. Just enough to remind us that we were very much in the minority.

I had a 'privileged' childhood (maybe not in the conventional sense) in that the innocence of youth and the era of 'multi-culturalism' (during the 1990's) allowed me to really 'get to know' how my friends and their families from different socio-economic backgrounds functioned. I had friends who were middle-class, friends who lived in high-rise council flats and everything else in-between. This really helped me to become adaptable and 'culturally competent'. I was the only black guy in my school year, but I refused to let the 'minority mentality' hold me back and accepted I needed to try harder than everyone else. I'm lucky that my environment trained me to succeed.

People would comment on how 'well-spoken' I am, or marvel at my 'cleverness' or being 'super cool', which I have always interpreted as a euphemism for "he's not like them other black kids is he?" I'm sure it is intended to be complimentary on occasions, but sometimes there are indelible undertones of condescending 'post-colonial white privilege'. I still get it as an adult now!

Ernest came back into our lives when I was a young boy - when his new wife had died. He was an old man by then and terminally ill himself. Amazingly, my family forgave him for his past transgressions and supported him for the remainder of his life. I didn't have a particularly close relationship with him, so I never really got to understand his personal journey in life. Ernest would rarely elaborate on his childhood in Jamaica or his life events. Neither of my parents are conversationalists in that regard either. I, therefore, have a limited knowledge of my family history despite my efforts. I learnt about colonialism and slavery from other elders, my peers, books like the ICE-T Opinion, films like Roots and music such as that of the Wu Tang Clan.

I'm now fully aware of how the spectre of colonialism has influenced my life and how the evolution of it continues to impact on my everyday reality. My personal strategy is to combat it with intellect, logic and militancy to educate hearts and minds for future post-colonial generations.

[*This was originally published as an article in Professional Social Work magazine in February* 2020.]

A pledge for social justice

- Sumita Verma

"I look to a day when people will not be judged by the colour of their skin, but by the content of their character" – Martin Luther King Jr.

I was appalled to see the barbaric killing of George Floyd, which broke all limits of cruelty in modern times. Many would argue that these sort of incidents are irregular, although thanks to social media, it caught the attention of the world - and the entire world rallied together in condemning this brutal act. As a consequence of global outrage, the Black Lives Matter Movement gathered momentum to shake up the system and to bring the predicaments of black people to the forefront.

Having chosen the profession of social work, any act of injustice disturbs me to the core and leaves me with a question: '*What kind of gratification do these kind of acts provide to the perpetrators?*' Being a bully to a stranger who doesn't conform to one's preferred skin colour exposes a disturbed mental state ('white psychosis?') Being Asian and having spent considerable periods of time in the USA and UK, I have witnessed and heard of numerous acts of hatred and insanity. Unsurpisingly, these brutal acts are not confined to any specific skin colour. Now it has expanded its wings and many people from diverse ethnicities face unexplained injustice at some point in their life.

Such an evil mindset manifests itself in the ideas of anti-Semitism, anti-Irish prejudices, Islamophobia and nonacceptance of any ethnic minorities - as well as the commonly observed anti-black mindset. This situation reminds me of a quote by Sir Martin Luther King Jr: "Injustice anywhere is a threat to justice everywhere". We must understand that all sections of society are intertwined, and that treating one section as an adversary results in social dysfunction. This is a very dangerous situation that threatens social cohesion. If left unchecked, this perpetuates into a cycle of hate and disharmony in society. It can be represented through the following chart:

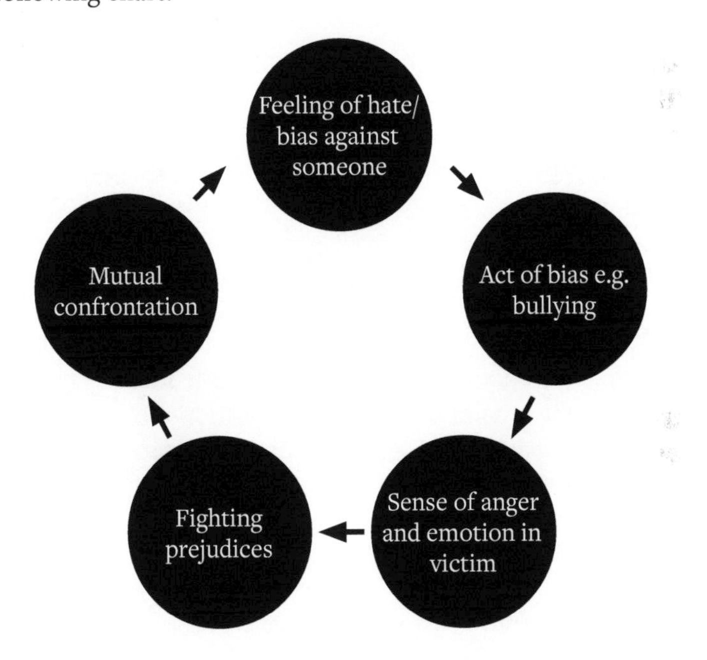

Sadly, many political leaders across the world have taken to divisive politics that endorse delinquent minds to spread hatred. This top-down divisive propaganda should be rejected by global citizens, who should act with maturity in rejecting such vicious leadership. The world has witnessed that in some countries, citizens have chosen inclusive leadership.

Age-old structural and institutional biases are prevalent in today's society. It resonates with the long-standing culture of "white privilege" and the disadvantages experienced by "people of colour". Structural and institutional racism is not restricted to just few organisations and professions. Instead, it has been a prevalent feature of the social, economic and political systems in which we all exist.

This is a very sad state of affairs when less privileged people are deprived of their rights and have to accept injustice as the norm. Creating biases and prejudices widens the gap even further, which translates into a vicious cycle of hate and social division. As someone who is passionate about social causes, I strongly suggest that an egalitarian system should be the mantra for an inclusive society. People should be given equal opportunities in all aspects of their lives and should be evaluated on the basis of merit and not their skin colour.

Coming from an ethnic minority background, I have witnessed racial intolerance in all communities. The tendency, however, is such that we generalise one's behaviour as a representation of the whole community - which is wrong. Our aim should be to treat everyone equally and fairly, rather than seeing them through the prism of race. I strongly believe that by promoting multiculturalism, we can take a step towards a more tolerant and accepting society.

It is crucial to recognise that multiculturalism can challenge oppressive systems and can address the issue of systemic racism. However, after witnessing the global support the Black Lives Matter movement has generated, I am very hopeful that we are heading towards a more just and equal society.

Determined by fortitude to overcome

- Ellah Kandi

I am who I am. I am a black woman. To some this might be a daunting expression, to others it may trigger different emotions and perceptions but despite it all, it does not change the fact that I am who I am. In the United Kingdom (UK) I am identified as 'black'; politically as a black African, culturally as a Pentecostal Christian. In addition, I was an asylum seeker.

Therefore, I am a part of several categories of oppressed groups. As a result of this, I have experienced multiple forms of oppression. Ward, (1991, 2000) suggests that due to the types of oppression being experienced through everyday events by individuals, it is important to offer new ways of "being" and living through developing practices that are empowering.

Masocha and Simpson (2011) argue that social workers are advocates for choice, social justice and autonomy with the desire to ensure that every individual is treated fairly. However, they find themselves working and enforcing decisions in a rather rigid and difficult political environment with a restrictive legislative framework (Humphries, 2004), for example, when supporting asylum seekers and persons from abroad. In the UK, asylum seekers are not allowed to work while claiming asylum or waiting for their status to be granted.

This means that people have no financial freedom and often can only access a limited number of services. I had no shelter, food, money, medical care or access to educational opportunities (despite wanting to). "*I have no hope*". These were the words that continually echoed in my mind. On average, asylum seekers in the UK wait 5 years to get an outcome of their asylum claims (Migration Observatory, 2019) - but I waited 12 years. While I was waiting for my outcome, I began spending my time in an allotment, just to escape and mitigate social isolation.

The voices of the oppressors did not cease. Their words were fierce: "you are not welcome here", "get a life", "don't you have anything better to do", "get an education", "get a job instead of being worthless", "go back to where you come from". These statements repeated until I became numb to them. My long wait to living a free life prompted a lot of questions, such as the length of time it took to process asylum claims. For example, there were reports of suicide attempts made by some individuals I shared accommodation with. This, however, was not a problem affecting only a handful of people. In fact, the Guardian (2018) also mentioned similar patterns found in UK deportation centres.

In the sections that follow, I will give an account of my personal fight for freedom and safety by sharing personal experiences of a BAME social worker; oppressive practices faced by marginalised groups in the UK and the use of empowerment as a tool to overcome challenging situations.

By understanding who we are, as well as having knowledge of our values and beliefs, we will effect change and empower others by rooting out our own internalised patterns of oppression - which can become our anchor. It is important for practitioners to have a sense of empathy, which is crucial as practitioners to seek to change injustice in reality - not just think it.

Social work approaches, for instance anti-oppressive practice, looks at power differentials in society. The Human Rights Act 1998 (article 14) addresses unfair treatment faced by certain groups. This may include black people in general or women of any racial group. As an African woman, I have experienced becoming an introvert as a result of internalising the oppressive experiences I encountered during my immigration process. I had experienced being placed in a jail cell and then moved to different detention centres. At this point in my life, I was disconnected from any form of social relationship which proved to be detrimental for my psychological well-being.

Advocate for the voiceless

Twelve years had passed and finally, the doors to a world filled with hope had been opened to me. I was destined for something great and after my enduring previous experiences; my determination to be a mediator and a type of advocate for the voiceless had become unparalleled. After obtaining my sense of freedom I welcomed the thought that education was the first step that I would take and therefore being even more determined to make that difference I embarked on a journey. One that was riddled with numerous stumbling blocks and hindrances, but at the end of it all, I graduated attaining a BA (Hons) in Social work - a dream come true. The aim was to advocate for those in need of services, being the voice for them that I never had, sharing information, providing a service that meets the needs of people often underpinned by legislation.

During my transitory journey as a social work student, I volunteered with the Chaplaincy team, mentored students at a local high school with the opportunities through the University. Also, I was very active being the University's Gospel Choir coordinator. Every role that I took on saw me having relations with people of varying backgrounds. These roles required that I adhered to the principles of confidentiality, data protection in light of the social work practice. It was imperative that I be open, honest, reliable and fair. I was able to apply my lived experiences, empirical knowledge and the foundations of my life in this role. As I studied to be a social worker and worked in these areas mostly as a volunteer. I learnt ways that demonstrated empathy, perseverance, authority, professional confidence and capability, working with people to enable full participation in discussions and decision making (Professional Standards - Social Work England, 2020).

I had tasted the bitterness of loneliness and homelessness prior to being looked after by a Samaritan family. These impacted me extensively and endowed me even more fervently with compassion for others who experienced the same fate. I had experienced grief and loss, had overcome sickness and through all of these, I was encouraged, and this empowered me to contribute positively to others. I looked for opportunities to make a difference, for example volunteering at a Human Immunodeficiency Virus (HIV) organisation in addition to supporting children with special educational needs. To enable me to communicate with deaf people, I learnt Sign Language to ensure their needs were met and were included in the activities they attended. In doing so, I won the East Midlands signer of the year in 2009. Having had the opportunity to volunteer at an afterschool club, I devoted my time to the children who had special educational needs - which led me to write a book titled 'Read Along and Sign Children's Bible' story book. I included sign language illustrations as I was determined for an inclusive approach within the group and wanted all the children to feel and know they were valued. My determination to cater for the welfare of people led to working with a small team providing meals on Christmas day.

Together with a friend, I had realised that many international students and home students remained on the University campus without family or friends. Evidence showed that a great number of people were extremely lonely, unhappy, and depressed during a time of great cheer and goodwill. Therefore, by hosting Christmas dinners, students and other members of the community got to join together and enjoy the company of each other, creating a community and perhaps a sense of camaraderie. This has become one of the key events in the University that students staying on campus look forward to as they have opportunities for networking and building friendships.

Spiritual Affiliations

My role in the university grew exponentially as my spiritual affiliations were a tower of strength. Considering that I was intent on being a social worker, all leaves of shyness dried up and fell away; I had to quickly bloom in a beacon of confidence. My role as a member and a coordinator of the gospel choir was effective in this. I have become acquainted with a plethora of people from numerous religious and non-religious backgrounds.

I have adopted a sensational amount of confidence, especially stage confidence, having entered a number of successful competitions with the choir. This includes winning the University Gospel Choir of the year 2016, BBC gospel choir of the year runner ups in 2015 and 2016; the choir Gareth's Best in Britain 2016 (East midlands and Wales winners and overall runner up in 2nd place) and being semi-finalists at Britain's Got Talent 2018. Indeed, such activities have assisted in shaping me to be the person I am today. Thus, being a well-rounded individual (who is able to observe with sincerity and impeccable communication skills), I am able to work with various types of people from different, races, ethnicities and social backgrounds.

Through competitions, I have had the honour of gaining the skills in observing people's behaviour and how to relate to each person, transferring these skills in how I complete care needs assessments and mental capacity assessments - according to what I have observed. This enables me to enhance my communication skills. With all this experience that I have had, it has enabled me to go beyond the barriers that were previously imposed in dealing with people of different ethnic groups and backgrounds.

I have attained extensive leadership skills through being a prime member of the choir; exceptionally convenient when dealing with my team and dealing with other professionals in the social work profession. Nevertheless, competitions bore only a minute significance to me being in the choir, even more rewarding was the exposure that I gained of the diverse communities in the UK, and further afield, as far as Jamaica. We toured Jamaica and learnt to appreciate more than the food, sun and sand. I learnt to take heed to the needs of the people, especially within the communities in which I ventured. Hence, I participated in doing some community work, as well as fundraised for resources that were crucial in keeping a 75-year-old school open to continue providing an outstanding education for children within the community. I gradually became more open-minded as my international volunteering and learning experiences took me to the Gambia, Philippines and afforded me a placement in Canada (for an organisation that supported women who experienced domestic violence).

Balm or an Olive branch

I am never one to hide my experiences, and therefore I share them as I am a firm believer that my life and the experiences I have endured can be of help to people. Perhaps a type of balm or an olive branch that can guide them to a better place.

To demonstrate that all things are possible if we only believe, I shared my story of resilience at the first-ever TEDx talk in Leicester 'My Journey' in 2016 and for the first time spoke publicly. The speech was delivered to an audience of people from numerous cultures. Through my story, I was able to give hope to so many who were affected as immigrants and who were also seeking a way to deal with their situation at hand.

This intertwines with my role as a social worker, as it is my duty to ensure that those who I serve are empowered and encouraged to attain the confidence that can lead to their independence.

My public speaking engagements expanded, landing me on the stage of the Leicestershire Police's Women's Inclusive Network conference in 2017. It was incumbent upon me to express my journey as a woman from an ethnic minority and once a dejected asylum seeker. Nevertheless, my woes had now ended, and the sun now shone brightly as I took my steps to a brighter future and superb prospects. If I could do it, others could too. A mere motherless child who came from Zimbabwe, who would have thought?

This inspired the growth of inter-professional working as my role in working with the police force started here. I was drawn to what the police did in implementing fairness and justice, which are key aspects in social work practice and found myself working with them inter-professionally. We shared a common goal and that was for a better community and society. This was an avenue for information sharing and signposting. I gravitated to this as I realised that with such interprofessional working, I was able to gain a wealth of information. Had I known such information before, it would have been so helpful but unfortunately, it was not the case. Nonetheless, all hope had not been lost as now I can help someone who might find themselves in the same position or worse.

Going Global

As mentioned, I have been part of international projects in Canada, Jamaica, Philippines, and The Gambia. During my undergraduate degree, my dissertation was about people living with HIV and I did not want to leave it on paper. I believed what I wrote and decided to act. In 2021 I will be launching an international charity to look after HIV Aids Orphans in Africa.

Considering that I lost my mother at a young tender age, I understand what it is like to grow without maternal love or needed attachment. My holistic experience that I have gained as a social worker has grafted me into a wholesome individual with so much to give. The charity I will launch is called EL-Kind; EL means God and Kind is kindness, therefore God's kindness. I want to make a difference in the lives of these young people who are often disadvantaged, catering for their needs such as providing medication (as they do not readily have this available like the first world countries). I want to bring hope to the hopeless, love to the loveless.

In essence all this can be explicated in the second verse a traditional song by Jon Cohen :

Make me a channel of your peace

Where there's despair in life, let me bring hope

Where there is darkness, only light

And where there's sadness, ever joy

Victory is mine

In 2019 - 2020 my team with whom I worked as a newly qualified social worker won the team of the year award in Adult Social care. To me this was a jewel added to my crown of victory and a reminder of how far I have come since embarking on my journey to freedom.

My lived experience is an example of how individuals from oppressed groups persevere. Difficult situations often shape us in becoming well-informed experts in empathy, love and care. The reason is that although society at some stage may hurl their self-fulfilling prophecies, seeking to predict our demise, these obstacles can become stepping-stones to success. These are only a few elements of my life that have influenced my decision to be a social worker. Additionally,

I have seen the need for there to be an increase of social workers who are of the black or ethnic minority.

These stories need to be shared with the youth who seek for positive and effective examples of progress. They can find in us, people to emulate. Our society needs advocates for critical consciousness, not afraid to challenge the structures of society around them (Freire, 2002). Black and ethnic minority social workers and the challenges they face have proven to differ widely. These lived experiences act as empowerment tools for the next generation of social workers: ambassadors of human rights, equity, justice, empathy and compassion. This is a mission that will forever be close to my heart.

I am proud to live in Leicester which is rich in diversity. Moreover, I appreciate and respect my profession, as it has led me to work for a local authority that endeavours to have a workforce that reflects the city in which we live. During my master's degree in Health and Community Development, I completed a core module concerning anti-oppressive practice, paying special attention to the Black Lives Matter (BLM) movement. The BLM movement has prompted us all to reflect on racism, and on the role of social work in helping to tackle inequality, ensuring we all uphold the principles: social justice, human rights, shared responsibility, and respect.

Being a member of an award-winning team has been an inspiration to me and I am proud of what our team hold dear. I am a firm believer in delivering diligent service to my community. I uphold positive work ethics, and this is agreed by my manager, who summarised:

"Ellah Kandi has joined the team as a valued member, BAME female, bringing her depth of knowledge and first-hand experiences to share with those around her. Ellah Kandi has demonstrated a clear passion to help address injustice and prejudice in society through the sharing of her first-hand experiences, which offer

a genuine patronal real insight, to her on-going support and guidance to her peers. As a result of the former, Ellah Kandi has helped to challenge stereotypes and offered invaluable learning opportunities for each of us to embrace. Hers is a real history and life story that encapsulates the depth of systemic discrimination and its impact upon the person. Her story reminds us all not only to recognise and value differences across our rich and diverse communities, but to challenge the impact of disadvantage and discrimination.

As a BAME female within the team, Ellah Kandi has helped those around her create a commitment to supporting the wider struggle around systemic racism and inclusivity in social care and beyond. Ellah Kandi has reminded us all that we each have a part to play, to engage and reach those around us more positively, and to remove the stigma and barriers often associated with deep seated prejudices."

For many, BLM may not mean much, but the light that George Floyd's murder shone on the worldwide racial injustices, has served as a painful reminder of the very real struggles that some experience. Struggles that are echoed, in the life experiences of those we know and love. We all need to ask ourselves and explore why this isn't high on our own agendas, at work and in our lives as a whole. I suspect the answer is that we are privileged enough for it not to feel like a need at this stage, but it is a real need that we all need to embrace.

References

Freire, P. (2002) Education for Critical Consciousness. New York.

Humphries, B. (2004) An Unacceptable Role for Social Work: Implementing Immigration Policy. British Journal of Social Work, 34(1), pp.93-107.

Masocha, S. and Simpson, M. (2011) Xenoracism: Towards a Critical Understanding of the Construction of Asylum Seekers and its Implications for Social Work Practice. Practice, 23(1), pp.5-18.

Migration observatory (2019) Migration To The UK: Asylum And Resettled Refugees - Migration Observatory. [online] Available at: <https://migrationobservatory.ox.ac.uk/resources/briefings/migration-to-the-uk-asylum/> [Accessed 20 March 2020].

Social Work England. (2020) Professional Standards - Social Work England. [online] Available at: <https://www.socialworkengland.org.uk/standards/professional-standards/> [Accessed 10 September 2020].

Taylor, D., Walker, P. and Grierson, J. (2020) Revealed: Two Suicide Attempts Every Day In UK Deportation Centres. [online] the Guardian. Available at: <https://www.theguardian.com/uk-news/2018/oct/11/revealed-two-suicide-attempts-every-day-uk-deportation-detention-centres> [Accessed 17 March 2020].

Ward, D. and Mullender, A. (1991) 'Empowerment and Oppression: An Indissoluble Pairing for Contemporary Social Work.' Critical Social Policy.

POETRY

Microaggressions

- Ahmina Akhtar

Your northern accent is so strong,
Have you lived in this country long?
Your name is so hard to say,
Can I just shorten it to A?
Can't you ever take a joke?
That's the problem with your folk.

I look around the room for an ally,
For someone on whom I can rely.
Someone to question why something was said,
To ask what was going on in their head.
But instead it is swept under the rug,
And met with a confused look and a shrug.
Sometimes it's too much to handle alone,
When others' inaction serves just to condone.

If I should respond will I be at risk?
Will I be perceived as being too brisk?
If I respond will it threaten our relationship?
Will my shoulder be seen as having a chip?
If I respond will it lead to a fight?
Will I just be told that I'm too uptight?
If I don't respond will it play on my mind?
Must I always speak as I find?

Responsibility leaves me weary and tired,
Losing all hope and left uninspired.
I tell myself it's okay not to always speak up,
As I know you can't pour from an empty cup.
At least then I can take some time to recharge,
As there's always tomorrow for the issues at large.

System Says...

- Brenda Herbert

System says – Why haven't you done all we told you to do?
Why haven't you achieved it all?
What more do you want?
We've put you in a room.
With your tormentor,
With those who scare you,
And told you what was wrong

World says – But she is trying
She doesn't understand what you are saying
She doesn't know what to do
She cannot speak

System says – But we have told her enough times
Domestic abuse – pfft – that's in the past
Too much dwelling on the past
She needs to get on with things
She's neglecting her children

World says – Where's your curiosity?
Where is the care?
Where is the working together?
Where is the humanity?

System says – But the child! The child!
She can't keep them safe.
And the Dad! The Dad!
He listens, he tries
He's doing so well!

World says – But the Help! The Help!
Where is the help?
Your ear! Your ear!
When will you listen?

System says – Too late, too late,
She didn't speak
She didn't learn
She spent her time in the past
World says – But the abuse, the abu...

System says – Too late, too late
We are going to court...

The African Immigrant

- Bright Mawoko

Hard, cold earth
Cold frozen river, sea and ocean
Wet gusts of wind,
The wasteland of Misery.

The story shall be told
Not by my mouth
But by my feet.

Did I ask whether I was on the move?
To some unknown destination
Whether I would see the walls and the roof
Of my lonesome home on that hill some day?
NO!

I am treading upon burnt-out desires
Stepping upon pieces of shattered dreams
Struggling amidst the debris
Of present "civilisation"
My head has grown bigger than my chest
My belly is fraught with gall.
I will stand up, stretch my stiff back
And stagger on to my unknown destiny.

The story shall best be told
Not by my mouth
But by my feet.

A Day in the Life of a Social Worker

- Elicia May

Eyes open

A commute on your tiptoes, dodging the virus
Meetings. Microsoft Teams. Masks.
Navigate a whirlwind of emotions, get placed on a pedestal, get knocked down, get back up, hold someone's hand, wipe someone's tears, wipe your own tears, wipe your colleague's tears, catch someone's smile, watch them grow, keep someone safe
The little steps, the small wins that keep you afloat
A day punctuated by;

- The to-do list that never ends
- The service-user who takes control of their life
- The government who oppressively tie your hands behind your back

Sip a cocktail of hope, determination and exhaustion
A commute on your tiptoes, dodging the virus

Eyes closed

Listen to Your Heart

- Farrah Khan

There's not enough time said the head to the heart
Heart: take your foot off the pedal, go right back to the start

Head: But what about things, everything and everyone?
Heart: you are just one person,
It will still all get done

Head: what about lists, places and time?
Heart: they will always be there, it will all be fine

Head: what about doing and fixing and all?
Heart: what about listening and caring, they're not small?

Head: How do I change and make it all right?
Heart: You've started the conversation, so there's no real fight

Head: How will I know, that I have got there?
Heart: you'll know when you stop and prioritise your self care

The Immigrant's Child

- Farrah Khan

Connecting to customs far and near
Knowing my path won't be clear
Made to feel like a foreigner here
The immigrant's child

Dressing in colours of the land
Spicing the food at hand
Knowing only I can
The immigrant's child

Valuing opportunity in sight
Believing for all that's right
Never giving up the fight
The immigrant's child

Embracing the wisdom in old
Holding family as gold
Fulfilling duty as told
The immigrant's child

6 Letters

- Jeremiah Johnson

Nigger!
Six letters
Five if you want to make excuses
You know
Subtract the ‘er’
And add the ‘a’
Claim that it’s a term of endearment
But it’ll be back to six when you realise who said it.
A white man in a white van.
Trust me,
Completely unacceptable right?
6 letters
1 word
2 choices
The answer is simple right?
My fists clench, grateful for the tension.
As my anger starts to ebb away at my confusion.
How dare he?
But the jokes on him
As the van stops at the traffic light
Same colour as my eyes
Well not quite
But I’m getting there.
I place my headphones round my neck
Ready to step to the window
He’s conveniently wound up.
I’ve convinced myself that any interaction can only go left from here.
If he apologises, I’m gonna put it on him

He dares to double down, then I'm gonna put it on him.
I've heard about Bermondsey
But I don't care if we're in Bermondsey
This ain't the 80s or the 90s
And my parents didn't slave away in this god forsaken city.
Just for me to accept this.
Conviction charged
I step towards the vehicle
Ready to give the racist
A piece of my mind.
And more.

The jingle of my lanyard
As it presses itself against my chest
Stops me.
I turn it over
Jeremiah
Social worker
There's two children and a teacher
Somewhere across the street
Waiting for my support.
But I'm right to be enraged
I tell myself as confusion ebbs away at my anger.
Am I?
Am I supposed to be a social worker
Before a human?
Aren't supposed to be human before black?
The light turns green

To his certain relief
He speeds away, taking my anger with him
Now I'm left to mull over the irony of being called a nigger, on
Jamaica Road.
Guilt helps me across the road
As my knees buckle under the understanding that
6 letters
1 word
Should lead to at least two choices
But the insidious, hypocritical, illogical
Nature of racism
Will always shift the paradigms
Of power and protection
in favour
of the perpetrator.

Black Lives Matter: No more silence

- *Maureen Mguni*

I write because I'm sad
I write because I can no longer be silent
I'm choking
It hurts
All the pain
I write, not just for George Floyd
I write for every black person
A story of oppression
Generation after generation
I'm weary
I'm overwhelmed
I can't breathe

"It's just the black men" they say
"No one kills the women!"
"So facile" I think
How can you not see
Killing my husband, my son
Killing my brother
Killing my voice
You have killed me...
Your feigned ignorance
Your denial
You shatter every piece of me
Every day
We can't breathe....

‘Protective Factors’

- *Mariah Wilde*

In mental health social work there’s a lot of talk of ‘protective factors’
It’s the strengths in one’s life play, supportive audiences and best actors.

This stage is set for every person with their own scripts to tell
Even I, the professional black worker, have my own story as well.

In a society where my race and gender is scrutinised and marginalised
I still have to empower others, to help *them* grow and realize...

That finding strength and support is a gift every human needs
The best social workers give to others, but also listen and receive

Because the masks I wear to visits these days aren’t the only ones I wear
I have to prioritise self-care because the yokes of racism are ones I bare.

Others that share the same skin as me are over-represented in the system
The stories of unsolicited strength in assessments are too many to even list them.
My hope is that as workers, we truly strengthen and empower each other

Because we need those protective factors too my friends.
Every sister. Every brother.

I know this work isn't easy, but there are also moments that make me light up.
But let's all remember to take care of ourselves, because we can't pour from an empty cup.

The Flames of Racism

- Narinder Sidhu

This racial fire has been burning for far too long, savagely engulfing those that deserve better.

Many watch blindly as the roaring flames of racism consume, exhaust and hide humanity.

I dare to wonder how far the fire will spread, for those who burn there is no comfort, no warmth, no love, no solace.

Those who watch silently, while secretly applauding, feeding this fire, this burning, this mighty destruction.

The pain shall linger and never be erased. Yet there are those who still seek to be healed and be part of your world, your society, your life, your heart.

These are forgiving hearts still struggling to be heard, to be seen, to be valued and simply belong.

Again, all you do is offer more pain, more systems, more barriers, more challenges, more suffering and more oppression.

While the fire grows deep into the forest of humanity, some fight for their future and some for their history.

Your hatred causes the fire to burn more intensely. Selfish greed, destroying our society. We deserve a safe place no longer built on the cruel pain and silence.

Those on fire must now hear our loud voices. Love is always the way, just ask those who have felt it.

Don't light the match, don't ignite more fires. We were born to love but we got lost amidst the fire.

Be our allies and let's put out the fire.

Tainted Dream

- S. Abraham

He tried to bully me from my dream to care
Even though service-users and colleagues would say "you can see a good social worker there."
This is not what he would see. What did he see?
Was it the colour of my skin or my sex?
The fact a mere student would do what she thought best?
What was it about me that made him wish to crush my dream?

Depressed whilst supporting the depressed
Oppressed, but still advocating

Sitting in supervision pandering to the man who had my life in his hands
My dream of social work slipping from my grasp like grains of sand
Sinking into the chair as I hear the words "Yes sir, no sir," roll from my mouth into the ears of yet another white man.
I complained throughout, but no-one would hear, could hear - care
Until that final day when I could get the hell out of there

His desire to crush me thwarted
My dreams of a social work career can now rise
Yet - with a scratch, a dent, a mark on the side
Tainted.

Each of Us Matters

- Sumita Verma

Each one of us matters
I matter, you matter and we matter
Our co-existence matters

The world looks beautiful in colours
So, why paint it in black and white?
Let us make it colourful as we all matter

Biases and prejudices are poisons
They spoil the beautiful fabric of our society
Let us keep that poison away as we all matter

Let us usher in a new world
Where no one has to say, "I can't breathe"
Let us make it a beautiful world where all can breathe
As we all matter

The Forced Silence

- Syra Shakir

What's the difference between you and I
The difference you state is all a lie
Are we not all the same inside?
But it's me you don't sit beside
A stare, a look, a horrid glare
I see it, I feel it; you don't care
And if I shout about my pain
Then all of us have lots to gain
But instead, you shut me down
And tell me just to stop my frown
You call me angry, a troublemaker
Get over it, you're just a faker
Now here I am all alone
Exposed and isolated it's all shown
So, don't speak out and use your voice
I'm too afraid, I have no choice
Be quiet, be silent, enforce the silence
Enforcers will ensure compliance.

Link to video and narrated poem: https://youtu.be/cYqkPcoZSFM

Diversity Acrostic Poem - Working with Diversity & developing Culturally Sensitive Practice in Social Work

- Vivian Okeze-Tirado

Decide to be a culturally sensitive practitioner

Invite people to talk about their cultures, values, beliefs & experiences

Value their history, individuality and differences

Explore clients realities & show curiosity

Reflect upon information & knowledge received

Scrutinise yourself – Personal SWOT analysis (Strengths, Weaknesses, Opportunities & Threats)

Identify strategies to aid your work

Train yourself to treat people / families individually

Yield to culturally sensitive practice

The revolution (A nod to Gil Scott-Heron)

- Wayne Reid

Dear brothers, sisters, allies & comrades

The revolution will not be televised, but it might be viewable on social media,
With footage of wrecking balls demolishing their revered statues - causing mass hysteria

The revolution will not be televised, because it's controlled by stealthy devils,
Devils who are probably quite happy to keep the imagery on the KCMG medals

The revolution will not be televised, but if it is - the spin doctors will try to spin it,
Distorting truths in biased ways and blinding us with 'science' to underpin it

The revolution will not be televised and the oppressors won't be feeling superior,
So, carry yourself with pride my friend, because in your areas you'll no longer be seen as inferior.

The revolution will not be televised, but it will enrich your cultural identity,
It will reveal a spectrum of racists and instantly deplete them of their energy

The revolution will not be televised, but watch those snakes
wriggle as they rattle,
Rattled to the core they will become unscrupulous in the
moral battle

The revolution will not be televised, but the gammons and
Karen's will be visibly outraged,
Perplexed by the surge of the uprising, their decibels will
rise several octaves

The revolution will not be televised, but we'll be free of the
'White privilege' abusers,
With bitter flavouring (and no seasoning), the goose will
finally cook in its own juices.

The revolution will not be televised, when their false reign
is in decline,
A long-standing battle will have been fought and won in
many hearts and many minds

The revolution will not be televised, but it will be
omnipresent when it arrives,
Society will be egalitarian and racial hatred won't survive.

[This poem was originally published in SW2020 COVID-19
Magazine on 14/07/20].

The Journey of an 'Other' to an Integrated Self!

- *Nushra Mansuri*

Growing up with one Brown parent and one White
I thought we were normal until we stepped outside
(**That's when the branding began...**)

The health clinic chided my mum when my sister would not speak
"That's because no English is spoken at home"
(**Lesson learned - diversity isn't good, don't stick out, just be part of a monolithic culture**)

Went to school and dreaded the register being called – I was first in line
The teachers could never get my name right much to everyone's amusement (I just died inside)
(**Internalisation: Angry with my dad- why couldn't he give me an English name so I could fit in?**)

In the playground, I wasn't the only 'other'. My friend D ran up to me upset
They called her chocolate concrete. I said call them rice pudding back
(**Observation: School dinners are now a colour chart!**)

Thought a boy in my class was my friend until he saw me out with my family at the weekend
Greeted me on Monday at the school gates, with "Nushra's dad's a Paki"
(**Impact: No nice warm feeling inside - just more stigma & shame**)

Big sis bought her friend home for tea after school
Next day she told the world we ate our food off the floor
(shades of Anita & me)
Later on she said her mum was in the NF so sister's friend beat her up
Sister now has a reputation as a 'hard girl' and troublemaker
(**Lesson learned – if you fight back, you are deviant**)

Went to friend's house for sleepover at the weekend
Told my family we needed to eat roast dinner on a Sunday and get a dog
Surely then we would belong? Oh wait, my dad doesn't go down the pub...
(**Lesson learned – we will never be the same**)

Same friend took me to join the Guides.
The Leader invited me to tea and changed my name to 'Tina'
(**Is that what Erikson means by identity crisis?**)

I was never 'Tina' - she never existed
(**Is that what they mean by social constructionism?**)

At secondary school, lots of boys shaved their heads and became skins
They looked at us differently the next day and chased us on the way home
(**Lesson learned: We are not safe outside**)

My best friend C from my childhood days followed the crowd
He put a firework through our letterbox which was very loud
(**Lesson learned: We are not safe inside. They tell us to go home but where do people of multiple heritage go?**)

Sister left school & started to apply for jobs
On the form she had to tick a box - White, Black or 'Other'
She crossed them all out and put Eurasian
(**Lesson learned – they don't define us, we do!**)

The beginning of my journey to pride in my identity... self-actualisation here I come ☺

The Lion's Everyday Flex

- Wayne Reid

When the lion roars, he cannot be ignored
Don't get caught in his jaws or swiped by his paws
He needs no applause
When feeding his pride or taking what's yours
He attacks for sport. He attacks with force
It's all normal and natural in the savannah, of course
Dismembering prey and challengers who surface
Warning off scavengers who might want to skirmish
A warrior king that is fearful of none
His strength more powerful than rays of the sun
At the water's edge, some antelope drank
Their tired hooves sank into the muddy riverbank
The prey tried to run, as a lioness crept
She was swift and adept, as her victims leapt
The hunters savaged the preys exposed necks
This is just part of the lion's everyday flex

STORIES

Into the Future

- Asmaat Khan

As I sit here, I scarcely know where to begin. I look around the coffee shop I'm in and let the smell of freshly ground coffee wrap around me like velvet, ebbing and flowing through the air. People sit and talk jovially, oblivious to the grey skies outside that swirl like a vengeful spirit, watching the living with contempt.

It has been 50 years since the Great War. Since then, things have been tricky, and it's been that way for a while. People of colour had begun to believe equality had been achieved, but this was far from the truth. The world had seen a Black president, companies used positive discrimination in their advertising. But people of colour are still being abused by the police. People of colour are still not being hired for senior jobs. People of colour are still more likely to be living in poverty. Things are far from okay.

The deaths and mistreatment of men, women and children at the hands of police officers rose, which had led to the Great War. A deadly virus has wiped out thousands of people across the world. During that time, another Black man died from police brutality. The people had had enough. People broke the pandemic regulations and took to the streets to protest. The initial protests drew no reaction from those in power, so the protests grew in numbers and strength. Looting occurred, which caused the Government to react with violence. Armies and Police forces were mobilised. This led to fighting and the War began with no one really declaring it - it just started. Tribes from the Arab and African worlds took to the fight too - using their military and weaponry.

The Great War lasted a whole year and ended with Black and other minoritised groups being worse off than before the War had started. The Government decided people of colour could not be trusted. Laws were passed forcing anyone 'non-white' into subjugation. Life became very different, anyone of colour in politics had to relinquish their roles and they were replaced with white counterparts. This happened in all sectors of business, healthcare, medicine, law, retail, music and entertainment, teaching and academia. If you were not white you essentially could not work, unless you had a low-level job.

The Government believed anyone of colour could not be trusted, which was fortified by referendums and elections - where it was decided the best thing was for Black and people from ethnic minorities to be stripped of all their rights and privileges. Anyone who was old enough to remember would liken this to history repeating itself. We had fought for our freedom tirelessly for years, freedom from genocide and slavery – only for it to only happen again. No one dared to speak this aloud. To share this kind of thought could mean imprisonment or, at worst, death.

Lists were drawn up of Forbidden Materials, which included: novels, poems, songs, paintings, literature or art of any kind created by anyone of colour that promoted education or equality. It was believed these were best destroyed, as they might embolden people of colour and encourage them to rise up again. Not everything had been destroyed. It was common knowledge that some people still kept books and records that were forbidden, but this was not something people openly discussed. If you quoted, referenced or spoke of any such Forbidden Material you could be imprisoned. If you repeatedly violated the rules you could be executed for insubordination.

I was guilty of this, not so much by choice, but because my daughter had bought them from the Dark Market. My children would be the reason we would be caught one day, I knew it. I had always told them to listen and do as they were told, but they were far too headstrong. Maybe it was my fault.

The Great War had hurt me viscerally and I had spent the subsequent years making my anger known to the point I risked imprisonment. After the Great War, I lost my job as a social worker, managing a team who carried out assessments for children. Instead, I worked as a support worker. That is until I was approached by NASW. The organisation that had previously been BASW (the British Association of Social Workers), but was now renamed to the National Association of Social Workers.

All people of colour employed at BASW had been dismissed and replaced with white counterparts and the organisation strictly followed the new government laws and policies. However, there was news that people of colour were grouping to form a resistance movement and the government was concerned about this. I was offered a role as a social worker with NASW - the first person of colour to be hired since the Great War. It was a great achievement, I knew, because this was a first. Indeed, it was historic. I knew there would be a price to pay as an Asian woman. I knew my colleagues would not like me and I was correct.

On my first day, I walked to the NASW office building tentatively. I looked up to the towering building before me, taking in the glass and iron structure shaped like a needle. The building itself was narrow but grew narrower towards the top until it ended in a point, jutting out oddly into the sky - as if it were piercing the heavens above. As I walked into the building, I noticed everything grew quieter, people stared as if the building were a holy monument I had just intruded upon.

"That's her!"

"That's the one, I told you didn't I?"

"Is she the one they're hiring?"

"What is she?"

"I heard she's just a support worker."

"She's so old, look at her."

Ignoring the whispers, I walked to the reception desk and gave my name.

"Good morning, my name is Nadia Mohammed. I'm here for my first day. I was told to report here. Please can you advise me on where to go?" I was trying not to let it show, but I was nervous - all too aware of my otherness and my colleagues.

The receptionist looked at me with disapproval. I noted how young she looked, a face smooth like flowing milk, no wrinkles at all and skin taut with the firmness of youth. She had to be very young.

"You need to complete this form," she sniffed.

"Right, thank you" I said.

I filled out the form and handed it back before being told to make my way to the 7th floor. I made my way to the lift, continuing to ignore the malevolent whispers hanging in the air like bad spirits. At home, I would tell my family it felt like nazar - evil eye. I knew my daughter would tell me to ignore bad juju, always being so much better than me at being her own person and taking pride in her difference.

When I got to the 7th floor I was greeted by another woman, extremely young again. She wore her sandy blonde curls down. Her pencil dress showcasing her ample assets and her makeup a bit too loud for an office. Her red lips shone brighter than the fires of hell and her blue eyes shone like the sea on a clear, sunny day.

"Hi, you must be Nadia. My name is Emily Jones. Follow me," she ordered in a clipped tone. I followed and listened attentively as she explained she was my manager and explained she was showing me to a cubicle that would be my workspace. We reached the cubicle and I set my bag down, noting the greyness of the cubicle walls and the ancient desktop, desk and chair. Before I could ask anything or thank her, she folded her arms and took a step closer.

"Let me make this clear: I don't care that you were pretty well known in social work before the Great War. You will do as I say, and I'll be monitoring your performance closely. The only reason you're here is because we need someone of colour, as only *one of you can* work with the Unwanted. You will find all their files in a folder on your desktop called Client Names and the paper copies are in a filing cabinet round the corner next to the printer. If you don't understand, ask."

She turned on her heels and left. I was stunned, I knew this was not going to be easy, but I hadn't expected such a frosty reception. I still found it offensive that children of colour were referred to as the Unwanted. After the Great War, many children of colour lost their parents in the fighting. Some families were completely wiped out, but the children had been difficult to rehouse, adopt or foster. People of colour could not earn the threshold required to foster or adopt and anyone white would not take in a child of colour. I shook off the hurt and the frustration and decided to go and make some tea before setting down to the Computer That Time Forgot.

As I let the teabag brew, I heard a voice from behind me.

"You must be Nadia, the new one working with the Unwanteds," a terse female voice said.

I turned and, despite my annoyance flaring up again, I smiled. *Do not let their microaggressions get to you.* "Yes, that's me," I replied politely.

"So where are you from?" she asked.

I loathed this question, knowing exactly where it was going.

"Sheffield, up in Yorkshire"

"No, I mean *really from*? You look Pakistani. You can always tell Pakistanis. I bet you miss it don't you? Miss the streets of Baghdad?"

I was utterly dumbfounded. Was she being serious? Was this a joke? I knew what it was. That ugly beast, rearing its ugly head again when I didn't want it - when I had done nothing to deserve it.

"Erm, well... Baghdad is not in Pakistan. I believe it's in Iraq," I shuffled. I hated this, but I knew to keep quiet. *Do not not let it get to you, do not say anything or everyone will think you're argumentative.* It was commonplace to see a brown woman and label her as problematic.

I turned on my heel and returned to my desk. The day passed in a blur until it was nearly home time before I was re-joined by Emily.

"Hi Nadia, I'm about to leave for the day, but I wanted to give you this new referral. It's urgent, this boy has lost his parents. There are no family members to claim him, but I need you to treat this with discretion," she said. Not one to mince her words or beat around the bush, I noted. Although it was odd that a referral needed such an emphasis on discretion.

"Why is this level of discretion needed? Is there something I need to know?" I enquired.

She shifted her position, not meeting my eyes. There was definitely a wave about to come. No, a torrent. Perhaps, a tsunami.

"The boy is Unwanted. But somehow, he seems to have slipped through the net. I don't know how this happened. If this was leaked to the media, they would have a field day," she massaged her temple. "The boy is a Half Breed. We know his mother was Caribbean, but details on his father are sketchy to say the least. They were Freedom Fighters. Information provided by the Department of Racial Segregation confirms his mother is the daughter of a tribal leader. Yorunda or something I don't know. I don't care either, but I just want you to deal with him and make sure it's quick. Get him off our caseload." With that she turned on her heels and left, small waves rippling in her absence.

I couldn't believe it. I opened the file and studied the face looking back at me. With skin like mocha coffee, with long natural hair, looking like it blew in the wind like the long, elegant branches of a willow tree. I looked at the treasure before me. His innocent dark eyes and full lips curved up in a smile like a cherub. The kind in Italian paintings from a time long gone. Not only was this child Unwanted, but he was a 'Half Breed'. If you were Black or brown it was dangerous enough to keep friends who were not, but it was illegal to have sexual relationships. Half Breed children were seen as outcasts, shunned by all. To add to it the boy was a Yoruba, a detail my colleague had gotten half-right. I ran a finger over the photo, thinking for a second there was a light around the boy's head like a celestial halo. It was not enough to make sure he went to a good home. I had to protect him.

When I returned home, I was greeted by the sound of some kind of remix of Earth, Wind and Fire's 'September' and a Pakistani song I used to know. My children were going to kill us all. I hung up my coat and threw my bag on the floor and entered the living room to see my son and daughter dancing and laughing. I watched as my heart felt heavy, knowing that we would never be able to be ourselves again. Never again would we be able to speak in our mother tongues freely. Never again would we be able to wear the clothes of our ancestors in public again.

I should have stopped the music and shouted at them both for listening to Forbidden Material, but I could not bring myself to stop them expressing themselves.

"So how was work?" my daughter asked. She followed me, kissing my cheek and throwing her arms round me like a warm blanket on a winter's eve. "I know you've had a bad day, because you look sad even when you smile," she added softly.

"You know me so well!" I exclaimed, taking out the remnants of dinner she had cooked.

"Oh, and I've had a bad day as your son is so rude and doesn't respect his elders and hits me and you say nothing. Always take his side," she huffed, rolling her eyes exaggeratedly - clearly for the added dramatic effect.

"I have a boy who's Half Breed," I blurted out. I couldn't help it. I knew my daughter would say nothing. If word got out about this child, there would be riots and fights. After the Great War, no one had given birth to a Half Breed. My daughter had been lucky enough to keep her job as a Police Officer after the Great War, mainly because her knowledge and strategical thinking was unparalleled. She would not breathe a word.

Despite her dark skin, a deep rich brown, like cacao beans after they have been soaking in the sun - the colour left her face.

"Half Breed," she breathed. "Mama, you must keep him safe. You know there are only a few of the Untainted who accept us. This boy needs safety, he needs security. There could be great things destined for him - I can feel it in my bones."

The Other Side of Paradise

- John Mapara

The Chavhanga Primary School was perched at the edge of the mountain, and its zinc roofing sheets glistened in the afternoon sunshine. This school was made up of a few buildings and the tilted boundary fence looked as if it were taking its time to decide on which side it should fall.

A low buzz emanated from the classrooms. Occasionally a curious child tip-toed to the window to look out at the sun and listen to the cicadas. It was spring, and the countryside was painted with the reddish hue of the Musasa trees. In the valley, the smoke could be seen spiralling into the sky as farmers prepared their fields for the coming rainy season.

The clanging bell marked the end of school, and the children stopped whatever they were doing and hastened to the assembly point - where the headmistress was already waiting with a stick in her hand. The young lady was wearing a crimson dress and her hair fluttered in the gentle breeze.

'Good... afternoon... Mrs. Mugano!' The children greeted in unison.

'Good afternoon children. How are you?'

'We... are... very... fine... thank... you!'

'Alright, tomorrow we are doing general work and you should bring your hoes, sickles and slashers. I am sure you all know what will happen to those who don't follow my instructions?'

'Yes... madam!'

'And now – where is Chipo Shiku?'

'I am here... madam!' The girl clad in a threadbare uniform raised her hand.

'That's good, I want to see you after assembly, but everybody else is free to go home now.'

The woman folded her arms and watched the youngsters as they scurried in all directions. Suddenly, her mind was flooded with thoughts about her own experiences at Chavhanga. When she first came, the place had looked so dreary that she had pestered the staffing officer for a transfer to a better school elsewhere. However, after about a month, her anxiety was dispelled, and she started to appreciate the local inhabitants who always seemed to have a smile and a few kind words for her.

In her spare time, the woman enjoyed climbing up the mountain to gather wildflowers and watch the birds hopping from one tree to another. When she reached the summit, she would gaze over at the *Pungwe* River, which coiled like a snake, as it flowed towards the distant sea. It was this river which had given her the confidence to believe that if she worked hard, she could also conquer the obstacles in her path.

A timid cough roused the woman from her reverie, and she asked Chipo to come where she was standing. The headmistress peered at the girl before she asked: 'What did your father say about Selina?'

Chipo looked down and scratched on the ground with her toes.

'Will you answer me? When is your sister coming back to school?'

'She... she is no longer staying at home... madam.' the girl finally answered with a wavering voice.

'Oh, God forbid! So, the rumour about her being married is true?'

Chipo sighed and nodded her head.

'When did this marriage take place?'

'It happened on Monday, last week.'

'Do you know the man who married her?'

'Um... not much, except that he is from *Nyafaro*.'

'I cannot believe this! No, this is not possible!' The woman struck her stick on the ground a couple of times. 'When you get home, I want you to tell your father that I will not let him get away with this! You can go now!'

In the forest, the cicadas kept calling and Mrs. Mugano felt as if the insects were pleading with her to rescue Selina. The girl had always taken the first position in her class, but not even once had she boasted about her intelligence to the teacher or her classmates.

On her first arrival, the headmistress was helped by Selina to clean her house and put her things in order. From that day a friendship was established between the two, and Mrs. Mugano often asked the girl for assistance in preparing her favourite traditional dishes like dried mushrooms in peanut butter soup or the bitter tasting Nyevhe.

When they were together, Selina talked a lot about her family - especially how her mother toiled in other peoples' fields to enable her to send her children to school. The headmistress was touched by Selina's tribulations and she encouraged her to persevere in her studies.

'Look, the Grade 7 final examinations are coming up soon and this is your time to show everyone that you are a star destined for great things,' the woman had told Selina on the last day they had interacted together.

Now, as she walked to her house, Mrs. Mugano's mind was in turmoil over what she needed to do.

The rain fell for the first time in a long while that evening. It was a heavy downpour and the room where the woman slept was constantly lit by the glare of lightning followed by thunder so strong that she quivered in her blankets. The storm seemed to have cast a spell upon the headmistress and, the following morning, she was not her usual self when she held a meeting with her staff to discuss Selina.

In her opening remarks, Mrs. Mugano argued that it was imperative for the school to do something to help the girl to continue with her education. Her speech triggered a heated debate that only quietened down when the deputy headmaster stood up to speak.

'My dear colleagues, this is not the first case like this at this school. I think we should just concentrate on the children that we have here, rather than this one who has already gone astray,' the bald-headed man said before sitting down.

Most of the teachers clapped their hands and shouted in agreement: 'You are very right! We are not the police! This is a case for the police!'

The meeting ended in disarray and no further action was taken to find Selina and bring her back to the school.

In the following months, the headmistress continued with her usual duties, but it was not difficult to see that she no longer felt the same zeal as before. A rumour swirled that she had been offered a transfer to another school in town, which was confirmed on the last day of school when a Mazda T-35 truck came to collect her belongings.

The truck driver and his assistant set about lifting the wardrobe, bed, television, radio, bags and other small accessories that a woman cannot do without. A curtain was stealthily drawn in one or two of the surrounding houses, but nobody came out to assist the two men. When they were nearly done, the headmistress went into her house to double-check nothing had been left behind. Then she heard a knock and, when she opened the door, the woman was surprised to find Selina standing outside.

She was wearing a flower-patterned dress with sandals and her hair was neatly plaited into cornrows. The headmistress gazed at her for a couple of minutes and she could not believe that this person, whom she had last seen as a mere child, had now blossomed into a lovely young woman. However, there was something that seemed to trouble her, and her eyes were red from recent weeping.

'Ah, Selina! I was not expecting to see you again!' The headmistress said when she could finally speak.

'I am sorry about what happened... madam. Anyway, I heard that you are leaving this place, and I've come to bid you farewell,' the girl said as she flung herself into the woman's arms.

For a moment, the two remained locked in a tight embrace and the headmistress felt a slight bulge at Selina's abdomen.

'You were so nice to me...' the girl said before breaking into fresh sobs.

'Don't cry, Selina!'

'Okay, I will try not to,' she said wiping off her tears.

When the driver finished covering his trailer, he got in the truck and blew the horn, signalling to his passenger that it was time to go. In the sky, dark clouds had already gathered and there was a growl of thunder.

The headmistress walked to the truck holding Selina's hand and, when she reached for the door, the girl exclaimed: 'Wait a minute! Will you kindly accept this small gift from me?"

'Wow! I don't know how I should thank you, my dear!' The headmistress said as she admired the copper ear rings.

Once again, the driver sounded his horn, but the headmistress ignored him and hugged the girl for one last moment. A few raindrops started falling and the woman finally parted from her former pupil and clambered into the truck.

'Don't lose hope! Goodbye! Goodbye... Selina!'

The vehicle began moving away and, in the rear-view mirror, the girl was seen slumping onto her knees and her silhouette became smaller and smaller until she disappeared from view. The headmistress then closed her eyes thinking about what the future held, not only for Selina - but for all the children of Chavhanga.

Jack and the Dancing Cat

- Mariah Wilde

He told me he had a cat that could dance.

"*I'm sorry?*" I asked politely, not wanting to come across rude but also wanting to entertain the fact that this could absolutely be a revelatory moment for me. An unteachable learning experience on my student social work journey.

I was sat in his crowded living room that seemed like the back of an auction house or collector's museum. Relics from a former life enclosed in on us like a ceiling of trees in the middle of a lonely forest.

Tall cuts of wood with splintering edges from unfinished DIY projects, the birdsong of records that were never played, on the 80s turntable - harking back to unsung DJ dreams. Light peeping through thick patterned glass tumblers, that had collected dust and never met the lips of dinner party guests.

Jack was a chronic hoarder who barely left the house, but the light of his world was his cat. It spurred him to get out of bed once a week to buy it food. In turn, caring for this living being fed *him* with a warm flame of hope. He had taught it tricks, including how to 'dance' on its hind legs and play fetch.

Videos.

Pictures.

Demonstrations.

...And several allergy sneezes later,

I had seen just about every trick he had trained his cat to do, and in the process, learnt about how Jack's mental health had impacted his life. Together, we imagined audacious dreams about how his life could look radically different in the future. A future where *he* was the professional and the expert. Where he wrote the prescription for his own happiness.

Jack once had a wonderful life with a partner and a successful carpentry business but felt a gaping hole in his stomach the day he found out he had lost it all. He filled that void with alcohol and retreated from the world to that very living room I was sat in on the day he told me he had a cat that could dance.

I remember feeling sad reflecting on what I knew to be true - that the rates of people accessing mental health services with additional substance misuse issues are high. That this combination creates a strong cocktail of challenges in systems with soberingly tight thresholds.

Dual diagnosis

Dual categories

One human yearning for more than these restrictions.

But in sharing those challenges and darkest moments, we mapped out a trail to get out of that lonely forest and into the light of day. I walked with Jack in his path to getting psychological help, practical support with housing and benefits, and together we fought for his human rights, where barriers seemed to block the journey we were navigating.

From that lonely forest, he transitioned to working with a community of volunteers in a garden allotment. He used his carpentry skills to create beautiful benches under a tree in the heart of a community garden, for his comrades to find shade under in the summer. He created artwork that was exhibited in local shows, poetry he read before audiences and lived out his lifelong dreams of going on holiday with estranged family members. Most importantly though, Jack reconciled old wounds and was reacquainted with past versions of himself.

I'll never forget the last words he said when we came to the end of our work.

"No one would know the struggles I was going through.

Such dark times.

It felt like waking up and every day was cloudy.

Life was one big cloudy day, but since we've been working together it's beginning to feel like sunshine.

I still get cloudy days Mariah, but now I see the shapes in the clouds. I deal with the changing weathers better."

Jack had changed, but in knowing him, his journey, and remembering his 'Cat that could dance' I had changed and grown too.

Memories and lessons from practice (a window into my heart)

- *Shabnam Ahmed*

I will be sharing four short stories, three inspired by my early practice and one by current practice. I never knew when I started writing these stories that they would ever be shared with the world, but I just knew that I had to write. I want to share something which describes my state when I write. In the musical *Hamilton*, there is a lyric, "Why do you write like you're running out of my time?" I resonate with this lyric deeply as this is exactly how I feel when I write. There is a warm feeling that comes from nowhere, my heart starts beating rapidly and I write, often in the notes section of my phone. Ten, fifteen minutes later, I have something to share. I am even more shocked when this is accepted for print! These stories have been written in the same state described above, like I am, somehow, running out of time.

The first three stories take me back over 20 years, when as a young Muslim woman, I embarked on my adventure to become a social worker. I like to refer to it as an adventure, as my mind has travelled extensively through the people I have worked with. I have grown from being a young graduate to approaching mid-age and many of the residents I have walked alongside, have grown with me, but are now in their resting places. A realisation and reflection that growth is usually not easy, from taking our first steps and experiencing falls, to puberty, through to menopause. It reminds me of the metamorphosis of becoming, just as the caterpillar transforms into its new state of existence – "The Butterfly". Unlike the butterfly though, who experiences this growth once, I am on a continuous journey of growth. Social work has given me and continues to give me lessons of life - ones which make me who I am today.

"The Overspill of Lipstick"

Are you intrigued when things are not quite in place? Do you live life with the overwhelming urge to bring order, to battle entropy, like straightening that painting, which is tilting to the left or wanting to disproportionately scream when your partner has left out some ingredients of a salad? Well then you will relate to this story - and understand my pain.

Ms Washington, a beautiful 81-year-old lady, who took her best china out to offer me tea, took hours to choose her outfit on the days I visited. She dressed and spoke like royalty. Her flat was her world, as were all her artefacts within. Everything seemed to be perfect in our relationship, except my constant discomfort with the overspill of her lipstick. I never saw her without her make up. The blue eye shadow on half of her lids, the circular rose blush painted on her cheek bones and then the red glossy lipstick - less on the lips, like it had been smudged while eating - if you know what I mean. I got the urge many times to wipe off the overspill and fill in the empty spaces or point it out as I do when my mum has worn her sweater inside out. What I also really wanted to do was give her a makeover - now that would have been bonding!

You might be pleased (or not) to hear that I never acted on my urges, unlike the time when I pushed a man off the train back to the platform (to save his head being crushed as the doors closed). I will never forget his perplexed gaze as the train moved on. Of course, I wish I had pulled him on the train instead of pushing him out.

The memory of Ms Washington's overspilled lipstick is etched in my mind forever. She was the kind of person where you were happy to delay writing your Transfer Summary report, as a visit to her was a perfect ending to a challenging week. You've all been there no doubt!

Ms Washington taught me two important lessons:

1. The beauty of social work is in relationships. People may need services, but what they really remember is the relationship. No matter if this ends after a few visits or years of connecting.

2. To control my compulsive urge to have everything aligned and orderly (If only temporarily).

Ms Washington sent me a letter when I ended my involvement. She wrote: "Dear Shabnam, I miss you. I have captured some of your energy in a jar and each time I feel a little low, I open the jar and unleash some of that energy into my abode."

This made me weep - firstly out of gratitude, I was extremely grateful for the feedback and secondly, I thought we are all like Ms Washington, drawing parts of our energy from relationships. This is what enables us to continue the cycle of giving and receiving.

In another life Ms Washington and I could have been best friends (Rest in peace).

"The Heart wants what the Heart desires"

This story is from when I was a social work student on my first placement many years ago and needed some de-construction and re-construction.

Never had I experienced sexual advances from the same sex before - and the combined impact of an upbringing where these things were not openly discussed, and battling with truly understanding what anti-discriminatory practice meant at the time - I was indeed a fish out of water!

Something did not feel right when Ms Murphy gazed intently into my eyes and seduced me with compliments. I felt uneasy, and remember thinking: 'Ok maybe she is just a very warm, loving, appreciative lady'. But it did not end here. She began stroking my hand and I cannot repeat here her offer, but by now my internal compass was pointing towards the door. My innocence and ignorance led to such discomfort and dissonance that this felt like the longest and most difficult assessment ever.

I asked Ms Murphy if I could use her toilet and whilst I was in there, the scariest thought ran through my mind: 'What if she locks me in like people do in horror movies?!' I quickly opened the door, she was stood outside, so close to the door I almost fell into an unwanted embrace - whilst thinking: 'Oh no, she heard me pee'.

All I could think of was that I needed to get myself out of there, but this felt difficult as she used my inexperience and naivety against me and held all the power. Her subtle, but manipulative approach had me trapped. I was sure at university we were taught we had all the power and we had to work on redressing this, so why did I feel like the powerless student? After what felt like many hours, I was free.

A few days later I had a very similar experience with a male client I visited, Mr Francis, and there was no difference in my feelings and discomfort.

Mrs Murphy taught me that what I needed to work on was my communication, resilience and confidence. Having the confidence to tell someone that their behaviour is inappropriate and being mindful of your safety is paramount in social work. One should not have to feel guilty or spineless for walking away from a dangerous situation.

I often wonder if I was actually beautiful and irresistible when I started social work or whether, as the title suggests, the heart just wants what the heart desires.

"Scents of Self-neglect"

When I qualified as a social worker, many years ago, I was not fully prepared to enter the dark side that involves covering your shoes with plastic bags and overdosing your scarf with perfume so that you can inhale the fragrance to block out the scents of self-neglect. Those of you who knew me then and know me now, would have noticed my silk blouses and pearls are history!

I recall a tip given to me when I was a student by a social worker who said, "Shabs apply some Vicks to your nostrils; it's the only thing that overpowers the scent of self-neglect." These were indeed wise words and the vicks does work if you are prepared and know about the self-neglect.

I recall my first ever visit to Mr Smith and the fear that entered with me. A carer opened the door to me and my journey through the corridor was reminiscent of a tunnel. The sky-high piles and piles of newspaper along the side of the walls left a narrow space in which to walk through to his living room. The living room reminded me of when I used to visit car boot sales with my father, so many different items, clothing, table lamps, decorations, and boxes full of carrier bags. The only difference was the quantity was far more than I have ever seen on any one stall of a car boot sale. Amidst the chaos, I could not see Mr Smith and when I called out to say hello, I was met with a faint response, "I am here". He was sat on a sofa right in the middle of the room, but the lighting was dim, and his flowery jacket camouflaged him into the flowery sofa. There was an aura of dampness and death, death of an animal perhaps. I attempted to navigate the space that was available and get closer to Mr Smith. As I drew closer, I sensed something run across the floor and my heart was racing, I suspected it to be a mouse. On coming closer to Mr Smith, I immediately caught sight of my dread – the largest dead rat I have ever seen. My instant reaction was a scream! Mr Smith shouted, "What's a matter with you, you stupid girl, you nearly gave me a heart attack. Get out of my house". No matter how many times I apologised, he repeatedly asked me to get out of his house. I scurried through the corridor and left in a hurry, fearful that the piles of newspaper in the corridor would fall on top of me and I would be buried under them. No one would find me as I had not written in my work calendar who I was visiting. That whole evening and night the scent of the self-neglect and dead rat stayed in the base of my nostrils.

I learnt though, that whilst my experience of the scent is short lived, the image of the self-neglect lingers and the curiosity of how best to support those that consume their life with it became an area of extreme interest for me. I knew that the best way for me to learn and grow in this area was to seek opportunities to work alongside people who were in some way self-neglecting, including hoarding. This caused me some discomfort, but in order to challenge myself I secretly started to request allocations, where there was an indication of self-neglect. Simultaneously I supported my learning by engaging with the research findings on self–neglect that Professor Michael Preston-Shoot and other researchers had undertaken. I learnt a lot through applying an evidence base, hands on experience, facing my fear and most of all through the relationships I built. Working alongside people who self-neglect requires patience and the ability to leave your judgements at the door and engage in a relational way.

I noticed that I was not alone in my fear when working with self-neglect and hoarding concerns and this was quite common across several services. I worked to overcome my fear and after some dedication and practice became quite skilled in this area of work. I then wanted to support my colleagues through their fear and I have done this through providing training in this area and developing a self-neglect checklist when working with people who self-neglect and hoard as a reminder to ensure key messages and learning from evidence underpins practice.

The scents of self-neglect will always stay with me from my time in social work, but instead of judging and othering, I now know that there is a unique story which unfolds behind each individual and it is those stories that I will always remember. Sadly, I never did find out Mr Smith's story, but I was privileged to get insights into many others.

REFLECTIONS

Muco-epidermoid carcinoma and I surviving the pandemic - A social worker's reflection

- Irine Mano

The letter which would mark the beginning of the rest of my life had come through the post whilst I was at work, in early July 2019. I read it with mild concern and pondered on its contents briefly, specifically the line below.

"The blood tests revealed that you have irregular blood cells which will need to be further investigated. Please make a further appointment so that a consultant can discuss with you in more detail"

Little did I know at the time, but the contents of this letter would impact me and my family significantly. I identified strategies that would help me manage the time in-between receiving this letter and actually meeting the consultant who would talk me through the contents as advised. Safe to say that talking therapies with the partner really helped me at this stage as he was acutely aware of the intermittent pain I had been experiencing in my chest and throat area for a few years prior to this point. Only earlier in the year had it been identified that I had a Vitamin D deficiency. This deficiency was attributed to the chest pain. The GP had explained that Vitamin D deficiency was common for a lot of adults who had most of their childhood growing up in Africa, like myself, and it was due to the lack of consistent sunny weather conditions in the UK which triggered the deficiency. Recent pains had warranted further investigation.

A tinge of anxiety and worry gripped me as being a qualified social worker, I am confident to manage risky situations as long as I am aware of what the actual risk is. In this case, it was a waiting game and the fear of the unknown gripped me for an instance, until I shook this off because I was aware too that this could ground me. As a mother of 2 teenagers, a partner and employed full-time as a lecturer in social work, there was no time to waste thinking about the unknown! Surely if this was a serious matter then they would have made an appointment for me urgently. I comforted myself and went about planning the rest of the days ahead and secured a meeting with the consultant as advised.

The day of the meeting came, and I attended by myself, as I had no inclination at this stage of the news that awaited me. The consultant looked at me with concern and verbalised that they had hoped I would come with someone. It was then that I knew something serious was happening. The bombshell was given to me in the most sensitive way possible, but yet this did not change the news they had just told me. I had muco-epidermoid carcinoma, a rare type of cancer of the salivary glands. The big C-word! Directed at me? Why me, why now, how – were all questions that swept through my mind. How come no one had told me during investigations that they were testing for cancer?

Needless to say, I cried out of despair, but knew simultaneously too that I had to be strong to come out of this. My life as I knew and loved would be changing and I would be the best resource to help me through it. I kept referring myself back to social work practice and how I would deliver difficult news to service-users. This calmed me down as I identified that the consultant was trying his best to make me comfortable. He even asked if he could hug me. Of course, I said yes as I sobbed away. I gratefully received this hug as a genuine show of empathy and emotion. Who said doctors cannot hug their patients? I was not just a statistic to him. He realised that I was by myself. Hearing the most awful news I was unprepared for; he established a rapport and built a professional relationship with me. This resonated with my social work knowledge and experiences. The good news was that my cancer had been caught early and my treatment plan would be on the curative pathway.

I questioned whether being black, aligned to the Vitamin D deficiency contributed to this diagnosis. Research suggests that women with low levels of vitamin D have a higher risk of developing breast cancer, same as development of prostate cancer in men. All the consultant was able to advise was that this was a very rare type of cancer and even more rare that I had been diagnosed with it as a black African female. Further reading around and research from cancer research UK reported that white males are more commonly diagnosed with muco-epidermoid carcinoma. Up to 720 people are diagnosed each year, less than a percentage of the UK population which stood at 67, 886, 011 in June 2020 according to the UN. I questioned what the chances were that I would be among those diagnosed. A stroke of bad luck huh!

It did not take me long to realise after receiving this news that I had to research all I could to maximise my chances of understanding what I was now faced with and increase my chances of coming out of it successfully.

As social work practitioners, we value working in partnership with those individuals accessing our services and how their voice needs to be promoted in decisions about their care. Knowing this, I found myself at a loss as I did not have adequate medical knowledge and found it difficult to contribute to decisions about my care appropriately, although I was asked all the way through. I queried whether some of the questions were tokenistic, as surely they knew I wasn't a medic. I wondered whether I had made service-users feel like this too during my own social work practice.

Due to a lack of knowledge, I relied more on the consultant team to guide me in making the best decision for my care. I remember being asked if I agreed with the proposed treatment plan - surgery to remove the cancer cells followed by intensive radio or chemotherapy or a combination of both if needed. I agreed with it on the basis of trust in their expertise. My life was really in their hands. Although the option of choice was given for me to reject treatment and seek a second opinion, I was also advised that I needed to make a decision soon in case the cancer spread so we had to move quickly. I could not waste any time and agreed with the treatment plan proposed. Subconsciously, I asked myself if I was making the decision under pressure. Then again, I felt reassured by the information I was given, and felt confident I was doing the best I could to maximise successful treatment. Is this how some of the individuals I have supported as a social worker also felt when faced with difficult decisions? I could only hope that the professional relationships I built with them helped them feel able to talk to me openly about their worries.

After each meeting, I researched the medical language that was used in order to fully understand and make sense of what would have been discussed. Then I would follow up with questions to the lead consultant or my designated Macmillan nurse. This gave me a sense of emancipation throughout the whole process. Thankfully, I have wireless broadband in my home and could use my research skills as an academic to gather further information and develop my knowledge about the diagnosis and the illness itself.

The research also helped me to formulate questions that would help frame my understanding of the prognosis as well. This process in itself heightened my empathy skills as a social worker because I understood from experience the importance of sharing information, policies, processes and potential outcomes with service-users to enable them to make informed decisions. In turn, researching also gave me hope and a reassurance that the consultants were doing all they could to help me. I had direct access to my treatment team via mobile and having access to the team settled my anxieties. Still, I queried myself how this would have been had I been a different person, perhaps one with limited access to internet, unstable job or with limited research skills. I often reflect how my situation may have turned out different. I will never forget the words when they told me:

"We are going to do everything we can to help you, but we are going to need you in this process because no matter what we do if you give up on us, there is not much we can do. You have to trust that we can help you and remain positive"

As individuals we hold multiple identities which overlap. When I heard this statement, I was the patient and it resonated with me that I needed to remain courageous to see myself through this. I had to trust the medical professionals helping me and feel able to question or challenge their views. The added layer to my identity was that I am a mother, and my children became a motivation for me to fight this even more so that I could give myself maximum chance of making more memories with them.

This was like how I felt with my partner too, although I also looked for additional emotional and physical support from him, whilst also exuding positivity (as much as I could), so that I would not bring his morale down due to this diagnosis weighing down on both of us.

I was then a daughter, a sibling and a friend; the most important relationships which helped me through this journey. I was reminded of systems theory and how these different categories of love and friendship interconnected to build what I call my 'framework of support'.

I also had a different identity, as a lecturer, for many black students who looked at me as a source of guidance in their social work studies and colleagues who looked for my contributions in the wider teaching team. I was fairly young at the time of diagnosis at 39 years old. Hence I could see the different sections of my life and how they impacted and contributed to my wellbeing. I consistently wondered, and still do, whether being black was a factor in my diagnosis. I think so, based on my own research, but this question has never been answered as the cause has never been detected, common with most cases of muco-epidermoid carcinoma.

During my recovery and phased return to work, in February 2020, Coronavirus cases were on the rise in UK and in March 2020 the UK went into lockdown. By November 2020, I had lost 2 close relatives and a friend to COVID-19 and experienced grief and loss. At the same time, I also had to adjust to my own recovery process after the neck dissection. The neck dissection left me with additional support needs that I had not considered fully in my recovery plan. The main goal really had been to stay alive!

Therefore, it came as a shock losing strength in my right hand. The right side neck and shoulder consistently requires physiotherapy to encourage flexibility and reduce stiffness. My neck dissection was on the right side and of course I had to be right handed too! Almost overnight, I found myself with a disability that did not quite fit the current definition under Equality Act 2010 of a disability, but nonetheless limited me regularly in my work and everyday life. Being a social worker, I was left questioning what else could be done in practice settings for individuals who may find themselves in similar circumstances, particularly when resources are limited. The answer has been to continue the conversation for seeking support and ensure the continuation of advocacy services where there are needs not met.

Although I knew that I was deserving of more support to help me work in my home during the pandemic (whilst navigating new health needs), I could not help but think of people more deserving of additional support more than me. I was actually thankful that I had a job, when so many other colleagues I know were either on furlough, shielding or had been made redundant. This in turn heightened my sense of gratitude that I had survived cancer surgery and neither radiotherapy nor chemotherapy was needed after the surgery - as the cancer had been completely removed.

I was still standing when many others in the country including 3 close loved ones, were losing lives because of COVID-19. I found myself going through the motions of grief and loss, yet this was also mixed with the worries of catching the virus myself and fear of loved ones catching the virus too - particularly those on the frontline. On the flipside, life had to carry on with work and parental duties taking priority. I know that I am not alone in this either, the whole country continues to face different challenges.

In my family, many are doctors, nurses and social workers and for most, they continue working throughout the lockdowns; navigating the challenges of adequate PPE and workloads that keeps increasing due to the unprecedented times the whole world is living in. *'At least I am able to work from home'* I always tell myself, but this also leaves me with mixed emotions.

I am thankful to be alive, yet also anxious of what would happen if I was to catch COVID-19 myself. Then I revert back to being thankful again because I remember the family members deceased because of COVID-19 and the cycle of emotion revolves. For me, recovery includes regular exercise, however gyms are closed and when I go out for exercise, I worry about catching the virus. I sometimes become anxious about leaving the house, which I connect to as my safe space even more now. I am acutely aware, however, that I cannot let the fear stop me from living - but it is a tough balancing act. At the point COVID-19 became a pandemic, I was advised that I needed to work from home and not expose myself to the risks of it, as I am now at high-risk by virtue of recovering from cancer. The most challenging aspect of this is framing my mind to accept the new me after surgery - with the additional support needs that I now have.

Overall, I believe this is crucial time where individuals' personal experiences need to be balanced with the professional expectations and compassionate support and supervision offered to help social workers. Research identifies how black people are discriminated against and face racism and oppression. This automatically indicates an added layer of needs for black people during this pandemic that cannot be ignored. For me, the significance of relationship-based practice is pertinent because it offers the opportunity for dialogue, thereby promoting anti-racist practice when working with black people.

The care and support that I received during my treatment and subsequent recovery, which I was involved in throughout, helped me to develop a sense of confidence in the treatment plan. It is pertinent to maintain transparent and honest lines of communication with service-users. Family and/or networks of support must be valued in interventions even more so.

The Comment

- Cosmas Maruta

As a little boy growing on the African plains, enchanted by the exuberance of youth and enveloped by the innocence of childhood, I walk through life with the swagger of one who has diamonds at the soles of their feet. Somewhere in the distance the future is a blur, encased in mystery, adventure and endless possibilities.

The nostalgia lasts until the first year of primary school when a devastating loss makes me a prisoner to grief, and captive to the ensuing trauma, a concept unheard of in these parts. Doses of tough love are prescribed with paediatric precision from family members when the topic of 'mum' is raised, and I learn from the hurt of others that this is a subject worthy of drawing life out of the people I love and systematically wipes the widest smiles off their once besotted faces.

In a culture where the land of the dead and that of the living is filled with taboos, black-magic, revered witchdoctors, eeriness and mystical existence, conversations around loss are avoided like the plague. Somewhere within my little heart, the fire of yearning for a mother burns so much that it sets my soul alight and places my life into a bewildering tailspin impacting on literally everything I say and do.

As if by chance, there arrives a gift from the heavens or the Gods perhaps. The gift of healing as time would later reveal. I come across the Sonnets by Shakespeare and the Canterbury Tales by Geoffrey Chaucer. Through the beauty of verse and prose I was mesmerised, immersed and captivated by the beauty of the English language and within weeks, I amassed the temerity to create a few rhymes of my own. Nothing resembling Chaucer of course but a stellar effort for a baby-faced novice, if I do say so myself. The archaic English is dense and unforgiving without a translation dictionary, not readily available in these parts, but its complexity is fascinating and enchanting in equal measure. The lack of meaning and deeper understanding does not deter me, I plod on to decipher the diction and the syntax and make sense of the words, which in their natural definitions would mean something completely different in modern day English.

However, to a fresh faced 7-year-old, looking for an escape in expressing deeply rooted familiarly contentious feelings, the fearlessness and desire to break boundaries spurs me on to romance with these tattered publications of these revered authors. I become brazen in the sweet refrain of poetry and before I turn ten, *Little Boy Poet Alomi & Other Poems* has been written on an eclectic mix of pieces of paper, shabbily bound together by thicker khaki outer paper - as if it were a manuscript ready to grace the loftiness of the most prestigious publishing houses on the planet.

Yet this little treasure is filled with renditions of loss and beautiful memories of the past, cradled in the arms of the cornerstone of my life. Captured in beautiful verse and prose are only ever recited to entrusted individuals who would understand the substance in the narrative without passing judgement on the discourse or discussing the nature of the meaning (which was usually hidden, indirect, and brought to life solely by the relationship between the reciter and the listener). My younger sister Tari would become the ever-willing guinea pig and self-appointed critique of the endless renderings of my suffering, free of derision or contrition, which meant she was a safe bouncing board for my disparaging verse and prose rooted in both grief and healing.

After many years of capturing thoughts and feelings, I begin the arduous self-designed healing process to heal from these early childhood burdens. I never forget the lingering feelings brought about by loss and how the need to open channels of listening and helping is paramount to avoid seeing any other child having to rely on the Gods to provide a timeous intervention, characterised by what for me would become a lifelong passion of writing the English language.

This interest in writing would later inadvertently spawn into the most powerful healing. I re-enter the university systems in the United Kingdom having chosen to become a Social Worker to be best placed to offer others support and guide them towards help when they need it. It is during this academic journey that I received 'The Comment.'

I submitted a piece of work for marking and a learned fellow returned the marked paper with a decent enough mark at merit level, accompanied by 'The Comment'. In the feedback section, the learned fellow wrote that my writing style is sometimes "over academic and reaching the point of unnecessary pretentiousness".

The comment cut deep, I had been caught with my defences down, my shield somewhere in the abys of my consciousness and the questions immediately started to flood into my head. What was I meant to do with this comment? How could I improve on my pretentiousness? What did this even mean for a person whose diction and syntax was embodied in his way of being.

The struggles of my childhood came flooding all at once and I felt as small as the Chaucer deciphering little boy, alone in a hurtful world where the reality of pain was enveloped with the failure to find answers to engender healing. I did not see it coming and in the blink of an eye I had been reduced to nothing in a single comment. Who was I kidding? Was I pretending to be English? Was I pretending to be white? Was I pretending to be a scholar; an academic; an equal? Whatever the answers were to these numerous questions I felt unworthy. I felt unwelcome and an undeserving academic, who by the entry requirements of the master's degree I expected to possess the requisite level of English to study at this pre-doctoral level, so being overly academic and pretentious was certainly not an expected comment.

The audacity to challenge this knowing the construction of the university hierarchy and the negative outcomes of black students at university level meant that I had an impossible choice. Grab a lion by the tail or put my head down until I found the recognition worthy of my work. For a student whose language was not based on the 'synonym' function in Microsoft Word, this was more than hurtful. For a few weeks I gave up. I felt betrayed by the defences I had built around me which had let me down. I felt betrayed by my misconception that I was a competent scholar, studying in a safe space at an English university - yet here I was nothing but a pretender.

I was at a crossroads in my studies, do I live by my academic sword and die by this very sword, holding on to my mum's favourite saying that 'If you don't have anything nice to say you should remain silent'? In this regard, I would be inclined to disregard this statement, or should I take this advice (if I can call it that) and deconstruct the very building blocks of my being?

I had been a competent student up until now and felt I owed this to my childhood passion for the English language, my early encounter with Chinua Achebe's '*Things Fall Apart*';

Andrew Marvel's *'To his coy mistress'*; Shimmer Chinodya's *'Harvest of Thorns'* or our local Southern African genius Dambudzo Marechera's powerful and controversial *'House of Hunger'*, but here and now, the seed of doubt had been planted. Its insidious roots had grabbed on my confidence, self-belief, trust in my abilities to mesmerise readers with the beauty of syntax as I shifted through multiple registers, confidently presenting cogent arguments, as one tutor would later comment.

The hypnotic nature of my prose and my mesmeric verse had disappeared into the ether, without a thought that I could recapture the fire that had even made me decide that I could academically compete at this level and even open doors for doctoral study in the future. Who was I to even dream, to dare, a black middle aged man, with children to look after, a wife to love and cherish as ordained by the union of marriage and the two jobs I worked seven days a week while studying for a full time master's degree in social work? Surely, I wasn't worthy. How could I be when I was only pretending?

As I critically reflected further on 'The Comment', I could not place its intention without forming an unsubstantiated opinion of the marker. By giving meaning to the words written and the remits of the tutor – student relationship, I felt strongly that the comment was harsh, uncensored, insensitive and without a doubt lacking in the wider understanding of who I was as a scholar and person. Its implications were far-reaching, as evidently the development of my language was woven into the tapestry of my being and my childhood exploits, which had left an indelible mark on the manner in which I express myself through my trusted prose, verse, diction and syntax. This in turn had allowed me to rid myself of the growing pains and learn valuable lessons about loss, grief and healing.

My redemption came in the later pieces of work where the comments from multiple markers at very high levels of their careers identified that I had a unique and fluid writing style that was captivating to the reader while maintaining academic integrity. Scoring precisely the same distinction mark for the whole of my second-year modules (including my dissertation), secured me an overall Distinction degree and the consistency of the markers in identifying my strengths and weaknesses allowed me to grow through constructive criticism which I could conceivably action. I became a positive statistic, and one that would tip the odds on the norm in terms of mature black students studying competently at this level with multiple responsibilities and competing priorities. Indeed, this could be said for all mature students regardless of colour, race or creed.

This module did not represent my lowest mark on this degree, it merely brought about a quandary which cut across my childhood, identity, confidence, sense of belonging and self-belief as an academic first - and then as a social worker. It questioned my belief that I was capable of offering guidance and support to others from an empathic frame of reference.

The overarching message espoused in this paper is that comments and feedback must be capable of being acted upon. They must be rooted in the rules of fairness and natural justice. Comments must be grounded in guiding and building, regardless of how harsh they maybe, because honesty can harvest transparency and provide an effective reflective space for learners and budding practitioners. Confidence is a very rare commodity for social workers in training and curtailing this already depleted resource does not build the next generation of confident and competent practitioners. Instead, it breeds a crop of workers unsure of their practice, entering a very challenging work environment seeking validation from senior colleagues and from users of services because of their assumed inadequacies, which in-turn could impact on coherent decision-making. Research has shown that when the challenges and realities of practice engulf newly qualified practitioners, especially in their early years, the likelihood that they will crash and burn at a very early stage are high.

If things had not turned out differently for me (as I decided to stick to what I felt I was best suited and sought advice from senior tutors and professors at the institution to improve my learning), I could easily have been one of the quitters or underachievers and a confirmation statistic that black students do not do very well at university.

The results of my assignment following 'The Comment' indicates that I took my eye off the ball with my confidence at an all-time low and this evidence demonstrates the power of words in professional development and mentoring. The final results of my course demonstrate that clear support from dedicated individuals who gave their time outside the university's expectations and the requisite 'pep talks' to boost my much-depleted confidence. I reflect humbly and with gratitude for those that saw something in me that was worthy of pushing to excel - this success and Distinction in my master's degree is for them.

Like I buried the last of my negative emotions working through my grief through verse, prose, diction and syntax, I bury this negativity by rewriting my last poem in my darkest collection from when I was eleven, dedicated to the one who gave me life, my mum:

A Rose

Where I used to lie, now lies a rose,

From the great vines of your sweet dreams, and the oasis of your sweet self.

Petals white, red; petals green, yellow;

Petals that belong to no one but a thorny heart.

I heard they saw you this morning,

Cold as a dog's nose with feet that belonged to no one.

But the rose lay besides your heart,

Singing no monotonous song nor sweet music.

Silent it glanced at you perish.

It saw your halo vanish into the stars,

Beyond the visual performance of its very sight,

Beyond its great zeal to witness your destiny,

Further beyond the pitiful thoughts of a rose.

Can I Speak?

- Anneta Pinto-Young

Can I speak now? Am I now allowed to have an opinion and talk to you about race and prejudice? Am I allowed to tell you what it feels like to be me, to be uniquely different? To experience the subtleties of ignorance and prejudice from people who feel superior to me?

I was nineteen when I first experienced blatant racism in South Africa. To be shouted at in a market by a South African who told me to: "Get out of his presence, to go home and not be around darkening up the place". He only shrunk back and withdrew behind his stall when I said, "Excuse me," and it was apparent from my accent that I was not from there. I was not a black South African, but a tourist who was not about to put up with his tirade.

It was on the same trip when an air host seemed disturbed by my ability to travel, and in an effort to amuse the group of young white females who stood behind him, insulted me and shouted about why my passport looked different. I was confused because I had all my documents. So, what was he on about and why did the girls behind me laugh in amusement instead of scold him for his insolence?

I was shielded in Jamaica by subtle classism and colourism and the well-entrenched colonialist slave master mentality, which kept us darker people in our places. You see if you are lighter skinned then you are "brown and pretty", and if your hair is anything other than African then you have "pretty hair."

We were not taught African history - and the only knowledge we had of Africa was of the starving and malnourished children that we saw on TV. We were supposedly rescued from Africa by the enlightened Christopher Columbus who discovered Jamaica and the Caribbean and brought us here for a "better and more civilised existence."

It is not by chance that some Caribbean's do not identify as being African. How can we when that part of our identity was stolen? Heads shaved and regarded as nappy and our skin tone frowned upon as black-like tar.

My trip to Africa was my enlightenment and my awakening to who I am. I lament for my people who remain in mental enslavement. To the absent reality of their ancestry and rich legacy of our African heritage and the kingdoms and inventions that characterised our history.

My heart breaks a little every time I see a black woman, bleached faced with long wig extensions, which has been defined as the idealism of beauty. I know what it is to feel the mental slavery of being trapped in my black skin and dreaming of having the blonde hair and blue eyes that I see on TV. I am grateful to have been liberated and set free by being authentically African.

I know slavery ended a long time ago, but how can you understand when you do not want to hear about how the history left scars on my psyche? Are we free to speak now that you have proof of what we have been saying for years exists?

Now that it has been recorded on camera and broadcasted for the world to see. Yet some of you want to keep your eyes and ears closed and stay blissfully ignorant to what I have to say. And posture arguments that all lives matter. Can I speak and will you hear me?

The Things I Couldn't Say

- Colleen Simon

In 1981 I was born on the outskirts of West London, well actually Hayes, Middlesex, real Londoners referred to it as "countryside". Hayes was not culturally diverse, I belonged to one of 3 Black families on a little council estate. It didn't seem as rough as the places we saw on telly. It was small and compact and surrounded by nice houses and middleclass folk. My mum was of mixed heritage (Antiguan and English). I didn't know anything about my dad, just that I never had one. I guessed, he must have been black, since my brother and I were a few shades darker than our mum.

Nursery was a placed I enjoyed, I loved dressing-up and being around people. I took a shine to a ginger-haired boy with big blue eyes called Steven. It might have been because like me, he stood out. One of my first favourite outfits was a white-two piece. One sunny day, as my brown skin glowed & glistened in the sunlight, for the first time, I realised I stood out, I was out of place and didn't belong. The parents/ teachers and the children often gave off a vibe. I didn't get invited to parties (including Steven's) or to play. I was often reduced to tears in the corner for any manner of slights, dirty looks or minor jibes. I was so sensitive to such things and even then, had an inkling life was going to be hard....... I was Black, poor and I had no dad!

Junior school was the worse period of my life, those on the lowest socio-economic pile stuck out. We just looked rough around the edges and inevitably were the "dinner ticket kids".

The minority, single parent/broken home, dole claiming, council estate kids. Some of us scrubbed up alright. Some were grubby or stank and a few of the boys were naughty. We appeared to have a mutual respect and understanding of each other. I was racially abused in the playground most days and called "academically lazy", by the teachers in the classroom. I was, however, encouraged to be; sporty, creative, perform, run, jump and sing like some sort of monkey. Lunchtimes consisted of gymnastics or practicing shooting in the netball post. As the tallest, I was stuck in goalkeeper but always wanted to be goal shooter. I really wanted to be Whitney Houston or a gymnast, own a shiny black leotard and a Marks & Spencer summer dress and have a My Little Pony lunch box. I wanted to have long flowing hair down to my bum like my friends Donna and Jemma. My mum would often tie my hair very tight, giving me a facelift and slit-shaped eyes. I was given strict instructions not to take it out, but since everyone was so obsessed with it, I often took it out so they could see how long it was. Even with my head stretched back, it never fell to my bum - only up and out. The moment my mum saw my Worzel Gummidge-looking image appear at the end of the day, I knew I was going to have to face the consequences. like many others I remember ranting "its not fair" my mothers' reply would always be "life's not fair", never a truer word spoken!

Another child called me the N-word one day. Since I had always viewed him as an ally, I remembered snapping. I pushed him from a step by the water fountain and he skidded across the concrete by his face. I was sent home with a letter from the Headmaster. I was convinced that my mum would understand my torture, maybe congratulate me for confronting a bully or console me, but she sent me to bed without dinner, which broke my heart. I was well renowned for being first in the dinner queue and found great solace in food. I felt betrayed that night. Associates of my mother's friends would often call me the N-word when she wasn't there. I hated life and wanted to be somewhere else and someone else. Some lunchtimes a group of us degenerates, would often congregate at the end of the playground and fantasise and dare each other to run away across the playground boundary - not sure where or how - with no money or plan. I just imagined having a new life somehow. Maybe finding my dad who would be this amazing big tall strong man who would love me and shower me with presents and affection and live in a big house.

At least, I got to play netball and sing, I was thrilled to get a part in the final production at Junior school. I played a solo by "Burlington Berty". When I excitedly went home to tell my grandparents, my Nan laughed and told me he was a tramp! My grandparents lived across the road from the council estate in a house. My grandmother was a White woman, who was quick-witted, passive aggressive, feisty with a pepper and potty mouth. My grandfather was a tall Black dark skinned jolly man. He was just my hero and was often sat in his armchair clutching a purple shiny can of Tennent's lager and cigarette between the fingers of the same hand. Upon entry he would always boom: "hello darling". They were always pleased to see me. I spent much of my childhood with them, making camps, out of bedsheets and clothes racks, eating biscuits, watching 'American Werewolf in London', running wild, learning to ride a bike. My grandfather served in the British Army in 1957 and frequented the Royal British legion, where his comrades called him "Chalky" & "Sambo". It was boring watching old men sat around drinking, but I got to drink Coca-Cola and passively smoke 120 Benson & Hedges cigarettes. My grandad never told me anything about the 365 beaches in Antigua and only ever returned their once. My grandparents were liberal carefree and soft. So much so, my older brother moved in with them when he was 16. I walked on eggshells at home. My mum always seemed tired or short-tempered and I often felt like an inconvenience.

When I was 9, I was allowed to get my hair 'curly-permed' for my birthday. Mum put Nan in charge and we went to the European hairdresser. I came home with an afro shorter than the one I entered with. I was holding back the tears in the chair, as the senior stylist chopped away. I felt so self-conscious, that I just couldn't talk and I often felt that way. When we got home, my cousin burst into laughter and took the piss, saying you look like one of the "Jackson 5". My mother was raging. When we went back to the hairdressers, she demanded a fix and a refund. After a good few months of growth, she then took me to a Caribbean hairdressers. I began to feel a bit grown up and could even wear my hair out from time to time - with a bit of curl activator. We moved from the council estate via mutual exchange and was to a 3 bedroomed semi-detached house on the main road (around 15 minutes away). Mum got a new boyfriend and seemed happier. I developed some puppy fat and grew to over 5ft, so was easily more intimidating in the junior school playground. When I was 10, mum announced she was having a baby. I was overjoyed. I had been very lonely. My older brother was 6 years older and showed me contempt most of the time. I decided a little sister would be amazing.

At my Hillingdon-based girls' high school, there continued to be the usual ethnic minority challenges, but I could more easily hide being poor and fatherless. There were more than 5 Black children and there was some power and strength in number. During the first few years I was studious, my mother had her baby girl, but broke her foot, so I took about a month off to help out. At around 13, I broke away from the studious 'geek crew' and become more of a "brand name" girl. We were the popular girls. Some of us had boyfriends from the adjourning boys school. Some smoked and we always got alcohol and got drunk at the park at the weekends. Music was life and boys were exciting. Money remained scarce so I got a job cleaning for a disabled lady with MS, called Pam. I got £13 a week and £20 if I cleaned the windows. Pam was pleasant enough but very lonely. I often got dragged around various part-time jobs with my mum. She had a strong work ethic. I accompanied her debt collecting and to cleaning jobs. At 15, I got my first job in Woolworths, I began to fund a champagne lifestyle on a lemonade budget. I raved, bought expensive designer clothes, trainers and jewellery. I so desperately wanted to learn to drive that I took the test 5 times.

I did ok at school. I found concentrating, remembering and English difficult. I excelled in Maths and liked drama. I'd made up my mind I was going to be an actress. My mother asked me to name some successful Black female British actresses. I could only think of Whoopi Goldberg and since she was American, she didn't count. My mum made it clear that this ambition was a pipe dream. My friend Toyah spoke of a college in Langley, that she had enrolled to do a GNVQ in Health and Social Care. I thought it sounded interesting, so I joined, but Toyah dropped out after 2 weeks. I continued until the end. This part of town was heavily populated with Asians and I joined a little crew and began to understand some of their cultural struggles. The 2 Black girls on the course flatly refused to acknowledge me. At the end of the 2 years we started to explore our future options. Up to that point I had never considered going to university, but they were all applying and so I decided that it sounded like a good idea for me.

I looked through some of the career options and decided that since I was social and caring, social work was a good option. I liked the company I offered Pam and what it did for her.

I set about applying and saw that London based Kingston University had a few interesting courses. This would be my first choice. Most universities had a minimum age of 21, which limited my list to Kingston and a few deferred places at some other places I hadn't heard of. Life continued as normal, raving boys etc until I got an interview letter to attend a university in Plymouth. I had only ever seen the place on the weather map and knew it was far away. I think I had only left the country once by then. I took the day off work and travelled down to Plymouth, taking the train from Paddington. I spent the night in a B&B alone and went off to the interview. As I walked through town, the déjà vu of nursery kicked in once again. Plymouth in 1999 was less diverse than Hayes in the 80's. I felt people's eyes burning through me. I attended the interview and remember 2 lecturers called Will and Louise continuously nodding. So much so, that by the end of my speeches about "wanting to help people", I had to say: "that's it". Before the interview, I had already decided that I was never moving to Plymouth for 4 years. So at the end of the interview, when they said do you have any questions, I responded by saying "Not many black people down here. Does this cause any problems?" Will nearly fell of his chair and Louise went a little red in the face. To this day I am convinced that curve ball might have secured me a place, but I guess I'll never know....

Plymouth made me an offer, which was the only offer I got, apart from a deferred place at Oxford Brookes, so I threw caution to the wind and accepted. Many people encouraged me, saying that it was a nice place and I could always come back. Money continued to be scarce, so there was no university fund. I was still raving it up like a true "garage girl" - living pay slip to pay slip. This was the first year of student loans. However, the university wrote asking for a few hundred pounds that nobody had. I sheepishly approached the Woolworths store manager Dave and asked if he would sub me until my next pay day. He kindly agreed without hesitation. The team also brought me, all of the household goods, I had been putting aside, which really touched my heart, I returned there for a few summers to work.

It turned out a lad from college called Dave was going to Plymouth. He was going to be living in the same halls of residence as me and only lived up the road in Uxbridge. Dave's parents kindly collected a few bulky items and drove Dave down. I'm unsure how, but I lugged two suitcases on a bus and two trains to Plymouth. When I arrived after the 4 hour journey, it was raining cats and dogs. Dave met me from the station and helped me drag those suitcases to the almost empty accommodation office. By this point I was emotionally drained, soaked to my underwear and ready to go home. I was on the verge of a full blown breakdown when a nice lady invited me to sit down. It seemed to have escaped her that I was drenched or maybe she saw something I didn't. I took a seat and she gave me my room key and reassured me that I could pay the rent when the student loan came.

I arrived at my assigned corridor to a sea of young White faces. Parents were fussing over them and filling the fridge and cupboards with food. I entered the bare room and had a little cry. Social class had just truly slapped me in the face. I dried off my tears, freshened up and had no choice but to go down to my local Woolworths to see if they would take me on. The usual Hayes struggles continued in Plymouth. The first 2 years were full of fun and frolics, nights out, fancy dress and listening to cheesy pop. I routinely enjoyed a good night out on a tenner, seeking out other friendly Black folk, discovering some of the local basketball scholarship students and servicemen, trying not to feel lonely and somehow pretending I fit in. The final 2 years of the social work course became more serious, I began to understand the gravity of the profession and what we could do. My first placement was at a children's centre. It was a difficult environment. The workers spoke of paedophilia so openly. My nights out pulled me through. I decided there and then, working with children was not for me. Much of the work happened with the parents and they appeared tricky. As part of anti-discrimination and anti-oppressive practice, my practice educator Gill, insisted that I ask a service-user his ethnicity during a direct observation. I found this largely humiliating at the time, since I was the only distinguishable person of colour for miles and he did not know what the word ethnicity meant! However, I do appreciate the fact that Gill, was able to spot my dyslexia in my 3rd year through a degree!, my final placement was in a Plymouth drug and alcohol service, I was absolutely taken with this area of work and would read and research, finding it all very edgy and interesting

Getting through my degree was a struggle, life always had an air of angst and seemed hard, I returned to my home town with a shiny new social work/graduate identity but everyone else remained the same, again I felt a bit like a fish out of water, but wanted to assume the role, travel into London for work and wear some sort of power suit and look important, I spent a year working locally in the voluntary sector and was largely unsatisfied with having to join the 'delinquents club' which involved kissing butt, during Friday night drinks for a promotion, my first social work job was in criminal justice and substance use, I travelled into London and enjoyed the variety of the job, I was in and out of London prisons, travelling the country visiting residential rehabilitation units and giving convicted and remanded people a chance to change, recovery and start a new life.

I always tell people I fell into social work, but deep down, I carried a lot of the psychological wounds and trauma of these experiences and felt outraged at some of the injustices I had experienced and how they made me feel worthless and less of a person. I resented the lack of protection, reassurance or the fact that I had nobody to truthfully share this with until now. Social work gave me the opportunity to be the cheerleader I never had.

A Closed Door

- Lorraine Singlehurst

Today, I cried.

It came from the pit of my stomach, and I couldn't make sense of it.

The last couple of weeks have been beyond difficult. As a woman of colour and nearly 50 years of age, I have experienced the fear, rage and upset that being a person of colour brings. No explanations are required for those who are "woke".

When a platitude email in my workplace was circulated, by the higher ranks of social work acknowledging George Floyd's murder, followed by the words "all lives matter" I was shocked, but still had hope.

When workers responded to this email, along with suggestions for the local authority, they were met with complete and continued silence. I hoped the organisation would somehow become willing to listen and learn from the brave voices speaking out. At a time when the streets were talking, I truly believed the door had been opened for my workplace to shine.

During a worldwide pandemic that placed people like me more at risk, I thought the organisation would acknowledge the additional risk to life and have a plan for our working environment.

When I realised the Government updates regarding increased risk for certain ethnic minority groups were being missed off the organisation's daily COVID-19 briefings and risk assessments ("BAME" colleagues data had been collected but they had no plan for managing it), the stark realisation hit home - with a weight that felt unbearable. These are my colleagues, my superiors, my friends.

Their cumulative responses in recent weeks speaks of their truth. It shows they are conducting themselves in a way that continues to pick at a gaping wound, that has little hope of ever healing if they refuse to wake up. Those gut-wrenching tears today were me saying goodbye to the last shred of hope I had that maybe a tiny bit of the world, my world, would change.

Whilst we have had 400 years of the fight, they too have had 400 years of NOT having to acknowledge their privilege, because of OUR fight. I guess even in the higher ranks of social work, they just aren't ready to give that privilege up.

For my own mental health, I have decided my time will no longer be spent trying to wake the walking dead within my organisation, only to be met with a closed door. I will, however, continue to stand for my truth and speak it.

Bridging the cultural divide - A social work legacy

- Lynrose Kirby

I am a black social worker. I was born in Leicester, to parents who were born in the Caribbean island of Antigua.

As I was growing up, Leicester was a very multicultural place - as it is now - and I grew up with friends from Caribbean, Asian and White European and British backgrounds. We were in and out of each other's houses, playing and socialising. My view of the future, had you asked me, was that it would be a melting pot, and racism would not exist to any significant extent. How wrong I was, as here we are some 40+ years later, having to remind the world that Black Lives Matter (too).

I qualified as a social worker in Bradford, in 1991, and have spent the majority of my career working in the field of adoption and fostering in local authorities, and the voluntary sector across the north of England. I have been promoted to the level of Team Manager and fulfilled roles of a Trainer / Consultant, and panel chair. I have worked with children and families from a wide range of cultural and religious backgrounds.

The fact that I am black has been relevant in my work. Early on in my career, in the 1990s, I was able to identify where white foster carers needed help to meet the needs of black children placed with them. A white colleague and I ran a group for carers with interracial placements which was quite an eye opener, as we discovered the lack of knowledge and curiosity that carers had about the backgrounds of the children in their care. Some carers were not able to point on a map to the area of the world where the children they were caring for came from. They had no idea about languages spoken in the country of origin or food commonly eaten there. So, we brought in maps to the group sessions and set them "homework" between group sessions.

I revisited this type of work as a Trainer in a more technical age using profiles of children with plans for adoption / fostering who had origins outside the UK. With the use of a smart phone, within 30 minutes the group was able to find the flag, name the languages, talk about the history of the country, play folk or pop songs, find and share pictures and recipes of common foods!

However, the group I worked with in the 1990s were carers, who were caring for children on a temporary basis, hadn't had any particular preparation or training in caring for children from a different ethnic or religious background to their own, and were therefore going down the route of treating them like any other child and were not realising that these children had additional needs due to their ethnic backgrounds.

The local authority I worked for took this issue on board and had development workers to support carers and children. They also recognised the need to recruit more BAME carers and worked to identify the barriers to this recruitment, leading to great success in this area.

Additionally, carers I worked with back in the 1990s were dealing with racism aimed at themselves because they were caring for, and sometimes assumed to be the birth parents of, black children. As carers who had come into fostering for largely altruistic, reasons they were generally lauded for the work they did, and they did not expect this response.

So in my later work in this area, I tried to prepare carers for the fact that they and their children are likely to face racism. I used quotes from transracially adopted and fostered people such as this one to link back to the experiences of children and young people.

"I guess my mother's only fault was thinking that my colour didn't matter, that it is only skin deep. I'm not sure what world she lives in, but it isn't mine."
Harris, 2006

The quote above is taken from "In Search of Belonging", by Perlita Harris, and there are numerous testimonies available from people like Lemn Sissay and Pauline Black who grew up transracially adopted by families, who loved the children they were raising but who did their best to ignore the fact that the child was black - and certainly didn't want the child themselves to bring it up or reconnect with their black culture / identity.

I am in my mid-fifties now, so anticipating the end of my social work career. I hope that part of my legacy as a black social worker will be that I helped to bring a better understanding some of the lived experience of black looked after children and young people to white British carers and workers and showed them that meeting these needs is not only, possible but necessary to the well-being of black children and will help them to grow into well-rounded psychologically sound and integrated adults.

References

Harris, P. (2006) In Search of Belonging. London. BAAF.

Sitting and Watching - a perspective from a mental health social worker

- Patricia Clarke

As the daughter of industrious and proud Jamaican migrants who settled in Yorkshire, who raised their children and lived in the UK longer than the land of their birth, the opportunity to offer reflections as a social worker in the UK at this time, is too good to miss!

2020 has been an extraordinary time for obvious reasons. COVID-19 has resulted in the global community grappling with a pandemic in which racial inequalities are more apparent in terms of victims. As if minority groups needed anything further added to their 'overflowing cup' of social exclusion, health inequalities, institutional racism and the long-term impacts of poor outcomes from mental health blighting the community.

The rapid and enforced retreat home – 'Stay Safe and Alert' apparently for those of us fortunate to have homes, requires a new negotiation in which families can stay safe at a time of isolation. Communities are subject to the removal of the already over-stretched checks and balances led by social care and very real fears about counteracting gender-based violence given the oxygen of isolation from public view. Consideration of the risks of trying to protect children and families already compromised by the loss of school life is also integral. A decade of 'austerity' symbolised by burgeoning cuts to social and health care, poor engagement of service users for varied reasons, and grappling with technology, has resulted in real tensions between agencies, the community in which they serve and the management of risk.

As a mother, wife and worker, I have gained so much from developments within my professional career in the north and busy south London borough within a mental health team. I feel that I have spent much of this year, sitting and watching.

'Sitting and Watching' is one of my favourite songs. The sweet sounds of Dennis Brown continue to offer solace after a tricky day at work, and establishing support is a fundamental part of caring for others. In my view, support has been historically underplayed for staff. Particularly black staff, for whom the baggage of managing fundamentally complex lives of people in need, is onerous enough. Navigating organisational culture is not exactly, an optional extra.

It was so painful "sitting and watching" vicariously, the murder of an untried citizen of the apparent Free World from an officer expected to "protect and serve". Sitting and watching passively, feeling helpless and fearing for the world that my 8-year-old son – who will need to be equipped to deal with a world where political leaders show us quite clearly who they are: racist, incompetent, and playing to the politics of the populist mob. Us and Them therefore prevails. Gil ScottHeron, powerfully told us that "the revolution would not be televised", but social media captured actions that I hope and pray are a sea-change to achieve universal justice.

Social care work, however, is far from passive, and more like "ducking and diving" than "sitting and watching"! Though trying to obtain balance really is the key.

Whilst it is demoralising to see supporters of the unjust even more comfortable in their ugly, frightened, venomous skins, there have been glimpses of hope too. Youth protests – Black Lives Matter – not just adjectives - the movement is about change. Change is central to social care too and professionals have a powerful place to work in authentic partnership to support adults in their complex social contexts and in a person-centred manner - valued by those they work with.

Sitting and watching continues when I consider the realm of politics. I have observed with disgust, fear and disappointment that the 'Leader of the Free World' retains much support in his overtly racist, misogynistic preening, in which the USA has been torn apart by policies that further subjugates divisions of class and race. At the brink of the 2020 election, which has implications for climate change, the UK relationship with Europe and the administration of law and order, I watch with wonder how the race to depose the least presidential of presidents' is still a favourite for another 4 years of dysfunction. The mismanagement of COVID-19 has led me to think that surely everyone can see the best is surely to come?

As a British citizen, I can't even be smug that matters are much better here. Lockdown the Sequel begins shortly - finally a recognition that social and economic equalities tasked with health risks of the pandemic must surely mean that "we are in it together?" Let's see.

This has been a time where in the words of the wonderful writer, James Baldwin, "peculiar language" used by the privileged view to position black people is so visible. Current parlance, BAME is so problematic and one of the impacts of the Windrush disgrace, which are still being felt by the sons and daughters who came to support the creation of the beloved NHS, is that I feel I am British. Until you are not! Apparently, politicians can define this for you, fail to be transparent about change, then remove civil rights. If we tolerate this, then your children (definitely) will be next, prophesised by the Manic Street Preachers.

The prevailing "peculiar language", which positions individuals in damaging and unhelpful ways also means that internal struggles within racial/ethnic groups, is problematic because people are in fact, diverse - and not monoliths. I find that James Baldwin so inspiring when exposing the fraudulent nature of "the system", and helpful in making us feel empowered and hopeful.

These current challenges are not new, but instead history lessons not heeded by those in power mean structural inequalities remain prevalent.

The sneaky, nasty ways in which this government contributed to the harsh treatment of human beings – deporting them without papers, changing citizenship rules and ignoring peoples' rights and justice - the challenge of being 'othered' in the UK continues.

The stench of their racism, injustice, ineptitude is so strong, that I have decided to "pinch my nose" and seek sanctuary elsewhere!

The complexities of social work – people's difficult lives, balancing budgets, working within organisations with "snowy white peaks" where racial issues are treated in a manner of a "season", rather than a universal, integral part of service development is tiring. Seeking sanctuary is a pre-requisite for safety for professional staff, who take the burden of arranging state care yet require nurturing ourselves.

However, once in my sanctuary (connections with loved ones, music, faith and space) I have realised that the different positions I have held within social care – project worker/ social worker/approved mental health professional and leadership positions (which I have really enjoyed and grown in a personal way) thereby develop my resilience.

By serving and trying to work in partnership with a range of families in distress - I can see that I have played a significant role in keeping people safe, offering justice and challenging inequalities within services, which remain largely monochrome, particularly in positions of real influence. It's definitely time for beautiful, energy-giving, collective, colour.

I could share so many different experiences borne often out of complex cases. Situations which initially caused me terror, raised feelings of hopelessness, but change finally did occur.

I have worked in social work education and worked for the government regulator – often being "the only black in the village". Whilst that was initially a lonely place; combating patronising people (often leaders) surprised by my intellect, confidence and skills it was very tiresome. I feel that my experiences of being an outsider (outlander) due to my heritage, have really sharpened my tools of resilience.

Thank goodness for that! With all the burdens placed upon the shoulders of people who look and sound like me, it's clear that we're going to need a rather large toolbox to thrive!

My Journey to Social Work as a Mixed Heritage Woman

- Rachel Pearce

As a child of a white British mother and Asian father in inner-city Birmingham, I experienced racism in the form of being "White". I learnt to be safe, to keep my head down, to not challenge and to be invisible. My parents separated when I was young and so I was "white", and discussing my heritage was painful - as I never knew it.

Moving to the South West, which is predominantly White-British, I again experienced racism in the form of being called "a paki". As a teenager, I could never quite fit anywhere. How can I be bullied for being white and for being Asian – as I was neither? As an adult, I always ticked the "White British" box because I didn't want to discuss my father, and admit I knew little about my heritage – it was embarrassing.

Becoming a new mother, I was confronted with the Paediatrician questioning my "White British" box ticking. I realised my heritage meant more now and needed to confront who I was. From that day on I became "Mixed Heritage". I did not want my son to be ashamed of his heritage. I was 21. My child's skin tone is darker than mine, and I have witnessed him being racially abused - which as a parent is just terrible. In early primary school, another child of Asian heritage was in his class and was disabled. My son was taunted for being just like that child. My son was puzzled by this and would say "*but mum I'm not disabled I don't understand*". The innocence of acceptance of skin colour for some and not others was there in brutal form.

As a social work student, I was the only person from a minority group on the course and in one lecture, around diversity, the group were described as White British students. I was confident enough to put my lecturer right on this and he was very apologetic - but what if I hadn't of been ok doing this? This has led me to question the experiences in schools and colleges of the people I support; children and adults and ensuring that subtle forms of racism do not slide by. I will highlight it.

Having spent time accepting who I am, this has enabled me to be more open and supportive with young people. I remember one young person in particular who was of Mixed Heritage (Black Caribbean and White). She had the lightest skin tone in her family, and this was a significant issue for her. I shared my Mixed Heritage background with her and she would ask questions around different ethnicities and actively seek emotional support from me. Our work became very focussed on diversity which was young person led. On one occasion she asked: "What do they think of us?" It was a really powerful thing, and I will always remember it. Questions that followed that were: "Who are they?" and "who are us?"

I will always go back to it. That feeling of being different is with you always. Depending on the support around you and what your experiences are, this can determine how we get through it and how to explore it. Positive relationships are so important to ensure there is scope and security for this exploration. It is so crucial to recognise that everyone has different levels of resilience and have potentially dealt with different forms of abuse – no matter what ethnicity they are.

My experiences have shaped the person and practitioner I am today, and I am thankful for this.

Visibly - Invisible: The Tale of a Black Female Social Worker

- Rebecca O.M Olayinka

I thought being a social worker would be a satisfying career, even though my own experiences with social workers were not that fruitful. I had two social workers when I was around 8 or 9. I was privately fostered you see. When things became ugly with my mum and my foster mother, the state had to intervene. It didn't do much good and I am still awaiting my personal files that have "gone missing".

I never thought I would be a social worker, when I was younger, too much responsibility it seemed like. Yet I had this desire to help people. My two brothers tried to discourage me from heading down this path, they didn't think of social workers as being right for Black people.

I was glad I chose the profession, as I like to help people. However, it felt like I was battling against an invisible force that was not just the social injustice and bureaucracies of local government, yet something more sinister. The misogynoir (racism and sexism) and microagressions I experienced was deeply embedded within the system, and in the clients that I served - and even my own managers. No one forewarned me that there would be other personal, and at times treacherous, battles that I would be fighting in some shape or form throughout my entire career.

I was taught at university to empower clients and to think of how I worked in an anti-oppressive way. It was always keeping the client in mind, reflecting on how there were power imbalances in relation to my role and the amount of power I held as a social worker. We utilised theories such as unconditional positive regard, solutions-focused theories and strengths perspectives. These theories were not reflected upon how other people viewed me - it felt like it was always a one-way affair. In truth, it left me feeling more disempowered than ever before, yet no one wanted to acknowledge or talk about this.

It felt like it was always in my imagination, my incompetence. I was even told it was my lack of confidence by one of my team manager's. When I questioned her further on this, she said that I "asked too many questions"! I knew there was something more to this, yet I was not able to prove it. I knew my confidence wasn't an issue, as a previous manager had often said that "I was quietly confident and hardworking".

My first social work role was in a rural area, where I was the one of two other Black women there - and there was something off that I couldn't quite put my finger on. In the whole 18 months that I worked there, I remember that I didn't see one single client who was Black - and only person from an ethnic minority. I remembered meeting client's families who were usually nice at the outset (on the phone); yet were often visibly surprised when they opened the door. My hair was quite colourful and "I didn't look as I sounded" said one client to me. I was newly qualified then and I didn't always think to challenge in the moment. I also had one client who, after I met her, "forbade me" (the actual words she used) from being her husband's social worker, even though she had put him in respite care and did not want him to return to the family home.

The lady called me up and was adamant that I wasn't to be the social worker. The only reason I got was that she "didn't know" me and that was it. My line manager at the time thought it was because the woman was afraid I would steal her husband!

This was not only an inappropriate and sexist suggestion, but it also failed to acknowledge an underlying narrative - it had racial connotations.

Race was completely exempt from the conversation; it wasn't even considered. I didn't remain the allocated social worker and the client was transferred to another worker. They thought they were supporting me. However, that was much further from the truth. By not exploring the potential underlying reasons (as to why the client's wife decided I shouldn't be the social worker for her husband), there was no way to ensure a more appropriate response going forward – should this type of incident happen again (to another social worker). At the time, I felt angry and upset, but I didn't really know why. Working in this particular council, issues like this were commonplace and not only from the clients and/or families - but managers as well.

I remember my line manager at the time, being very critical of my work, sending assessments back to me due to some slight spelling mistakes. I remember her scolding me for telling the truth to another Local Authority (LA), as we had not managed to review a package of care in a case that was being transferred and her becoming angry about this.

There was always something I was doing wrong, like not working fast enough. Even though I was usually on duty twice per week and was frequently out doing assessments about urgent safeguarding concerns or emergency placements - which also meant typing up a whole assessment and finding a placement all on the same day.

There were two other senior practitioners in my team. Sometimes, one of them would look at me then go to the other and whisper in their ears whilst looking at me. My line manager would sometimes take me into a small room and chastise whatever it was I was doing or not doing. She once even went as far as telling me that my skirt was too tight. I was wearing a mid length skirt that looked smart and had a nice material. I wore tights and it finished just below the knee, so I didn't understand at the time what the fuss was all about. It wasn't the first time I had been "rebuked" for not adhering to the phantom organisational dress code.

"Your skirt is too tight." My line manager had said.

I replied that: "I could still walk in it and it wasn't any of their business".

She continued in her admonishment and said that I couldn't wear it. She asked: "What would you do if you had to visit a prison on duty and someone tried to grab you because of your skirt?"

I was shocked, not only was I being told what to wear, but that I was even being threatened with a very unlikely scenario to try and scare me. Also, quite worryingly it appeared that there would be little protection for me if anything was to happen and it was deemed my fault. I couldn't believe it. This wasn't something I had come across before. The funny thing was there was no actual dress code. I even looked up the relevant policies and procedures and there were none.

Supervision meetings had become a distant memory. When I went to my team manager about this, she made excuses, even though there was one period I had not had supervision for 5 weeks! I did not enjoy supervision at the time and even dreaded it, yet I recognised it was important for my practice development to keep this up.

I finally left the team, as I felt like I was slowly being pushed out. I also started to have panic attacks when I arrived at work, I knew this was not normal and having time off with anxiety was not a long-term solution either. I thought it was best to get out and move on. I had built up some good relationships within the team, but I didn't feel supported enough to stay. The place was stifling, like being slowly suffocated little by little the longer I stayed. I used to think: "I don't want to live this way", which prompted me to look for another role.

Later, when I'd been offered another job and references were requested, my senior practitioner criticised me for not telling her that I had applied for another job. It seemed to be a big deal to her. I wondered if it was really about power and control for her. I finally said to her: "I do not like the way you have been treating me."

She pretended not to understand and tried to reassure me that we "had a good working relationship."

However, I was adamant otherwise. I wasn't going to be gaslighted anymore. I expressed my concerns and explained how I felt. She didn't really listen. Although, I felt like a weight had been lifted off my chest - like I could leave the place with ease.

Things got better, when I moved, although in my next role, I was the only Black social worker in my team. The team were supportive, yet no-one discussed race, it was never brought up or questioned when there were difficult interactions with clients and families. It wasn't really acknowledged at all. It was like they wanted to be so polite in not mentioning it, that it became (at times) the elephant in the room. I had started speaking up for myself more and it was easier to manage difficult conversations.

I had to read up and learn techniques myself, as my social work training did not equip or provide me with any of the tools needed to be assertive as a Black female social worker. I found that I had to be quite proactive in educating myself. I did mindfulness courses, although I hated meditation. I was always reading articles to help me to develop and improve as a person. I was so critical of myself. I didn't realise (at that point) that it stemmed from a lack of self-love from my own difficult past.

I thought: "If I can just empower the clients I work with, this will compensate for everything else." There was no training, for Black social workers specifically to deal with the difficulties of being just another Black face in a sea of white spaces. No mentorship and no real encouragement to help me make a difference as a Black social worker. The clients remained predominantly White-British, although it was more diverse than where I had worked initially.

My new line manager was very knowledgeable within her role and well versed in the law. It was the first time anyone took an interest in my professional development. It boosted my confidence when she arranged supervision meetings. The panic this previously provoked in me, started to dissipate, although it never properly left until a considerable time after. Race however was still not considered in supervision and team meetings - and neither was there much about equality and diversity generally.

I received a lot more comments about my hair, as I like to show my personality through my hair. It has in the past worked well in breaking the ice with clients who at times have been otherwise reluctant to engage with me. However more personal and intrusive comments have come from colleagues. There was one colleague a fellow social worker, who seemed fascinated with my hair. I didn't think that much of it at the time, but she asked further personal questions, such as: "How did you get it like that?" and "is it real?" I liked her at the time and didn't think too much of it.

I was good at looking past things like that when I was younger. I just wanted acceptance. This same colleague and I used to socialise from time to time and I thought she was a good friend. Yet one time, when I expressed frustration at a friend of a friend who had sung along to the N-word at a party, she said she didn't understand the problem. She explained she did not know why the N-word was derogatory anyway, as it was the same as "Bitch." She added that she had sung along to it too many times. We were in my car at the time, and I got so angry I pulled over and told her to get out of my car! She was angry too, although I didn't understand why. I admit it wasn't my finest moment; but I felt gaslighted and my feelings seemed worthless. It was like I was unable to get upset at what had occurred because her white privilege allowed her to deny my plight.

My next career move was more promising as I had, for the first time, a manager who was willing to have open discussions with me (and the team) about race and intricate issues that are not usually talked about. This manager was courageous, unafraid to learn and always wanted to ensure she was doing right by the clients we serve. My manager, before she left, expressed that I challenged her in an unintentional way to look more into race and the subtle forms of racism which are embedded within our society. I wonder if I was listened to more because I am now a senior practitioner myself?

I practised as a social worker for 7 years and only then did I have a manager who really wanted to listen to my experiences as a Black female social worker – and wasn't tokenistic in their approach. My manager was able to sit with uncomfortable conversations, such as why it wasn't appropriate to touch or comment on my hair. She was shocked that people said and did these things. I explained that it is always white women who seemed to be fascinated with it (looking at me like I'd just stepped out of an alternative universe, where they have never seen such a thing before). I have had numerous colleagues trying to touch my hair and far more who think it is subject to their approval. They would say: "Your hair is nice, I like it". I reminded them that my hair is not subject to their approval and neither am I.

My social work career has felt like I have needed to prove myself, not just to clients - but continually to my employers as well. Unconscious bias has rarely been talked about until now, and issues around race have been seemingly swept under the carpet until now. I feel I have experienced slightly more discrimination from management than clients. I have experienced bullying and racism from other Black senior managers, which when I have aimed to discuss this with White managers, this has somehow fallen on deaf ears. They made excuses like: "They picked you to move roles because you would get things done." I have questioned this, as they didn't actually know me that well and when they fell short in providing a coherent answer, I could tell that they were acting on their own biases.

I never thought race would be a substantial issue within social work, one that worryingly is not discussed and is often dismissed. I had thought that as part of our values we would automatically be looking at being supportive, not just to clients, but to social workers as well - particularly those who may face additional stigma and challenges due to their ethnicity.

I took for granted this would not be a problem, since there is a large percentage of frontline workers who are from Black and ethnic minority backgrounds. However, with so few in positions of management, the obvious question is - how do we provoke real change?

2020: Perfect Vision

- Chris Parker

18 March 2020

2020. Perfect vision. An opportunity to reflect and revise personally and professionally. I was ready for it. I had plans for the New Year. What was even more exciting is the energy I felt around me. It seemed that everyone I knew also had plans of their own. I knew this year would be different from all others and I just couldn't figure how or why I knew this...

19 July 2020

Who could have predicted that this year would be comprised of working in my living room and wearing masks? Who could have known that I would be working in a profession which thrives from human contact, building relationships through empowerment and addressing injustice for the most vulnerable during a pandemic? Since lockdown was declared, I have struggled to control my emotions. Anxiety and fear increase as I watch the news. Images of body bags being rolled onto trucks, quiet cities and politicians attempting to provide a solution to a growing problem have become my daily exercise. Just when I thought things could not get any worse, another senseless death of a Black man in America by police has happened. This was no ordinary murder. It was a perfect storm which had been taking shape for a number of years. This death emphasised the realities of oppression, inequality and classism. It was painful to acknowledge the impact of a new virus in which a lockdown was needed. There were no scientists or public health officials discussing trials or even a vaccine for this seemingly incurable illness. The emotions I am feeling are like an inescapable wave was crashing down on me. Media outlets continue to show familiar images of various Police-related deaths of Black and Brown people over the years. The call for justice is deafening. The protests continue and have a different energy to them. They have spread across the world in response to this tragedy.

04 August 2020

There are correlations between the virus and those impacted by its seemingly indiscriminate grasp. Black, Asian, Native Americans and Latinos seem to be the targets of both viruses: COVID-19 and racism. The protests continue. However, it seems the reminders of racism and oppression are too painful for many. This has created a variety of distractions, designed to shift the narrative and view the responses of many as inappropriate. It has created divisions among families and friends whom we were already having difficulty seeing due to lockdown. Ironically, physical distance has become more than just a way to reduce your chances of contracting the virus. There is a loss of control, which has caused some people to resist the advice given by the government and public health officials. The idea of wearing a mask for protection has become a political statement. How did this happen?

07 September 2020

As all of this is quite overwhelming, I am reminded of why I became a Social Worker. The decision to oppose injustice and inequality as well as advocating for the most vulnerable people in our society. I am expected to perform my professional duties, whilst being faced with the reality of my own vulnerability to COVID-19 and racism. I questioned how I would be able to continue empowering others when I needed support maintaining my own emotional health. I'm ready to talk about the issues of racism, but few of my work colleagues want to broach the subject for fear of saying the wrong thing. It seems easier to discuss COVID-19 and the return to work plan. The opening of shops and schools in an attempt to promote normalcy seem premature, if there is no real acknowledgement of the racial injustice faced by people of colour. This new normal has forced us to think differently about our lives. It has encouraged compassion and selflessness. It has also highlighted the danger both viruses pose and the consequences if we persist in refusing to take action. 2020. Perfect vision.

31 December 2020

COVID-19. Lockdown. Work from home. George Floyd. Protest. Masks. Hand Sanitiser. Economy. Disproportionality. Restrictions. Isolation. Bubbles. Mental Health. Politics. Division. Tier 2. Tier 4. Anxiety. Exhaustion. Vaccines. Uncertainty. Hope. Words and phrases which defined the most unforgettable year of my life.

As the hours of the final day of the year conclude, I am grateful that I have had the opportunity to reflect on all of these words and phrases. Although I spent most of the year feeling quite anxious, I have noticed a shift in prioritising what is important versus what I can actually control. I have lost friends and gained a perspective on the value of time. I have also gained friends and realised the importance of love. I feel that my relationships with my family are stronger due to the imposed isolation. This has made me wonder how one of the most isolated times in history for many of us, promoted so much division. I am quickly reminded of the amount of control we have had to surrender this year. There is also the reality of inequities, which have been highlighted through protests and the systemic impact of disproportionality. As the aggressiveness of the virus has prohibited my involvement in protesting, I have become more involved at work in developing virtual presentations to address these matters with my colleagues. I have been surprised at how many people I work with who were not aware of the structural differences, but I have been encouraged by their enthusiasm to learn and change.

In essence, the many words and phrases of 2020 have influenced me to accept inevitable changes in my personal and professional life. I have seen what anxiety unchecked looks like and realise that being vulnerable at times is not such a bad thing. The concerns I have had throughout the year have been acknowledged by many people. Experienced lows have profoundly challenged longstanding practices of discrimination and inequality have energised a new generation to mobilise. There is hope that despite difficulties, there is resolution if motivation is present. 2020 also re-introduced a variety of virtual methods to satisfy our need for connect with others. As this is not a substitute for in-person interaction, these platforms offered alternative ways to conduct meetings, play games and share moments with family and friends. Being connected has definitely been a godsend.

So this is it. The countdown to begin another year. 2021 will without doubt be filled with uncertainty and at times, it may be difficult to leave much of 2020 behind. The unfinished chapters of 2020 will leave us with reminders of what was and what could have been. For now, the only thing I can look forward to is a new year with a touch of continuation of the present. I guess I will be the only person to know how much of yesterday I will leave behind and how much of tomorrow I will embrace.

Lockdown Chronology

- Sheree Von-Claire

Lockdown has been very difficult. I've found the depletion in my resilience to be determined by many factors. I am a single woman living alone with a workload that's been disabling, and the news is full of statistics for black people posing a greater risk of dying from COVID-19. This knowledge serves to intensify my fears around the virus.

I voiced worries around my competence to Ingrid – not because I felt incapable, but because I was exhausted by work pressures and not enjoying good health -yet continuing to work. At the same time, I was exposed to so many challenging situations at once with my Carers... M's illness, Z's allegation, and the breakdowns of placements for 6 young people.

My daughter having the Coronavirus at the same time my Mum had an accident was so worrying. Supervision should have been the forum to take how I was feeling, yet there was seemingly no place on the agenda to discuss emotion in my supervisions with Ingrid.

I'm not a senior SSW, but I have the highest caseload and contend with much that requires management intervention. Ingrid failed in her duty of care to me by making supervisions a tick-box exercise during which she presented as tired and indifferent and had only once asked how I was during the past year.

Since lockdown began, I've been self-alienating, alone most of the time, working like a machine and not allowing myself to feel. In ordinary circumstances this would have been fine; however, during lockdown, I've been unable to balance such a maladaptive coping-strategy with my usual opportunities for regular social engagements. I'm currently doing a 10-hour Open University course online titled, "Supporting and Developing Resilience in Social Work". It has helped me to recognize my experiences of emotional burnout. It's disheartening that it's taken a suspension for me to allow myself time to engage in this very useful course.

6th to 10th March.

- Leave cancelled March due to heavy workload. Worked on Saturday 7th March to support a new child moving in.

10th March.

- Last day in the office. Advised to work from home due to electrical problems.
- Caseload of 24 children and 8 Carers.
- Struggling to manage and told Ingrid I was behind with recordings. Asked for 2 weeks support to get straight.
- Had a physical meeting with Ingrid and colleague Paige requesting a new SSW.

12th March

- Thea, (daughter, 22), visiting for a few days to see her niece. Thea not feeling great - tired and a little giddy.

Weekend 13th to 15th March

- Regular monthly weekend with Lexi, (granddaughter). This one is ahead of her birthday on Monday.
- Got call from Jamaica. Mum's had an accident - she was making porridge and fainted face first into the pan. Serious burns. She's 82, but fit, able, and independent. A shock to

realize no matter now young she seems; the years are still there. Doctors can't tell why she fainted.

- Lexi is unwell with a chest infection. Crying all the time. Not like her.

- Saturday night realized Thea has Coronavirus.

- All following week Thea is frighteningly unwell, she's burning one minute yet so cold the next needed to heat her with the hairdryer; vomiting, piercing headache, struggling to walk as bones hurt. Hospital say, with 99% certainty, that it is Coronavirus but won't allow her admittance until 7 days have passed. Ingrid allowed me 2 days off. By day 11, Thea much better. Managed to get her home the day before lockdown.

April

- Workload heavier than ever. So many risk assessments and policies to urgently change due to Coronavirus.

- I live by myself and lockdown is very lonely.

- Rounders season cancelled.

- Church are doing services on Zoom. Church and speaking to friends / family are my only social outlets.

- Diagnosed with Sciatica. Continued to work.

- A member of my Church family and a friend's Mum passed away from Coronavirus.

- 5 annual reviews to type, doing them out of hours as no time during the day.

- Managing allegations for Z Family.

- No time to switch off. Exhausted.

May

- Broken wrist on 3rd trying to roller skate. Work is so constant, I just wanted to do something fun. In a lot of pain and not sure I can continue to work; told Ingrid. Working anyway and using the voice recorder for some things.
- Paige's hen weekend and Church weekend away now cancelled. Paige's wedding not until next year now too.
- Got a mole on my chest checked. I'll monitor.
- Stressed. Made error allowing Tatum back before the meeting. Sad no recognition of the 2:00am finishes, just what's done wrong.
- So very tired. Asked again for 2 weeks to get straight. Ingrid dismissive.

24th May

- Ingrid sent incorrect medical information about my wrist, written up by Deborah. Told both what was wrong with document. I won't sign until changed. Why has she only sent this now and added a fabricated conversation between me and the hospital?
- Breakdown of placement for H girls after 8 years. So much work on this. Glad in respite at least.

26th May

- George Floyd. As a black woman it pains me to see this. Things still do not change.

June

- Ingrid seems to be panicking about things not done. She keeps calling. Denying conversations have happened. What's that about?

- 5th suspended. Why call me at 6:30pm? Shocked. Bereft. I can't pay my bills without being able to use my degree. Being a social worker is the career I struggled to put myself through university to achieve. I've been working like a machine towards outcomes that seem impossible. Feel broken.

- Mole looking bigger. Video appointment first, then GP asked me to go in physically. I have an emergency hospital appointment on 19th June – directly after my disciplinary hearing. Terrified but, sadly, my suspension isn't allowing time to think about this.

- Flat tyre from puncture - just add to the list...

- Main holiday to Caribbean with my closest friends cancelled. Nothing to look forward to this year now.

- Suspension ongoing. It feels like a foregone conclusion – Supervising Social Workers are 2 a penny by comparison to those higher up the scale.

- It feels almost traitorous to have not gone to the Black Lives Matter rally at the weekend. An important issue I should have supported; but I feared potentially being caught up in troubles and having that as another weapon wielded against me...

DISCLAIMER: This chronology is presented creatively and subjectively. It is documented purely to reflect my thoughts, opinions, and emotions and not those of my employers or anyone else. All names and other identifiers of people the reader may choose to link to me in a working or personal capacity have been changed.

Reflections - A Day in the Life of an Independent Reviewing Officer (IRO)

- Sherifa Adenmosun

7.15am

Check emails. Re-read report for today's review. Make sure laptop & mobile is charged for day ahead. Carry water and snacks.

8:00am

Leave home. Head to Euston to begin the 10hr round trip to North Wales. Mode of transport for the day bus, underground, overground rail and car.

9:00am – 1:00pm

My activities on the train consist of the following:

Reading whilst travelling and listening to music intermittently. Checking my diary for the next month is up to date. A key aspect of this role is the need to make use of travelling time. Thinking about the young man whose review I'm about to chair. I have not seen him in a while... It was his 16th birthday earlier this week.

Reflecting on my week so far, I chaired initial reviews locally for 3 & 4-year-old siblings now living with their Uncle. It is the 3rd set of care proceedings for these young children. There are 3 possible outcomes at Court: reunification with Mum, remain with family under connected person arrangements or adoption. The children are safe now and their needs are being met. This must be long-term, so they have a good foundation in their formative years and beyond. Mum has her own unmet needs, as she requires support around to be able to evidence change and the ability to sustain the changes to meet the needs of her children. The children's timeframes are key in such matters, particularly as proceedings have been ongoing for 3 consecutive years. The Courts prescribe a tight timeframe of 26 weeks in order to prevent drift and delays.

Today's review is my 25th in 4 weeks; this means 25 IRO Looked After Child (LAC) Review Decisions/reports to be typed up and circulated within 20 working days. No two days are the same in this role, but like most jobs the ability to prioritise, work to tight statutory timescales and manage time effectively is key. This week I've had 3 'admin days'; 2 of which were at home - a necessity for the ongoing report writing, monitoring cases and reading with this role. I go into the office on Wednesdays for brief meetings with Social Workers. I was thrilled to bump into 2 of my colleagues for a quick catch up. Us IROs are like ships that pass in the night, but that said, we have incredible virtual/telephone support and excellent Managers. This enables us to share a wealth of knowledge and allows us to check in with one another. We are going through a major shift as a local authority in terms of how we conduct LAC Reviews, to ensure they increase child participation and are less procedural. The feedback so far is positive especially with reports now being written *to* children instead of *about* them.

As we pull into another station that I cannot pronounce, I think about my caseload - currently at 61 children. Some of my children are turning 18 in the next few months. Some have had final LAC Reviews. I hope that they are prepared and still supported as they ease into adulthood. Fortunately, the Local Authority has an excellent Leaving Care Team. The staff are passionate and invest in the young people, which supports this crucial transition.

At the other end of the spectrum, I think about 2 babies who I've overseen for about a year as their IRO - since they were new-borns. I've chaired their reviews since they moved to their respective adoptive placements within the last 4 weeks. The children and new parents are doing well. They cease being LAC once the Adoption Order is granted by the Court.

Ping! Email alert. 30mins until I disembark. A Social Worker has sent me all the final evidence needed for 2 brothers in proceedings. He wants the IRO view on his Final Care Plan recommendation. The email has 14 attached documents for Court. I search my calendar for a slot to prioritise this task within the week deadline. I may get a chance to start reading when heading back to London later today. I hope so - as it's over 100 pages to decipher.

1:00pm - 2.30pm LAC Review Meeting

I arrive at a remote train station in North Wales, the child's Social Worker and I have a chance to briefly catch up. He had already produced a report for the meeting beforehand in accordance with procedures. Our car arrives for the 1hr 10min drive to our location. It took the scenic route high into the Welsh valleys. It made sense now, why this young person was doing so well over the past 6 weeks - at this distant crisis assessment centre. The chance of absconding was reduced significantly - this was his biggest vulnerability factor.

Upon arrival, I see the young man, we chat, he looks very well. He told me that he enjoyed the peace and quiet of being away from London. He just wanted to sleep... Staff appear very hands on, the support and boundaries in place are high and attuned to this young man's needs. My view is aligned with his Social Worker's, essentially that long-term this placement isn't sustainable. However, it does provide an opportunity to assess his needs and plan appropriately. The

Care Plan must take into consideration him living in the real world, but not necessarily London for now. The crisis centre was a place invested in promoting his long-term stability and safety whilst also hooking him into meaningful learning.

During his meeting, the young man was able to articulate his views and participate fully in his LAC Review. I commended him, as this had been the most engaging in the year that I had known him. As the meeting concluded and the decisions formulated, it dawned on me that this Social Worker really knew this boy. From his explanation and understanding of the boundaries and his expectations of the young man to their genuine banter. I saw the Social Worker exercise care and control with this vulnerable child with amazing skill. Us IROs are always pleased to see this. I know the value this holds for a child, both now and in their future.

3:00pm - 8:00pm

I reversed the journey and headed back to London. I had to take one additional train, due to issues, this happens... I'm always prepared for late arrivals when travelling long-distance.

I read reports and check/respond to emails. I'm almost back in London just after 7:00pm. People sometimes ask: "Why do you go all that way for a meeting?"

My response is always the same: "The LA placed [the child/ young person] in [location], so our legal duties remain the same wherever they are placed..."

To conclude, I hope this has given you a brief insight into the IRO role. I do this job because of my interest in the outcome and experiences of Looked After Children. One day I can only hope they will have the same stability and support that is afforded to the non-LAC population.

Sept 2020 – Reflections post lockdown

The above piece was written in July 2019 pre-COVID-19. Oh, how times have changed... We are all, as a profession, in a very different place to where we were last year due the impact of the pandemic on society as a whole. This pandemic has literally turned our personal and professional lives upside down. The full extent of the physical and emotional consequences for society is not yet known.

The vulnerable children that we work with are often largely unseen by society, and their outcomes in life are poorer in every sphere. These same children are now generally 'visited' by their workers through screens, which can exacerbate feelings of isolation in foster care/residential or semi-independent placements. In other ways, I'm thankful for the internet connections via Google Meet, Zoom and Microsoft Teams and the versatility and creativity this has provided when chairing virtual Reviews during lockdown. It's been a much-needed lifeline to stay connected in both professional and personal spheres.

I'm a keen advocate for "*seeing children*" where it is safe and possible to do so. I want to highlight the concept of the corporate parent. It is a responsibility that is sometimes overused within children and families Social Work. Since the lifting of lockdown, I have seen the reverse of this. I don't know of anyone who has been happy to say to their friends/family "let's just continue to see one another online only, as it's much easier and cheaper...." I say this because suddenly now, despite lockdown restrictions being lifted, some professionals (who are fit and able to work/travel), are losing sight of the importance of real human contact.

Intrinsic within Social Work values are the concept of human dignity and worth of human beings. Whilst holding on to this key value, I have seen some colleagues within my Local Authority carry out *child-led* doorstep visits (at a social distance) during the height of the pandemic. This clear message that a child is worth a face-to-face visit speaks volumes to the children and young people that we work with. I for one hope that we can hold on to this. Let us not forget the core of our professional values.

Breaking the Silence

- Syra Shakir

I am a woman of mixed ethnicity - Pakistani and Irish. I was born and spent part of my early childhood in South London, then spent my high school years in the North East, before moving to West Yorkshire, where I began university and I remain to this day.

I qualified as a social worker at the end of 2006. I began my career as an agency social worker. I was probably more than your average Newly Qualified Social Worker (NQSW) at the time and so I had a hefty caseload. I worked hard as I could with everything, to avoid disappointing anyone and I always attempted to show I could do anything. I certainly did not look like your 'average' social worker, if there really is a 'type', and I knew that. Wearing silly stiletto heels and eye shadow - what was I thinking in those early days of my career? But despite the heels and the makeup, you could see my brown face, and thick, usually frizzy mane of hair.

My social work career progressed, and I worked for different local authorities and for a residential family assessment centre. I worked for three different West Yorkshire authorities during my whole social work career, with people from all walks of life. Across a variety of different areas: urban, suburban, the lush green Yorkshire countryside and the inner-city concrete jungles. In all my 14 years of working in social work (on the frontline), the last 5 were as an Independent Reviewing Officer. Sadly, the most horrific, heart stabbing and gut-wrenching overt racism and maltreatment came from other professionals.

Ok, there was the odd occasion when I was working with a couple of families who were active English Defence League (EDL) members. I can't say that I didn't feel some level of hostility - but I was never treated as inexplicably as I was by other professionals.

So, it's all about multi-agency working, co-operation and teamwork? Well try speaking to me in a normal voice without that foul contempt, and at least have the decency to look me in the face when you are directing your poison. They always assumed I was incapable or incompetent before they had even begun working with me.

As I moved into academia (and what is the white world of higher education), I thought I would move in the circles of those who are enlightened! How wrong I was.

I've spent many years of my academic career being referred to as a student. Yes, you could say my appearance makes me look younger - but after 12 years and 3 kids later - come on people! Sitting through meetings where, despite being the lead on new and innovative projects, I was overlooked. It was my white colleagues who were spoken to directly. I was patronised and spoken down to, on regular occurrences. Always the lecturer, but never the senior, was the story of my academic career, for almost 12 years of being there. Despite all the hard work, commitment, project work, success and income generation I had undertaken and been involved in.

I always remember the day the senior leadership team presented their concerns about differential outcomes for students, racial inequalities, and what the university were going to do about this. It was like a lightbulb had finally gone off. I felt emancipation had finally arrived on the whitewashed campus.

I then remember speaking to a white colleague about other matters, but at which she decided to rant about how offended she was by the senior leadership talk. That she and all the staff had been accused of being racist and that no-one at the university was racist, how dare this accusation be directed towards staff. If this wasn't enough, she then went on to tell me about a black lecturer in the team had blamed her poor module review results on the fact she was black as to excuse her shortcomings.

You know the fight, flight or fright scenario we discuss in social work, well this happened to me like a lightning bolt that shook my body to its core. Despite my strong internal workings for social justice, I froze in her office. I could hardly move my lips and all I said was something pathetic like, "that's a bit strong" and "one would not really know how these things would feel unless one was someone of colour". To this day, I still beat myself up for not having said anything more and not challenging her. Around 6 years later, I have still not set a foot in her office and I never will.

However, here I am today writing this story and having been promoted in 2020. I also have a lead role at the university in addressing racial inequalities. I do not hold back anymore in speaking out about social injustices and challenging those who discriminate and persecute. Racial inequalities continue to exist and manifest, but the fight against them will go on.

My social work practice has taught me just how effective one can be in using the right words to fight racism. Be yourself, always speak up, speak out and keep it simple when you want to bring about positive change and never ever lose hope or optimism.

Digital Rhythms

- Biant Singh

I am a social worker and Community Musician and I'm at my happiest when combining the two. I was born and bred in the inner city of Nottingham, where my family were directly exposed to complex issues of race, poverty and disability. From an early age, I grew up steeped in the traditions of Indian classical music.

I chose to train as a social worker, because I wanted an opportunity to support people to develop their independence and make their own choices and decisions. These principles were (and remain to this day) central to my belief system.

I am committed to community and passionate about service-user involvement.

Over 3 decades I have developed a facilitative practice where social justice, music, performance and the wellbeing of people intermingle. My work takes me into many situations: as trainer, consultant, academic, musician, percussionist, social worker and friend. Depending on what the moment requires, we are united by a common purpose; to create an inclusive environment that energizes, enlivens, heals, and brings people together to feel better.

Drawing on my cultural and artistic influences from the Indian classical traditions of 'Guru Shishya Parampara', the drum has followed me every step. It has allowed me to retain a creativity in times of harsh realities, including austerity and increasing bureaucracy and proceduralisation. I have drummed my way into the heart of social work practice with individuals and community groups communicating in a free-flowing authentic way. The process has been like a simultaneous leap of faith from a world of thought and reason into the world of expression.

It has been a challenging period during the COVID 19 Pandemic and lockdown to deliver crisis intervention and preventative work with individuals and the community whilst working remotely from home.

Embracing digital technology has not been easy but is becoming the 'new normal' using Teams and Zoom platforms to support individual's health and wellbeing and promote inclusion. The Drums that were once placed in front of people to create Beats and Rhythms now are in a virtual world of sound transmitted the through the screen. I have gained a lot more experience and a lot more thinking time and doing time with activities that have opened themselves to me.

A recent virtual session with young people, who have been facing huge amounts of social isolation and are becoming further marginalised as vulnerable young people in our society, involved an experience using everyday kitchen utensils. With wooden spoons and tins of beans as their Drums we created digital rhythms in the name of knowledge and skill by using ancient drum patterns to stimulate a musicality, imagination and creativity. We took a simultaneous leap of faith from a world of thought and reason into the world of expression. These objects become their islands of personal identity, stimulating an active interest in their wellbeing. We called this session Object, Rhythm, Alchemy.

During the Pandemic my practice and learning have placed it in a wider context of social work practice the overall experience has made me think about the impact that I have made and am making to service users across all sections of the local community using digital technology to support wellbeing, developing digital health hubs with trusted organisations like the local CVS and District Councils. It's not just about my own processes but it is a continuous learning and thinking that has directly come from my practice.

You cannot just rely on your experience you have got to keep moving forward or at least sideways!

Footnote

In many Shamanic societies, if you came to a medicine person complaining of being disheartened, dispirited or depressed, they would ask one of the 4 questions:

1. When did you stop dancing?

2. When did you stop singing?

3. When did you stop being enchanted by stories?

4. When did you stop finding comfort in the sweet territory of silence?

The Black Social Worker

- Winnie Lwanda

I am the "black social worker" and need only be known by my first name, as I stand out. My surname being "unusual" or "exotic" is spelt phonetically, but is commonly mispronounced or written incorrectly.

People see the colour of my skin before they see me as a person. A visible other operating against invisible barriers. Working twice as hard, yet rarely celebrated. Understanding that my face does not fit, opportunities are limited and progression is not encouraged. Seen as "angry", "bitter" or "playing the race card", by not playing their game and knowing my place within hierarchical systems.

But I refuse to accept the limitations defined by ignorance and apathy towards racism that is systemic, insidious and a societal problem. Racism is centred on a power imbalance and that power does not lie with people of colour. Black people have lived in Britain for centuries; not that our stories and contributions are typically found in history books and not that there is understanding of the British Empire. So how many more centuries will it take to achieve racial equality?

Being the lone black figure and the only black voice, my experience has been of diversity being discounted and the equal value of life being denied. I am deeply saddened by people professing anti-racist and anti-discriminatory values inconsistent with their actual behaviour. I ignore the most common microaggressions of emails addressed to: 'Hi Surname'.

Every day I work amongst people who make me feel uncomfortable because of the way in which they relate to me. I let you touch my hair. I hear you referring to me as "coloured" and say nothing. I hear troubling conversations about immigration amongst particular groups of people and dare not speak. I remain in stunned silence when a colleague with an appreciation of hip-hop music uses the N-word or stereotypes are used within the context of appropriation. I have my Britishness questioned mindlessly and do not respond.

When Human Resources tell me there is no policy which covers racism towards employees by members of the public, I do nothing. I have been called a "nigger" and had my skin colour likened to excrement. And I quote: "you are a public servant. This is Britain. Go home to your own country". "What's the world coming to when a black woman and a gay man are taking your kids off you?"

I gracefully accept that further incidents will not lead senior managers to address this issue. I overlook my employer's statement on equality and diversity on its website omitting on the grounds of "race" or "ethnicity". I was shocked when asked by a manager if my sickness absence within my newly qualified year was due to a black doll being placed on my desk, despite my fit note stating work-related stress and two colleagues raised specific concerns about this. Social work is renowned for high levels of burnout to which no-one is immune, with varying levels of support.

And when I do speak out or act against what is unjust, I am maligned.

As the "black social worker" this is a reality from which I cannot escape and poses a constant challenge to my general wellbeing and sense of self. Yet what demoralises me the most is knowing the that prejudice and bias seep into practice.

The person oppressed by white privilege understands the power of the social worker. If you fail to see both, please ask yourself who am I empowering? Am I part of the solution or part of the problem?

Ambition Navigation

- Wayne Reid

Starting position

My grandparents originate from Jamaica and they moved to England in the 1950's. I am 2nd generation Black British. I come from a working-class background and I grew up in 2 predominantly White-British council estates in Sheffield. I'm proud of the principles instilled from my upbringing.

As far back as I can remember, I know that in some situations I've been considered as an anomaly, enigmatic or a bit of a novelty (depending on the context). This is still reflected at times in how people perceive my Yorkshire accent, aptitude, dress sense and personality. At secondary school, I remember asking teachers for extra homework to the absolute horror of my classmates. However, I couldn't easily be categorised as a geek, as I had a wide circle of friends and I was decent at football (which was a matter of life and death at the time). I knew I wasn't regarded as a 'stereotypical' black guy though – which had pros and cons for me.

I left school in 1996 with decent grades (9 GCSE's A-C), but with little direction and found myself drifting aimlessly in junior administration roles. As a young man, I lived for the weekend and enjoyed the music scene with my friends and DJing at clubs. My perspective was youthfully short-term, but I felt worldly. At the time, the whole vibe just seemed multicultural to me. There was even an optimistic socio-political outlook, the era was encapsulated by New Labour's election soundtrack: "things can only get better". Of course, inequality still existed, but there just seemed to be more of a shared understanding on some race issues (at least in the company I kept).

My family were skint and accessing post-16 education was not routine, so the academic route of college and university seemed unrealistic to me. My parents are grafters. So, I accepted an apprenticeship at a local 'Business College' and had several short-term placements. I completed 2 NVQs in Business Administration and Customer Services and bounced around different administration roles. I later made the unpleasant discovery that the qualifications were basically equivalent to the qualifications I had already obtained from school... Even later I found out the 'Business College' was closed for malpractices...

In retrospect, I realise I was just lazily shepherded into administration roles, without any meaningful career guidance. I think my parents and schoolteachers were just relieved (and surprised) I'd left school with decent grades and without a criminal record, children or both – unlike some of my peers.

Fostering

My social care career began in 1998, when I applied for "just another admin job" at a private fostering agency as a Placements Officer. I quickly discovered the role was far more interesting than I'd first anticipated. It involved undertaking the 'initial matching process' for potential foster placements, including identifying children's needs and cross-referencing them with potential foster carers' knowledge, skills and expertise. I worked closely with Supervising Social Workers and other professionals to progress potential placement options.

I was enlightened and inspired by the experience. Becoming a Supervising Social Worker and supporting foster families seemed such a rewarding and satisfying career path. The thought of having a work mobile phone, company car, working from home was enticing... However, my daydream quickly evaporated when I realised the role was unattainable without a university degree - which I couldn't afford, and I also doubted my academic abilities. At that time, I didn't realise that subconsciously becoming a Supervising Social Worker had become my primary career ambition.

After about 4 years, aged 22, I felt I needed a fresh challenge. My career progression prospects at the agency were limited beyond administration (without a social work qualification), so when an alternative administration opportunity, with better prospects, arose at the National Probation Service (NPS) I applied - just on the off-chance.

National Probation Service (NPS)

When I arrived at the NPS interview panel, I was glad to see it was being chaired by a Black male manager. I subtly observed he was pleasantly surprised to see me, and I knew this could be an advantage. I was mindful of maximising this, by being charismatic and professional and not appearing aloof or nonchalant. It worked. The next day the manager called to offer me the job. He was complimentary about how I'd interviewed, whilst being 'constructively critical' (in what I came to later understand was his particular feedback style - a combination of 'tough love' and Caribbean swagger). He elaborated that because I had interviewed so well, he wanted me to interview for the role of Probation Services Officer (which involved working directly with offenders). He asked me to prepare a brief presentation on engaging offenders to deliver at another interview later that week. I sensed the brother favoured me and I was boosted.

I prepared and delivered the presentation and was swiftly offered the role - which I accepted. It involved working on a specialist intervention project, aimed at intensively controlling and changing the offending behaviour of repeat offenders (aged 18-25). I worked with partnership agencies to deliver wide-ranging community interventions. Also, I frequently prepared and presented court reports at Magistrates and Crown courts throughout South Yorkshire.

It was all a steep learning curve for me. I had no prior knowledge or experience of working directly with the public, never mind the intricacies of the criminal justice system. Well, only what my friends who were TWOCKERS had told me! I was a young Black male in a white-dominated institution that I knew was culpable for the disproportionate criminalisation of young Black males just like me. I remember early on visiting a local prison with a Black colleague to co-facilitate a 'Black prisoner group' and saw many Black friends and family members I had grown up with who were now incarcerated. This was a jarring experience and my first real experience of the tensions between my personal and professional lives.

I was in grave danger of becoming overwhelmed by my duties/responsibilities and the situation I had found myself in. I was very fortunate that a knowledgeable (older White male) colleague informally mentored and schooled me on the basics of criminal justice and the remit of the project. I'm forever indebted to him for taking the time to do this for me. I've never understood his motives for doing it. Paradoxically, I soon came to find the Black male manager from the interview panel (who was now my line-manager), did not get on with this White colleague. I came to realise that some of my manager's behaviour was controversial. However, as the person who gave me my 'big break', I was always grateful to him. I respected what he had achieved (despite the challenges he must have faced as a senior Black professional during his career) and his stature as an elder within the local Black community – regardless of our personality differences at times.

One clash between us was more public than either of us would have liked. There was a miscommunication between him and I regarding an innocuous training request I had submitted. Being the confrontational character he could sometimes be, he approached me (in the middle of the office) and to my disbelief he began to openly admonish me about it! Given my admiration and respect for him, not only as a senior, but as a Black elder – I tolerated his monologue the best I could – but after a while I found myself challenging some of his comments. Our exchange provided avid viewing for our nearby (mainly White) colleagues in the open plan office – who were all deathly silent (but no doubt attentive).

As our debate escalated, my manager somehow became more aware of our surroundings and signaled me to a nearby office - where he continued to talk *at* me and accused me of being "disingenuous". I have to admit, I 'lost it' at this point and became both angry and tearful – something I've not been at work before or since. The situation was soon interrupted by another manager who entered the office and politely informed us that our raised voices could be heard by everyone on the (open plan) floor... My manager later apologised to me and we moved on. It was difficult navigating our tempestuous relationship at times – but my admiration for what he had accomplished as a Black professional outweighed my views about our personality differences. For me, this highlighted the diversity *within* cultures, as well as *between* cultures.

The NPS project was successful and was later integrated into the mainstream provisions of the service. The end of the project meant I was then expected to work with offenders aged between 18-65. Since I was still in my mid 20's, the routine of sending predominantly White middle-aged men to prison for breaching their court orders became too patronising and tedious for me and I knew it was time to move on.

Youth Offending Service

In 2005, I was offered a Youth Offending Service (YOS) Officer role in the 'bail and remand team'. My role was similar to the project role at the NPS, but it involved working with young people (rather than adults) in a multi-disciplinary environment. I had been selected over one of my White colleagues from the NPS, who subsequently behaved quite childishly and refused to speak to me. It soon became apparent my ex-colleague was expected to get the job as she often socialised with my new YOS team outside of work. This strained my working relationships within the new team and communication was *proper awkward* from the outset. They made it clear I was unwelcome and my work was overly-scrutinised. I worked efficiently – but there was an unmistakable divide between me and the team. This became deep-rooted over time, but it was more about our incompatible characters and personalities, rather than a racism issue (I think) – but nonetheless I was isolated and marginalised. I found solace by listening to Tupac Shakur ('Can't C Me' and 'Open Fire') routinely on my drive to work each day for motivation.

It wasn't all doom and gloom whilst working at the YOS. I became a father in 2006. Also, I was fortunate to befriend an older White male colleague who was on a 'phased return' to work following a serious motorbike accident.

Despite his ongoing rehabilitation, my colleague was very perceptive and empathetic of the challenges I faced (within my team and in life generally). He was unconventional, but uncompromisingly professional. As a revered Practice Teacher, I considered him the 'Obi-Wan Kenobi of Social Work'. We would sometimes have private meetings to enable me to offload and he became a good friend/mentor as my career progressed. As an originator of 'race panels' and social work activism on 'anti-oppressive practice' in the 1980's (and an ex-boxer and boxing promoter), my friend/mentor was a formidable advocate of Black rights and understood the barriers to racial equality. Our relationship continues to this day and I consider him a demigod and an infallible ally.

During my interview for the YOS role, I had enquired about the possibility of being sponsored to undertake a Social Work degree. I was advised there was "a queue of staff ahead of me, but I could wait my turn". I accepted this position and took up alternative training opportunities in the interim. After 2 years, the YOS announced plans to only support youth justice-related qualifications. I was advised by the Head of Service that "the goal posts had moved" regarding my prior agreement. I was enraged by this change in service delivery and the limitations it was placing on my career prospects.

I articulated my complaints to the Head of Directorate and took advice from my trade union. Following an investigation, I gained approval to apply for sponsorship, but my application would only be accepted based on merit. I applied and was selected to study via the Open University route alongside my full-time job. However, the offer was conditional – I had to leave my job at the YOS and move to the Leaving Care Service – due to the closer relevance to social work. I was unhappy with this, as I loved my job (despite my misguided colleagues) – but begrudgingly accepted my fate.

Leaving Care Service

When I arrived at the Leaving Care Service in 2008, I received a much warmer welcome – despite my resistance to the move. The staff team were from more diverse social backgrounds and the work was more varied. I worked as a Young Person's Advisor, supporting 'looked after' children/young people with their transition into adulthood. I undertook this whilst studying in my own time and returned to my substantive role in-between completing 2 intensive social work placements.

Placement 1

I engineered my first placement, through an ex-colleague from the YOS who had moved to a Community Mental Health Team. He persuaded a colleague to undertake the relevant training to become a Practice Educator and accept me as a student. She was an Indian lady, known for her detached and unambiguous presentational style - who couldn't quite work me out – but I got through the placement unscathed and learned a lot about working in a different multi-disciplinary setting with people with long-term continuing needs.

Placement 2

When I returned to my substantive role (in the Leaving Care Service), I was told by the Head of Service that my next placement would be in a Child Protection team – which I was dismayed about. As a new father, I was reluctant to expose myself to potentially extreme child abuse and neglect – but I had no choice. Sure enough, the following year the move was organised and I moved teams with trepidation. I found the whole experience, including the working conditions and the volume of work, very challenging and it is the only job that has noticeably affected my well-being. Although the experience later benefitted my career, I was more than relieved to return to my substantive role again upon completion.

Post-qualification

A few months later, I qualified and registered as a Social Worker. I decided I wanted to become a Supervising Social Worker in private fostering. I earnestly sent my CV to various fostering agencies and waited to see what came back. My ego was massaged by the volume of interest I received, including the agency I had previously worked for as a Placements Officer.

Inadvertently, I received an email from another agency (from a company director addressed to an internal manager), that basically read: "Here's a CV from another newly qualified social worker (NQSW) without much experience. Just fob him off gently..." Due to my cultured professional experiences at this point, I was slightly miffed, so I contacted the director and thought I would politely correct them (at the very least) – regardless of whether they had any vacancies. I did just that and spent the next 40 minutes speaking with him! By the end of the call, he was brimming with enthusiasm and indicated they might offer me a job! I had an informal interview the following week to firm up their offer, which I readily accepted. I had achieved my dream of being a Supervising Social Worker!

Fostering (re-visited)

My SSW role was home-based. I supervised and supported foster placements across the north of England for several years. I worked with a range of local authorities and professionals to meet the holistic needs of children/young people and provided appropriate advice/support/supervision to foster carers. Also, I was actively involved in foster carers recruitment, assessment and training.

Unfortunately, after 8 years, the fostering agency was purchased by a larger fostering agency. I was uncomfortable with the significant change in company ethos and the increasingly overbearing nature of my line manager. So, based on these circumstances, in 2017 I applied for the job of Professional Officer at the British Association of Social Workers (BASW) - just on the off-chance. I was doubtful about securing the role as I knew there was a lack of diversity in the upper echelons of social work. I was wrong-footed when BASW offered me the role.

British Association of Social Workers (BASW)

I don't mind admitting that initially I found the versatility required in my role at BASW overwhelming. I remember needing a post-work nap in those early days! My diverse national role includes: recruiting and supporting members (Social Workers); mentoring Social Workers; engaging with wide-ranging stakeholders; building branch networks; formulating policy/position statements; organising events; collaborating with universities; responding to complex social work enquiries and coordinating national consultation responses/surveys. I support national groups that focus on: Students & NQSWs, Criminal Justice, Mental Health and Professional Capabilities & Development. I have reported publicly (on various high-profile media platforms) regarding social work issues affecting children/young people, families and adults.

In 2020 (following George Floyd's murder), I proactively spearheaded a movement to reignite anti-racism in social work via my role at BASW. Possibly akin to the horse that bolted. I have been privileged enough to represent my views on anti-racism in print, online and on international platforms. I'm honoured to be the founder of the BASW England Black & Ethnic Minority Professionals Symposium.

I strive to lead by example, whilst recognising my imperfections. I hope to improve the public profile of Social Workers (and the profession), in a way that inspires people from all social backgrounds and ultimately benefits society.

My philosophy is to have a dream and be dogged in how you navigate towards your ambition.

The story of my career is captured in this YouTube recording: www.youtube.com/watch?v=ZTJJuxsZ5oo.

Lessons learned

Based on my experiential knowledge, my advice to aspiring professionals is:

- Be resilient. Use your passion to fuel your determination to succeed and bounce back when needed
- Utilise the advice/support of your formal/informal networks and identify suitable mentors and positive role models.
- Don't be afraid to ask questions!
- Recognise the compatibility of personalities is key in developing effective professional relationships
- Know your rights and assert them when necessary
- Do your homework, be prepared and be proactive (geeks prosper)
- Don't dwell on the negativity of discrimination. Maximise any opportunities for 'positive discrimination'
- Be self-aware and recognise the ways you can be easily labeled, stereotyped and categorised – as well as your own inescapable 'racial lens'.

- Don't be deterred by rejection. Mishaps, mistakes and misfortune are good learning opportunities. Always seek feedback and consider on how you might do things differently next time.
- Be authentic and stay true to yourself

(This list was originally created for the Black & Ethnic Minority Symposium 'SMASHING the Glass Ceiling' event on 2/12/20).

Finding My Brave

- *Shabnam Ahmed*

"The river needs to take the risk of entering the ocean,
because only then will fear disappear,
because that's where the river will know
It's not about disappearing into the ocean, but of becoming the ocean"
(Khalil Gibran)

Today, I feel ready to share with the world, how a middle-aged Asian woman – that is I found her brave! One of the valuable tools that social work has given me is the habit of reflection. Reading my reflective diaries in January 2020, which I started as a social work student in 2004, gave me the nostalgic feeling, one like when you visit your old photo albums and are filled with both comfort and discomfort, sometimes at how much things have changed, and sometimes how much nothing has changed. For me, reading through my journals in 2020, felt like an MRI scan. For anyone who has had one of those, the technician see's beyond what I believe any other x-ray facility has the ability to do. Even the bits you do not wish to be on show. Usually the bits that caused discomfort are the ones the technician highlights and there is some kind of revelation. In a similar way as my eyes, heart and mind x-rayed my scribbles, something prominent that caused a lot of discomfort became clear. This moment set a spark towards me finding my brave.

In March 2020 when the prime minister of Great Britain told everyone to stay at home and we experienced our first lockdown the world came to a stand hill. Fear and uncertainty gripped the nation. As a manager of a large team at the time, I not only heard the emotions and worry of staff about themselves and their families, but for those that they had so passionately come into the profession to support. Breathe was a theme and a worry. To quote a sentence from my reflective diary "*Corona – the invisible beast, that goes after your breath*" (Diary date entry – 1st April 2020).

The world was further shook on 25th May 2020, when even if we did not want to watch it, most of us did. A beast attacked again, this time it was visible and murdered a human being, whilst others watched. Police brutality and racism was brought to the world through the words "I cannot breathe" accompanied with "sir". This was a decisive moment and an awakening for many. To think that even in his moment of death George Floyd referred to his assailant as 'Sir 'reveals the extent of the powerlessness created by years of white supremacy and inequality. So both the invisible virus and visible virus attacked breath and particularly the breath of Black and Ethnic minorities.

Three distinct events connected for me:

- My reflective journals and what they revealed for me up to March 2020
- The pandemic
- Murder of George Floyd

What connected these three things were my thoughts and questions about 'Belonging' and 'Space'. What spaces are Black, Asian humans allowed to occupy? Where and when are our voices heard, and when and where do we feel we belong? I am not the one voice for this group of people but the journey back through my reflective journals led me to think about why and what has been preventing me from living out some of my dreams. Why has it taken me so long? When I am seen, how much effort do I have to put in to be seen, how have I been supported and who has enabled my visibility? This was a difficult personal journey to take back to the past, bringing me here to the future and it was indeed very revealing. I cannot compare my experiences in any-way to the murder of George Floyd and those that have lost their lives in the pandemic. I am still here, breathing, but this was exactly what led me towards finding my brave and using my breath whilst I still have it. If not now, then when Shabs, was the question I asked myself.

As events unfolded in 2020 and a shared language emerged in relation to anti-racist practice, terms such as Microaggressions and Microincivilities became popular. Many of my reflections in my journal reflected just how I had experienced many of these and unseen them at the time. However, from where I was standing now, I could no longer, unsee, unhear many of what had become the unnoticeable wallpaper around me in the past. This understanding further fuelled my enthusiasm to represent. To use my voice to be the person I want to be and to turn up my volume so others like me could hear and feel represented. It is interesting that in the last year most people who have said to me that I inspire them have been Black or Asian. Could this be because there is some resemblance to me or to what I represent? I want to share some of my truths with you, which helped me to understand and put into perspective my self-doubts, as this journey of introspection is what enables me to share what I share today.

Taking you back into my teens, an experience at college, where as a mischievous 17-year-old student, whilst doing a presentation on a washing powder detergent with a group of friends; we could not hold a straight face. We laughed throughout the presentation. After the lesson, my teacher held ONLY me back and suggested that if I was considering applying to university, I should not and instead I should find a job in fashion, as I was not cut out for studying. I never shared that comment with anyone until 2019 when applying for my doctorate. At each graduation, I say 'Thank you' in my mind to that teacher. Whilst her comment did not deter me from going to university, it has never left me thus starting my doctorate was a decision that I delayed for several years and even on starting it, I often find myself experiencing the 'Imposter syndrome'. Do I belong here? I hear a reply from my Professor Jo Finch "yes you do Shabs". Which is most comforting.

Another example I wish to share is something I have heard many Black and Asian colleagues say and relates to invisibility. This is when suddenly something you may suggest, initiate and even complete takes the position of 'We' or 'I' and is no longer yours to claim, and even you start believing that it was not yours in the first place. Over the years now, many of my contributions are not mine to own. I do not think people have intended to do this deliberately, but I need people to know that when you do this, you steal something more than an idea, you make that person invisible.

Not seeing people like myself represented enough in the places I want to be in, over 22 years of practice, never having a manager who was not white sent clear messages to me about where I belong and where I do not belong. It is no surprise that it took me 20 years to consider applying for a manager's position. These and many more insights about my truth, made me uncomfortable and I realised that silence was not an option anymore. I started to feel a sense of comfort in my discomfort, if that makes sense. I could sit with my insecurities and let them silence me, or I could try to use the life I have, the spaces I occupy and become visible. I decided to the latter. I listened to the words of Maya Angelou repeatedly "Courage is the best virtue, have courage". This is when The School of Shabs was born. In August 2020, I launched my educational social work YouTube channel. A dream that I have had silenced for many years.

Events in 2020 gave me the push I needed to start living out some of my dreams. Through my channel I want to represent, I want people like me, to feel whatever their talent they can achieve their dreams. Through my videos, I want to share diverse voices, show casing their talent and contributions as well as my own. I hope that by using such a large social media platform, I am accessible and I can offer some of my practice wisdom freely. I hope that people will read this and then see me, know it was not easy, but take courage in attempting to do the things they want to do and be who they want to be. I found my brave and I hope you will too.

"Let yourself be silently drawn by the strange pull of what you really love. It will not lead you astray" Rumi.

You Matter.

RUMINATIONS

'Ruminations' is the name of a mythical book written by one of my personal heroes KRS-One (the hip-hop pioneer). It is a much-revered, but rare, book that has evaded me for years - but I'm forever hopeful of obtaining a copy.

This section of OUTLANDERS is based on my ruminations. It is a selection of the articles I have produced whilst working for BASW England. The murder of George Floyd had a profound effect on me. Overnight, I became the proverbial 'horse that bolted' at BASW and proactively reignited the anti-racism in social work movement pioneered by the likes of Gurnam Singh, Kish Bhatti-Sinclair, Claudia Bernard, Angie Bartoli and others. I was determined to do everything in my power to counter what I (and many others) perceive as a relentless and omnipresent attack on Black lives globally.

Up until George Floyd's murder, I had enjoyed a fruitful (but low-key) career at BASW, but that atrocity forced me to step outside of my comfort zone to expose the multi-faceted examples of white supremacy that exist in social work in a solution-focused way.

In my opinion, the reality is that all organisations, institutions and structures are influenced by white supremacy. It is just a question of HOW MUCH, not IF it exists. Therefore, I developed the Anti-racist Commitment Framework, as from my observations there appears to be no clear national accountability or strategy for ensuring anti-racism within social work. You will see the framework is located after the article on 'How to promote an anti-racist culture in social work'. The framework is my slapdash attempt to explore potential solutions. It is not perfect (by any stretch of the imagination), but it does provide a basic foundation on which to build layers of anti-racist cultural and organisational practices.

My plans for the future on anti-racism include: enhancing my anti-racism presentation; emboldening the BPS; campaigning for anti-racism, anti-oppression and anti-discrimination to be included in the regulatory standards; challenging the disproportionate representation of social workers of colour at fitness to practice hearings; developing initiatives on 'authentic allyship' and I have plans for another book... These endeavors are not an exhaustive list. I have some other embryonic ideas, but I also want to actively listen and support my colleagues and peers, to develop anti-racist innovations that they are nurturing. I do not undertake this work in isolation, my colleagues (and collaborators including Siobhan) have fully embraced and supported this work - particularly in BASW England.

My mantra of 'pure, proactive and unapologetic' is an indication of my combative and militant mindset when it comes to Anti-racism in Social Work. My strategy is to move through different phases to promote anti-racism, such as : shock and awe; edutainment; promoting allyship and other further phases which are in the pipeline.

Ultimately, my desire is for this anthology to be considered a valuable resource to educate, empower and equip Social Workers from all backgrounds in policy, practice and education for decades to come.

'One world, one race... the human race!'

Wayne Reid
BASW England Professional Officer & Social Worker

Twitter
@wayne_reid79
@BASW_UK
#CrushingStereotypesDaily

Black Lives Matter: social work must respond with action - not platitudes

The murder of George Floyd is the latest in a long line of atrocities and brutalities endured by the global Black community.

This has a long history – longer than is sometimes convenient for honest acknowledgement. I notice some commentators are referring to George's 'death', which is a dilution of what occurred. George was brutally murdered by a police officer and the world has seen the evidence.

The context to George's murder is emotive and cumulative: endless examples of police brutality cases in the US and UK, modern-day systems of oppression and the historic and ongoing suppression of the effects of slavery and colonialism in mainstream education.

These factors can accumulate and create an acute sense of anger and rage. These emotions can manifest in civil disorder and criminality. It has been evidenced that anarchic extremists are infiltrating protests to covertly fuel acts of looting and violence, which is then reported by the media in such ways as to discredit the protesters. This detracts from the causal factors that have triggered the protests – and if we want to discuss looting, how about the longstanding looting of Africa's natural resources?

As a Black British male social worker, I write this article on Black Lives Matter wearing numerous hats, as this issue affects me deeply, both personally and professionally.

Clearly, my opinion cannot and should not be understood as representing all Black and ethnic minority people or practitioners. We are not a homogeneous group.

It was important to me for my employer, the British Association of Social Workers (BASW), to publish our organisational position statements before I wrote this article, as I refuse to be the tokenistic 'Black voice' of BASW. I'm one of many Black voices in social work. It is my reality, that my role enables me to be heard more broadly than others.

I'm proud of the authenticity and candour of BASW's statements responding to George's murder and in support of the fight against racialised discrimination.

Those who follow me on Twitter, or who are on my mailing list, will have observed my campaign to educate, empower and equip Black and ethnic minority people – and importantly our allies – with various information and resources.

Disappointing responses from social work leaders

On occasions, I have been outspoken about the delayed/weak position statements and responses from prominent social work leaders and organisations. Given that social work's core values and ethics are deep-rooted in anti-oppressive practice and social justice, this eventuality has been particularly disappointing for me and many others within the profession.

Sadly, these values and ethics appear sometimes to have been taken for granted, diluted or ignored in recent years/decades. Perhaps austerity has desensitised us?

Overall, I'm sure Black and ethnic minority social workers and service users will welcome the late (if weak) acknowledgements and platitudes from some of the social work elite. The statements will send a necessary message to employers and other stakeholders across the profession about the relevance of current world events to social work policy, practice and education.

However, I think some of the statements could be strengthened by providing a clearer commitment to systemic reforms to eradicate all forms of racism through specific, measurable, achievable and realistic targets.

'I'm not a racist'

During the furore surrounding George's murder, some individuals/organisations have recoiled at the suggestion they may be racist.

"I'm not a racist!" is the common response, the accusations seemingly worse than the facts.

I would argue that racism is not an absolute mindset; instead it's a rather fluid one. There are degrees of racism. I imagine very few people reading this article would identify with extreme right-wing neo-Nazi racism, but many will have stereotypical views about certain ethnic groups which they project in everyday situations if they are honest and self-aware.

There is a structural and lazy acceptance that 'lower-level' prejudice and oppression are somehow separate – with the former being considered a less important issue. However, I believe that tackling such prejudice would engender a real decrease in the overt, violent forms of 'race-related hate'.

In my view, the spectrums of white privilege and white supremacy are also broad – not absolute.

Fundamentally, there are a range of behaviours and oppressive systems that are socially acceptable, which we must address and redress to tackle racism effectively in all its ugly manifestations. For example, the statement 'all lives matter' is covert racism, as it ignores the history and current circumstances of Black people globally. Physical colonisation and slavery may no longer be acceptable or legal, but colonisation and slavery of the mind has been the norm since their abolition. Black lives matter applies then, now and always.

The recent misdemeanours of Dominic Cummings show us there are clear double standards; not just from a class perspective (which was perpetuated by the media), but also through the lens of white privilege. I wonder how Raheem Sterling would have been portrayed flouting the lockdown rules.

Re-examining 'BAME'

Terms such as 'Commonwealth', 'hostile environment', and 'BAME' need to be re-examined. BAME does not describe who I am. BAME is a clumsy, cluttered and incoherent acronym that is opportune for categorising people of colour as a homogenous group – when we quite clearly are not.

Of course, I cannot speak for all people of colour. I understand that 'BAME' can be operationally helpful when exploring the overarching effects of all things racist. However, it misses so much nuance and subtlety, and can be seized upon by those who wish to deny racism as a white problem.

Routinely, I hear people comfortably stating that BAME people "can't even agree amongst themselves". This sloppy reductivism leads to terms being invented such as 'Black on Black' crime. I have not heard about "White on White" crime – ever.

Some quarters consider having a small minority of people from Black and ethnic minority groups who reach positions of power (including within the current Cabinet), as progress, in and of itself. I respectfully disagree and would go so far as to say it is actually unhelpful.

I think a contingent of these people only seem to identify as being people of colour when it is expedient. Often, they have championed policies that in fact would have previously disadvantaged their own families – which is basically 'pulling up the drawbridge' and morally bankrupt.

In some ways it is worse than having a 'conventional racist' at the helm. To quote Malcolm X: "I have more respect for a [person] who lets me know where [they stand], even if [they are] wrong, than the one who comes up like an angel and is nothing but a devil."

Politicians have form for allowing their personal ambitions to override ethics and morality. Their denials can play beautifully into the hands of those who seek to maintain the existing order. As black and ethnic minority representation is disproportionately very low, these people do not necessarily use their power for good and structural inequalities remain unchanged.

'White allies' and what they can do

At this current juncture in race relations, there has been much discussion about how 'White allies' can be 'anti-racist' and supportive to the cause. Of course, allies can be personal and/or professional. So, what is really behind those awkward smiles and sugary sympathy? Actions most definitely speak louder than words. It's time for all well-intentioned platitudes and recycled rhetoric to be converted into meaningful activism and 'root and branch' reform.

It is imperative that social workers evaluate their roles and (moral and regulatory) responsibilities. Current race relations require social workers to be proactive and do our homework to stay contemporarily astute as allies to Black and ethnic minority colleagues and service users.

There are various opportunities through BASW to develop your expertise in this area with our equality, diversity & inclusion group, events, branch meetings and training programmes. Also, I will be leading a Black & ethnic professionals symposium for BASW members in the coming weeks, so do contact me at wayne.reid@basw.co.uk or @ wayne_reid79 if this is of interest.

We all know that organisations are at times avoidant of these issues, but as social workers we must recognise that silence on racism is complicity with the oppressors. BASW will not remain silent on this issue and we implore you to do the same.

'One world, one race... the human race!'

[This article was originally published as 'Black Lives Matter: social work must respond with action – not platitudes' by Community Care magazine (online) on 12/06/20] https://www.communitycare.co.uk/2020/06/12/black-lives-matter-social-work-must-respond-action-platitudes/

How to promote an anti-racist culture in social work

Following the constructive feedback received on my last article, I've been keen not to rest on my laurels. Kind words and superlatives are, of course, pleasant and healthy for the ego – but they won't eliminate the barrage of everyday multidimensional racism. Whilst pausing the platitudes, I've been ruminating about clear actions that social work educators, employers and key stakeholders can take to promote anti-racism. My aim in this article is to outline some practical (and skeletal) ideas for social work organisations to consider. I will use the terms people of colour (POC) and Black and ethnic minority interchangeably for ease. Again, I write this article from my own viewpoint, not on behalf of all Black and ethnic minority people or social workers – as we are not a homogenous group. Also, I'm by no means an expert in organisational development/leadership, but I do consider myself as an 'expert with lived experience' of personal and professional racism in life and in social work. These are purely my opinions. Contemporary scholars include: @gurnamskhela, @consultancy_hs, @kguilaine and @muna_abdi_phd (Twitter handles).

Black and ethnic minority social workers cannot and should not be expected to 'fix' racism

Black and ethnic minority social workers cannot and should not be expected to 'fix' the racism in their workplace. However, those of us who are confident and capable enough (with the right support) can have a crucial role in educating, empowering and equipping ourselves and (potential) allies and influencers to enhance and shape anti-racism initiatives in our workplace settings.

EVERYONE has a duty to combat racism (and other forms of discrimination) in the spaces they occupy. This includes reporting racist incidents when they occur; forming like-minded alliances with peers to tackle key issues; raising awareness and making suggestions for positive reform. However, this article is aimed primarily at social work employers, educators and key stakeholders.

Typical organisational responses to tackling anti-racism:

From my cultured social work experience, the responses below generally indicate an organisation's prioritisation and level of commitment (or not) to anti-racism. However, before any meaningful change can be achieved, social work educators and employers must acknowledge the inherent and intrinsic nature of 'whiteness', 'White fragility', 'White privilege' and white supremacy as subconscious default positions in most (if not all) institutions, structures and organisational cultures. Individual and organisational awareness is an imperative first step for social workers, social work employers and social work educators to address workplace racism effectively. "In a [multifaceted] racist society, it is not enough to be non-racist. We must be anti-racist."

Broadly, there are 3 typical organisational responses when attempting to tackle racial inequality:

1. Keep silent, keep things the same and "hope all this Black Lives Matter (BLM) 'stuff' just blows over". This kind of inaction and paralysis of fear correlates with and reinforces perceptions of 'White fragility', 'White privilege' and white supremacy for some POC. This type of organisational response usually commends staff for being resilient and deflects attention away from the essential redesign of systems that routinely make people suffer.

2. Publish lukewarm organisational statements that recycle and regurgitate previous rhetoric on workforce unity with predictable (and borderline offensive) platitudes – often proposing only superficial changes. For example, publishing a sympathetic, but non-committal kneejerk brief statement; possibly delegating responsibilities to an already overworked Equalities Officer or proposing minor changes to already vague policies/procedures on 'valuing diversity' with little or no accountability. Approaches at this level are usually well-intended, but tokenistic and overlook the nuanced obstacles and pitfalls POC face every day. Unfortunately, this response is common.

3. Publish an authentic anti-racism action plan outlining significant reforms that commit to specific, measurable, achievable and realistic targets (suggestions below). For example, publishing a strong mission/position statement condemning George Floyd's murder and racism in all its forms and committing to BASW's Code of Ethics, anti-oppressive, anti-discriminatory and anti-racist practice. This approach interlinks with the 'Anti-Racist commitment framework'.

The acid test is to share this article with your social work leaders and see what response you get.

Covert, entrenched and everyday racism in the workplace

If the recent news of police officers taking 'selfies' beside the bodies of 2 murdered black sisters; the recent far-right violent protests in London or the racist comments by Suffolk councillors do not outrage you or alert you to the fact that racism is thriving in this country right now – then you really need to consider whether you have sleepwalked into being an opponent of anti-racism. At the very least, we must be self-aware and honest (with ourselves and others) when our boredom threshold is reached. This can be subliminal and counterproductive to anti-racism at every level. Everyday microaggressions (including 'banter' in the workplace) can fuel violent racist incidents.

The covert, entrenched and everyday racism in the workplace sometimes indicates the lack of quality cultural diversity and multicultural education and training available (to all staff). Surprisingly, it is rarely acknowledged in social work that race is simply a socially constructed idea with no scientific validity - invented and refined principally to oppress POC. This has modern and everyday ramifications in the working environment. Throughout the Coronavirus pandemic, Black and ethnic minority practitioners have reported to the British Association of Social Workers (BASW) that Personal Protective Equipment (PPE) has clearly been prioritised/ withheld on occasions for their white colleagues. Others explained they were made/ordered to visit service-users with suspected COVID-19 (with no PPE and no guidance/support), whilst white managers stayed at the office with 'their' supply of PPE and engaged in racist banter. These perverse experiences can be impossible for victims of 'naked and slippery' everyday racism to articulate to others or reconcile internally themselves. Furthermore, these incidents are normalised and subsumed in many workplace cultures, with limited opportunities to 'professionally offload'. In some cases, it's really not hard to see who the direct descendants of slave-owners are. With some people, it stands out like a beacon, regardless of what they say and do.

As outlined in my previous article, there is a long [history] of atrocities and brutalities endured by Black and ethnic minority people globally. 'Black lives matter' is an acknowledgment that our lives need to matter more than they have, that society should apportion them equal weighting. That is why the retort of 'White' or 'All' Lives Matter in response to BLM is not really comparable or relevant. Would it be right to ask: "What about colon cancer?" during a discussion about breast cancer? Or advise a bereaved mother that 'all lives matter' at her child's funeral? "Save the whales" does not mean other sea life is unimportant. This is not complex stuff and just requires us to revitalise our basic human qualities – compassion, empathy and humanity. Factually, unlike the lives of Black and ethnic minority people, white lives have always mattered. So, to keep proclaiming 'White lives matter' adds excessive value to them, tilting us further towards white supremacy. In hard times, surely it is right to protect and support certain groups – particularly vulnerable ones. This does not devalue, disadvantage or discredit any other groups; it just raises general awareness and improves the support available to specific groups that require immediate attention. BLM has its critics, but it is unclear why a movement that promotes equality is demonised by some people who vehemently claim they are not 'a' racist.

Anti-racism in social work must be fully considered and dismantled through collaboration with Black and ethnic minority social workers in roles as 'experts with (personal and professional) lived experience'. This is the only way that Black and ethnic minority social workers' basic needs can be properly met and their wide-ranging expertise fully utilised. Of course, this approach can only improve the experiences of black and ethnic minority service-users too. It really is just a question of how much of a priority is anti-racism in social work?

So, how can social work employers implement 'anti-racist practice' in the workplace?

What might an anti-racist working environment look like? What can social work employers do to promote anti-racism in the workplace? What would the experience be like for Black and ethnic minority social workers? Here is my vision of how this might work in reality:

Recruitment

Anti-racist recruitment targets are set to employ Black and ethnic minority senior leaders and educators to better reflect local communities and the workforce (where necessary/ possible).

The 'Rooney Rule' is adopted, similar to senior recruitment in American National Football League. This involves at least one POC candidate being interviewed for each senior leader vacancy.

Operations

Anti-racism is: explicitly promoted in mission/position statements (good example here) along with other forms of anti-discrimination; included in relevant polices/procedures and forms part of employees' employment contracts to underline its importance.

The data on workforce diversity and 'protected characteristics' (ethnicity, gender, religion, sexuality etc) informs the support available for minority groups; training for all staff and organisational policies and procedures. The workforce is encouraged to self-declare their identity and individual/group wellbeing at work provisions are developed in partnership with them. Creative wellbeing at work provisions are developed for those who have experienced workplace trauma associated with racism (and other types of discrimination). This includes peer-led support groups for members to reflect fully on their personal and professional experiences. Personal wellbeing is a mandatory agenda item for supervision meetings. By using this 'identity dashboard' approach, organisational efforts are more focussed and genuine; progress is properly managed through a cycle of reviewing data output and periodic verbal/written feedback from the workforce.

Safe and informal systems are introduced for Black and ethnic minority social workers in the workplace. For example, discriminatory practices or constructive solutions are made anonymously in an 'honesty box' to empower POC without fear of reprisals. Arising issues are then explored in supervision, team meetings or with senior leaders (if necessary).

Annual ethnicity pay audits ensure that any anomalies and discrepancies for Black and ethnic minority staff are properly reviewed and resolved.

The COVID-19 risk assessment is consistently used for all staff (particularly those from Black and ethnic minority groups).

Education

Anti-racist education is recognised as being at the heart of developing a more cultured and inclusive workforce and healthy workplace.

Education providers 'decolonialise' social work training programmes with the input of black and ethnic minority academics, social workers and service-users integrated at all stages of programme development and delivery.

Anti-discriminatory, anti-oppressive and anti-racist practice form a fundamental and mandatory requirement of social workers professional development and registration. This includes a range of educational tools and training opportunities (for different learning styles) to ensure *quality* cultural diversity education is prioritised and valued. Staff continuously learn and better understand microaggressions, stereotypes and how they can demonstrate 'anti-racist practice'.

The expertise of specialist external trainers and consultants is instrumental in shaping effective anti-racist approaches – with no reliance on tokenistic online courses.

• **Allyship**

Anti-racist allyship is understood by senior leaders, educators and practitioners to be vital in combating all manifestations of racism. Educating, empowering and equipping allies to actively support colleagues from marginalised and minority groups is common practice.

Allyship actively promotes ways in which managers and staff can become allies or become *better* allies to support their Black and ethnic minority colleagues. Social work employers and educators demonstrate they are willing to keep listening and learning from POC to instigate any meaningful change.

• **Reverse mentoring**

Anti-racist 'reverse-mentoring' enables Black and ethnic minority social workers to mentor senior leaders and educators on anti-racism (especially those with identified 'anti-racist needs'). It is important reverse-mentoring allows mentors some autonomy in their approach. Furthermore, mentoring agreements (considering confidentiality, power dynamics and conflict resolution) are agreed and signed by both parties at the outset.

• **Leadership programmes**

To combat 'glass ceiling racism', various professional development opportunities are available designed to provide advice/support colleagues from different ethnic and cultural backgrounds to enhance their career progression.

'Positive representation' recognises the disadvantages and obstacles for POC and provides opportunities (mentoring, nominations, secondments, shadowing etc) to support them in reaching their full potential.

Due to the representational imbalance, ring-fenced investment and operational resources to support leadership programmes is in place. This addresses the lack of Black and ethnic minority social workers in senior roles and provides support for those who are.

Unsurprisingly, I cannot be detailed or too prescriptive above due to limited space. Also, the demographics/dynamics in each work setting will vary. However, my suggestions can be cross-referenced with the 'Anti-Racist commitment framework'. The framework' provides more detail on: accelerating diversity; educating, empowering and equipping people; leading by example and building transparency. The framework is also compatible with BASW's Code of Ethics, Working Conditions Wellbeing Toolkit and mentoring scheme.

Ok, so what needs to happen nationally?

The existing national frameworks and initiatives to support Black and ethnic minority social workers are fragmented and optional. This can create confusion and dilution in their coherence and implementation in practice. Social work has a long history of committing to anti-discriminatory practice, but less in the way of practical mandatory implementation or robust challenge on these issues. Now is the time for the profession to properly address this. I (and no doubt many others) would welcome the prioritisation of sector leaders (including the Chief Social Workers, Social Work England, Directors of Social Services and other key stakeholders) to meaningfully and purposefully move this agenda forward to establish a mandatory 'anti-discriminatory national framework' that is universal across social work - in collaboration with BASW.

An important first step, would be to explicitly reintroduce anti-discriminatory, anti-oppressive practices and anti-racist values and ethics into the professional and qualifying education and training standards. This new regime should involve partnership working between key stakeholders to enforce these values and ethics across the professional landscape. Key aims/objectives would be to: ensure consistency, introduce mandatory requirements, emphasise 'anti-racist' values and be universally applicable to all social workers like the Professional Capabilities Framework and the professional standards.

We all know that organisations can sometimes be avoidant of anti-racism, but as social workers we must recognise that silence (or inaction) on racism is complicity with the oppressors. Unfortunately, as a profession we have been complacent and have much more to do to cultivate equality, diversity and inclusion in the workplace and society.

BASW England is able to provide advice/support; facilitate consultation and deliver training (where possible) to assist social work organisations in implementing the above approach and embedding the 'Anti-Racist commitment framework'. For social workers, there are various opportunities through BASW to develop your expertise in this area with our Equality, Diversity and Inclusion Group, events, branch meetings and training programmes. Also, BASW England will be leading a Black and Ethnic Professionals Symposium (BPS) for BASW members from 23/07/20 and a forthcoming anthology, so do contact me at wayne.reid@basw.co.uk or @wayne_reid79 – if you are interested in any of these initiatives. Many of you will also be aware of our campaign to change the imagery on the KCMG medal and our open letter to the Queen. BASW will not remain silent on this issue and we implore you to do the same.

I sincerely hope this article resonates with those with power and influence within social work to rigorously combat racism by integrating a mandatory 'Anti-racist commitment framework' (see following). I am confident that this will embed anti-racist values and ethics into practice (not just theory). Also, I also hope anti-oppressive and anti-discriminatory practice can be reaffirmed generally, as sadly, these have slid off the agenda significantly in recent years.

As a footnote, the Criminal Justice Act 1991 (Section 95), contains a section requiring the Home Office (changed to the Ministry for Justice) to annually publish the results of Criminal Courts in England and Wales. This makes it unlawful for those employed in Criminal Justice System (social work educators and employers) to discriminate on the grounds of 'ethnic background'. This is a powerful tool, possibly under-used, by black and ethnic minority professionals and white officers (allies) who identify racism – particularly in social care generally. This has the potential of legislative support for operational staff who raise the issue of racist practices (where perceived).

Let's not forget, "when you're accustomed to privilege, equality feels like oppression". The only real enemy of progress is ignorance. Social justice must prevail.

'One world, one race... the human race!'

[*This article was originally published in Community Care magazine (online) on 17/07/20.*]

ANTI-RACIST COMMITMENT FRAMEWORK		ACTIONS FOR CHANGE
ACCELERATING DIVERSITY WITHIN	Build a workforce more reflective of the communities we serve by promoting opportunities for Black and ethnic minority people to enter and advance within organisations.	A **fast-track scheme for high potential people from ethnic minority backgrounds**, fuelled by targeted recruitment for senior leadership and work with partners to help grow diverse talent pools. Selected staff will be mentored by a member of the Senior Leadership Team as they progress through different opportunities designed to build their career foundations. This will be maintained by ensuring there are diverse shortlists for every senior management role across the organisation.
EDUCATING, EMPOWERING and EQUIPPING PEOPLE	Transform the working culture to zero tolerance of discrimination. Introduce new immersive training to enhance awareness and support, to underpin inclusive management approaches and meet various learning styles.	**Race and culture awareness training will be mandatory for everyone.** This will go beyond routine online training by: offering guidance; peer support groups; recognising local issues; providing support to equip managers to champion diversity and utilising external specialist advice/support as/when necessary.
LEADING BY EXAMPLE	Ensure that every senior leader has a greater understanding of the issues faced by ethnic minority communities and are equipped to lead the fight for equality.	**Every senior leader will commit to either having an ethnic minority reverse mentor or providing professional support** to a community organisation serving ethnic minority groups
BUILDING TRANSPARENCY	Any gaps in data collection will be addressed, ensuring that senior leaders can be held to account for the progress made in tackling both discrimination and equality of opportunity.	Staff will be encouraged to self-declare their identity, enabling a rich profile of the workforce's diverse needs to be built. This will underpin the introduction of an **annual ethnicity pay audit**, backed by any immediate action required. An 'ethnicity dashboard' will help to track progress across the colleague lifecycle and set targets for senior leaders. This will be published internally annually.

‘When you’re accustomed to privilege, equality feels like oppression’

Black History Month has passed but we must not stop ringing the alarm on racism in social work.

The level of inaction from many within the profession’s establishment is both deafening and revealing. To quote US novelist and activist James Baldwin: “I can’t believe what you say, because I see what you [don’t] do.”

Being ‘let in’

I write this article from both personal and professional perspectives. I do not speak on behalf of all Black and ethnic minority people or social workers as we are not a homogenous group. Also, I refuse to be the tokenistic ‘Black voice’ of BASW. I’m one of many Black voices in the profession. I realise that I’ve been ‘let in’ (to some extent) to express my views because, to quote Black historian and TV presenter David Olusoga, I “won’t scare the horses”: I am supposedly well-spoken and middle-class or so I’ve been told.

For the record, I’m not aspiring to be a ‘nice guy’ when it comes to combating oppressive regimes and systems. ‘Niceness’ is often weaponised against people of colour. My motivation is not for career ambition or financial gain. It’s for the cause, not applause – and the cause is Black Lives Matter.

My narrative is based on my lived experiences and those of other people who are routinely judged on the basis of their skin colour.

Minimisation Street

The prevalence of anti-black racism and the stealthy manoeuvres to gloss over our contributions and downplay our legacies is discombobulating. Some of us learn to live with the burden of our exposure in white spaces, even though it punctuates the rhythm of our everyday lives, and some do not.

Most Black and ethnic minority people recognise early on that we are forced to try harder and tolerate multi-layered oppression for our endeavours and to be recognised. This is evidenced by the tiny number of Black people honoured with a statue or trophy name; the groundswell of racism aimed at Marcus Rashford for campaigning to provide meals for disadvantaged children and the avalanche of complaints and relentless racism targeted at Ashley Banjo for leading a BLM-themed dance.

Interestingly, some people have likened Black actor John Boyega being cut out of the Chinese launch of a perfume advert to a photo tweeted from a Guardian Social Care Lives 2020 event in which I was cut out as a panelist.

People must make their own minds up about any similarities. The reality is the list of minimisations and omissions (accidental or otherwise) for me and other Black people is endless and normalised.

Critics argue that politics is for politicians and Rashford should 'stick to football' and Banjo should 'stick to dancing'. These modern-day revolutionaries are accused of 'playing the race card' by some. Reducing our life experiences to a game of cards serves only to undermine the importance of what we say.

This minimisation strategy disturbingly correlates with attempts to de-politicise social work policy, practice and education. Have social workers been 'dumbed-down' to simply become agents of the state? This debate has continued for decades to a point where social workers are now regarded by some as agents of social control. Being politically and socially aware is essential to promote social work values and ethics – otherwise, surely, we are just automated robots.

To quote Black activist Guilaine Kinouani: "Any attempt at portraying [social work] (or any scholarly discipline) as an apolitical, decontexualisable and 'neutral' field of knowledge production which can operate outside of the realm of politics and ideology is not only ill-informed, it is naïve."

Does the automation of tasks that social work has become in some places stifle this type of critical and free thinking? I'd argue it does and that there has been a silent (but deliberate) shift to devoid social workers of their political nous and social activism.

I'm not talking party politics here, but all the local and national activities through which people make, preserve and amend the written and unwritten rules under which we all live. The activities associated with making decisions for groups, power relations between individuals and the distribution of resources or elevated status by central government.

From this perspective, politics is inextricably linked to the phenomena of conflict, cooperation, fairness, social justice and human rights.

It's a bad state of affairs when those in power use the media to corrupt our societal world view, so that to be 'woke' or to 'do-good' is considered something to sneer at. Accusations of 'virtue signalling' and 'victimhood' do not evoke compassion or humanity, but provide an insightful measure of their sensibilities.

For those politicians of colour who deny 'white privilege' and denounce critical race theory, 'Skin folk ain't always kinfolk' is an apt mantra from my upbringing.

Nowadays, I take the view that some white wolves exist in Black sheep's clothing. Let's be clear, these people are cleverly disguised gatekeepers and handlers. White supremacy is often more palatable when it is communicated by people from Black and ethnic minority backgrounds. Of course, the incentives of money and power are enough to seduce most human beings regardless of their ethnic background.

I'm Black all year round not just for one month

Black History Month (BHM) is not really a celebration of Black history. It's more a filtered window of remembrance to pacify us. If those in power were serious about Black history, they would integrate it into all aspects of mainstream education.

There is a very real danger of BHM, the BLM movement and anti-racism all being caricatured and side-tracked by the insidious multi-dimensional forces that exist to suffocate them. Namely, different manifestations of white supremacy and institutional 'whiteness'.

This is why we have 'bigger fish to fry' than Rule Britannia or whether Adele should have her hair in Bantu knots! Examples of this suffocation in social work include: racial harassment, gaslighting, and marginalisation. When white people attempt to police the dialogue and language of Black and ethnic minority people (based on what they view as palatable), this is how the 'psychosis of whiteness' is socialised and teaches perceived entitlement and superiority over Black people. An example of this can be seen in the responses to rap music and Black culture.

Also, there are attempts to derail, discredit and devalue Black lives through social media, including through auto-generated 'bots' which is deeply sinister. The mission to educate, equip and empower hearts and minds on anti-racism has never felt more urgent in my lifetime.

The mainstream media and politicians think BLM is old news. However, since the resurgence of the BLM movement, BASW has been at the forefront of anti-racist social work activism. BASW England has championed anti-racism in social work on a scale unrivalled by any other organisation in the profession.

As an organisation, we also realise that we are not immune to the perils of white supremacy and institutional 'whiteness'. However, BASW has shown a willingness to address and tackle these issues internally and in the profession more broadly.

Cringe position statements, feeble blogs and noteworthy silences

Since my last article in Community Care on promoting anti-racism in social work, there have been some decent position statements from some organisations and prominent social workers. However, there have also been some cringe statements, some nauseatingly feeble blogs and some noteworthy silences.

Unfortunately, there remains a scarcity of cast-iron and explicit actions and/or commitments to anti-racism. Lightweight placatory comments like: "we are against racism and oppression in all its forms" is just not good enough anymore. Also, shamelessly flogging a blog from the only non-white staff member is a glaring attempt to tokenise the issues at hand. This is semi-skilful subterfuge to avoid addressing the real-life cause and effects of racism in social work.

What message does this really convey? Far from transformative, this approach is performative allyship or lacklustre window dressing at best. You know it, I know it – we all know it.

To quote Kinouani again: "When organisations perform anti-racism, it does not take long for the mask to fall... When performative committees are formed, they soon give themselves away. Justice is actually hard to fool." Less fakery and more authenticity please.

Here is a reminder of the three typical organisational responses to racism that you might want to cross-reference with the white identities table by social work academic Gurnam Singh. How does your organisation match up?

- **Keep silent,** keep things the same and hope all this Black Lives Matter (BLM) 'stuff' just blows over. This kind of inaction and paralysis of fear correlates with and reinforces perceptions of 'white fragility', 'white privilege' and white supremacy for some Black people. Such an organisational response usually commends staff for being resilient and deflects attention away from the essential redesign of systems that routinely make people suffer.

- **Publish lukewarm organisational statements** that recycle and regurgitate previous rhetoric on workforce unity with predictable (and borderline offensive) platitudes – often proposing only superficial changes. For example, publishing a sympathetic, but non-committal brief statement; possibly delegating responsibilities to an already overworked equalities officer or proposing minor changes to already vague policies and procedures on 'valuing diversity' with little or no accountability. Approaches at this level are usually well-intended, but tokenistic and overlook the nuanced obstacles and pitfalls Black people face every day. Unfortunately, this response is common.

- **Publish an authentic anti-racism action plan**, outlining significant reforms that commit to specific, measurable, achievable and realistic targets (suggestions below). Examples include publishing a strong mission or position statement condemning George Floyd's murder and racism in all its forms and committing to the British Association of Social Workers' code of ethics, anti-oppressive, anti-discriminatory and anti-racist practice. This approach interlinks with the Anti-racist Commitment Framework. It sees white allies fully involved in challenging, deconstructing and dismantling racist systems in solidarity with Black people.

It is fantastic that Brighton & Hove Council are recruiting a lead practitioner for anti-racist practice on a permanent contract. My hope is that other social work employers will follow suit. At BASW England, we hope to work with employers to promote these types of innovations.

Equally fabulous news is that De Montfort University have developed a fully-funded PhD Studentship on BLM, which seems like a pioneering opportunity. Also, the progress being made on Frontline's Racial Diversity & Inclusion Action Plan is encouraging. Social work organisations must build on this impetus and swiftly (and proactively) embed anti-racist strategies into how they operate.

BASW England are pleased to be working in partnership with the chief social workers for adults and various cross-sector stakeholders in developing the Workforce Racial Equality Standards for Social Care (WRES). The aspirations for the standards and interest from local authorities is promising. At this juncture, I'm unaware of any national provisions in the pipeline specifically for children's services.

Dr Muna Abdi, a leading anti-racism educator, says: "The work of anti-racism is to fight racism wherever you see it... even in yourself. The struggle cannot be found in the pages of a book. You can't read yourself into activism. Sooner or later, you'll have to make a choice... Do what is safe or do what is right."

I will continue with my own activism. If my contributions remain that of a muzzled, side-lined agitator, on the fringes, throwing rocks at the throne - then I'll just continue to be authentic and stay true to myself.

I do not want to appear ungrateful, but I can live without the acclaim, the 'likes', 'retweets', plaudits etc. I want revolution! So, brothers, sisters and allies – if you know your herstory, if the ancestral spirits live within you, if you know right from wrong - then now is the time to show and prove yourself. What have you done to enforce anti-racism and promote Black liberation lately?

Let's not forget the saying, "when you're accustomed to privilege, equality feels like oppression". The only real enemy of progress is ignorance and 'wilful blindness'.

'One world, one race... the human race!'

[This article was originally published by Professional Social Work magazine on 11/12/2020] https://www.basw.co.uk/resources/psw-magazine/psw-online/%E2%80%98when-you%E2%80%99re-accustomed-privilege-equality-feels-oppression%E2%80%99

Anti-racism in social work: no more questions - just actions please

A senior social work manager joked to me recently that I "was the only authority on anti-racism in social work". Although she was jesting, it did make me wonder what accountability and protections actually exist to support social workers of colour within the profession, given what we know about the omnipresence of racism. It didn't take me very long to conclude – very little.

I write this article from my perspective, not on behalf of all Black and ethnic minority people or social workers – as we are not a homogenous group. I refuse to be the tokenistic 'Black voice' of the British Association of Social Workers (BASW). I've had a diverse social work career and anti-racism is in all our interests. I'm one of many Black voices in the profession. It's just my reality that my role at BASW enables me to be heard more broadly than others. Also, I realise that I've been 'let in' (to some extent) and 'won't scare the horses', to quote the playwright and critic Bonnie Greer, in relation to the historian David Olusoga. I use Black and ethnic minority people here for ease.

Yes, social work is institutionally racist

Sensible people know racism is not just an isolated event or incident. It's also a reflection of institutions, structures (including micro and macro socio-economic and socio-political factors) – which all interact with each other and shape the lived experiences of Black people. When will we accept that the philosophy of white supremacy runs deep in most organisational cultures? It really is not that hard to see.

Since my previous article on promoting anti-racism in social work, there has been some decent position statements from some organisations and prominent social workers. However, there has also been some cringe statements, some nauseatingly feeble blogs and some noteworthy silences. Unfortunately, there remains a scarcity of cast-iron and *explicit* actions and/or commitments to anti-racism.

Clearly, anti-racism in social work is not universally accepted as high importance or as urgently needed. The response from the social work elite has been about as coherent, convincing and speedy as the government's response to COVID-19, the A-Level fiasco and the Windrush scandal combined.

However, the social work profession (like many others) is not broken. What we are experiencing and witnessing has been designed. If we truly want an equitable and inclusive profession that really encourages critical thinking, prioritises social justice and truly values diversity of service users and staff, then we need to reimagine new structures, new systems and new discourses. A paradigm shift! Anything else is just papering over gaping tectonic plates.

Yes, social work is institutionally racist – but so are many institutions, organisations and professions (not just the Police) when you consider Sir William MacPherson's definition from the 1999 report of the Stephen Lawrence Inquiry. There is evidently a "collective failure to provide an appropriate and professional service to social workers of colour based on their colour, culture or ethnic origin". This is visible in "processes, attitudes and behaviour which amount to discrimination through unwitting prejudice, ignorance, thoughtlessness and racist stereotyping" which disadvantage ethnic minority people.

This correlates with the over-representation of Black and ethnic minority social workers in fitness to practise cases;

reports from the Social Workers Union of Black social workers being failed on their assessed and supported year in employment (ASYE) and various other detrimental career outcomes. Basically, the modern-day social work equivalent of lynching.

I observe many key social work leaders asking the same old tired questions, then promising another exploration of the long and gruelling wilderness we meandered through in previous decades. Just like another government enquiry into, well... take your pick! The ongoing Windrush scandal? Stephen Lawrence? Stop and search?! The tactics deployed by our oppressors generally involve seek and destroy; smokescreens and mirrors or deafening silence.

Is there appetite for real change?

The question is not: '*Is* social work racist?' More incisive questions are: 'As racism in society becomes more overt, what is social work actively doing to promote anti-racism?' Or, 'When will social work commit to (something like) a *mandatory* anti-racism commitment framework?' With respect, in my previous article, I literally outlined a blueprint for large-scale anti-racist organisational change. I feel like I've done the class bully's homework and then still taken a bashing on my way home. My ideas are not perfect (by any stretch of the imagination), but your homework is done for you, nonetheless.

We must now ask, whether there is really the appetite for real change? Is there the actual *commitment*, *intention* and *motivation*? Because if not, why not? Financial investment is not necessarily a major hurdle here – it comes down to the priorities and values of the existing leadership. I'd rather have some meaningful action, even if it is not perfect, as long as it is genuine – rather than this neverending paralysis of fear and/or indifference. Let's have more clarity about what your change looks like and the timescales for implementation. If not, it's all just performative window-dressing and pitiful. No more questions – just meaningful actions please.

Disappointingly, neither Social Work England's education and training standards for 2019 or 2021 nor the professional standards for social workers explicitly refer to anti-discriminatory (ADP), anti-oppressive (AOP) or anti-racist practice. The professional standards refer to "challenging the impact of disadvantage and discrimination, promoting social justice and helping to confront and resolve issues of inequality and inclusion".

But is that really explicit enough? How can social workers be properly educated and held to account on promoting basic human rights for marginalised groups with the bar so low? Or is this just not a priority for us anymore? Social justice in this context feels like another catch-all to me – like BAME or EDI (equality, diversity and inclusion). Without explicit inclusion of these principles how can we ensure they are applied in policy, practice and education? Simple answer? We cannot. Why is this no longer important?

There is a long history of ADP, AOP and anti-racist principles being intrinsic to social work values and ethics. The legal backdrop and framework is built on the Human Rights Act 1998, Race Relations Act 1976, Disability Discrimination Act 1995, Sex Discrimination Act 1975 and Equality Act 2010. Therefore, it's almost incomprehensible in my mind that these hard-fought principles are omitted from today's regulatory standards and supplementary guidance.

Regressive social work standards

The previous social work standards, regulated by the Health and Care Professions Council (HCPC), were stronger, expecting practitioners to "be able to practice in a nondiscriminatory manner" and "use practice to challenge and address the impact of discrimination, disadvantage and oppression". Prior to that, the General Social Care Council's (GSCC) codes of practice required employers to "put into place and implement policies and procedures to deal with dangerous, discriminatory or exploitative behaviour and practice" and social workers to use "established processes and procedures to challenge and report dangerous, abusive, discriminatory or exploitative behaviour and practice".

Therefore, the current social work standards are regressive and do nothing to advance the principles set out by their predecessors – despite the desperate and obvious necessity. Many believe these principles are now diluted and de-prioritised beyond the point of complacency. Similar concerns have been raised by the chief social worker for children and families, with regards to the teaching of anti-oppressive practice in social work education.

Social Work England's professional standards do acknowledge the impact of "difference and discrimination" on service users, but what about how these factors impact on minority groups of social workers? There has been a silent shift to sweep the protected characteristics under the carpet of 'equality, diversity and inclusion' (EDI); which we know masks individuality – much in the same way as 'BAME' does to Black and ethnic minority groups. It conveniently rolls off the tongue – but subtly dehumanises and 'others' us.

The importance of incorporating these values and ethics was highlighted by BASW England in our response to Social Work England's (SWE) consultations on rules and standards in April and June 2019 (prior to Social Work England's inception). Unfortunately, our recommendations were not included. Reminders were issued to Social Work England (via Twitter) on 17/06/20 and 23/06/20. As of yet, there has been no response. I refer to these facts to underline the importance of these fundamental principles and how their omission in social work regulation is a travesty of social justice in itself. Without explicit inclusion, how else can social work educators and workers be properly educated and held accountable on ADP, AOP and anti-racism? There are real concerns about the standards being superficial, cold-hearted, corporate benchmarks, as opposed to empirical and evolutionary cornerstones of social work that advance human rights and social justice.

I still find it astounding that social workers are so heavily regulated and that their employers are not. The Local Government Association's (LGA) employer standards, are not mandatory and insufficient accountability exists A few other equality frameworks and 'innovations' exist or are in the pipeline, but again the big questions are: Are they mandatory and enforceable? Do they apply to all social work employers? Do they explicitly embed ADP, AOP and anti-racism in social work policy, practice and education? Not as far as I can see. So, the provisions all seem very piecemeal and one-sided to me and rather oppressive for all – especially Black and ethnic minority social workers.

Do Social Work England and the chief social workers support the idea of the LGA's employment standards becoming mandatory and universal? We know from BASW campaigns, research and our ongoing discussions with members that the working conditions for social workers remain diabolical in many organisations. However, there is little evidence of this being taken into account and appropriate action taken against employers (when necessary) as part of fitness to practise cases.

No more questions – just actions

Community Care has reported that Black and ethnic minority social workers are "over-represented in fitness to practise cases [and] adjudication hearings are disproportionately white compared to the profession". This evidence needs to be categorised and scrutinised in the context of social work employers (public, private and third sectors). Also, these conclusions are not new. The GSCC and HCPC have historically reported on this too. So, what efforts have been made to address these longstanding issues of poor working conditions and inequality? Again, how much of a priority is it? Why are we continuously asking the same old questions? No more questions – just actions please.

As reported in another Community Care article, how much of a priority is given to employing ethnically diverse workforces and senior leaders? I think most Black and ethnic minority professionals (and their allies) would be keen to know what is *actually* being done to reverse these trends.

Since George's Floyd's killing and the resurgence of the Black Lives Matter movement, BASW has been at the forefront of anti-racist social work activism. BASW England has championed anti-racism in social work on a scale unrivalled by any other organisation within the profession. Our activities have involved: the publication of numerous articles; incisive and timely position statements; a campaign to change the racist imagery on the KCMG medal; establishing the Black & Ethnic Minority Professionals Symposium; developing the Black & Ethnic Minority Social Workers Anthology (working title); several podcasts and webinars; a response to the minister for equalities' report on the disparate impact of COVID-19 on Black and ethnic minority communities and presentations on anti-racism in social work (specifically designed for social work organisations) across England (and internationally).

The KCMG campaign is ongoing (at the time of writing). We have received an acknowledgement from Buckingham Palace and our letter has been redirected to the Cabinet office. However, in a bizarre twist, the original tweet (which went viral) has now been deleted from Twitter. We have asked Twitter to explain this, but no response has been forthcoming. We know silence on racism is complicity with the oppressors. I think silence can also be construed as blatant racism in some scenarios. It seems when our oppressors choose not to attack us, the wall of silence is their other favoured tactic. Open dialogue has remained a prominent source of conflict resolution for good reason – it works! It helps to positively undermine any covert or overt power imbalance.

BASW England will continue to educate, equip and empower social workers of colour and allies. As an organisation, we realise that we are not immune to the perils of white supremacy and 'whiteness'. However, BASW has shown a willingness to address and tackle these issues internally and within the profession more broadly. We will consider all anti-racist proposals from partnership organisations and specialist collaborators that will potentially benefit social work. I like the idea of an Office for Minority Health, as proposed by Professor Dinesh Bhugra, to promote proper accountability and ensure people from Black and ethnic minority backgrounds have their holistic health (and social care) needs considered.

You can't read yourself into activism

Anti-racism in social work risks being perceived as radical activism or anarchic ideology. Our social leaders must reverse this flawed belief system. I live in hope that social work policy, practice and education will now begin to properly recognise and reflect that 'race' is a socially constructed idea with no scientific validity – invented and refined principally to oppress Black people.

Race remains an unstable concept because it is superficially based on physical appearance. When race was constructed people knew very little about DNA, genetics and human origins. It is an outdated colonial invention that still permeates modern society. Intellectually and morally, as a profession and as a society, we must see beyond what was pre-determined for us centuries ago.

So, if society is built on plantations of racism, still celebrates racist history and traditions and reminds us daily of the inescapability of white supremacy, it's not enough for social workers (and social work organisations) to be 'colour-blind' or 'non-racist'.

We must be PROACTIVELY anti-racist – otherwise anything else is just tiresome lip-service. If anti-racism in social work does not exist for social workers, can it ever truly exist for service users? Anti-racism is absolutely integral to social work, so when will it be given the credence it deserves? Without standing up for our defining values and ethics, what is to stop us succumbing to the pervasive and pernicious post-modern sleaze?

"The work of anti-racism is to fight racism wherever you see it... even in yourself. The struggle cannot be found in the pages of a book. You can't read yourself into activism. Sooner or later, you'll have to make a choice... Do what is safe or do what is right." (Dr Muna Abdi).

Ultimately, if my destiny is to try and fail, then I can live with that. I'd rather die trying, thanks. Otherwise, how can I look my kids in the face or even look myself in the mirror? My scruples dictate that I must do what I know to be right (personally and professionally). My only wish is that more people did the same. I do not want to appear ungrateful, but I can live without the acclaim, the 'likes', 'retweets', plaudits etc. I want revolution! So, brothers, sisters and allies – if you know your *herstory*, if the ancestral spirits live within you, if you know *right* from *wrong* – then now is the time to show and prove yourself – **RISE UP!** What have you done to enforce anti-racism and promote black liberation lately?

Let's not forget, "when you're accustomed to privilege, equality feels like oppression". The only real enemy of progress is ignorance and 'wilful blindness'. Social justice must prevail.

'One world, one race... the human race!'

[*This article was originally published by Community Care on 16/12/2020: https://www.communitycare.co.uk/2020/12/16/anti-racism-social-work-questions-just-actions-please/*]

Fast-Forward The Rhetoric & Replay Multiculturalism

Oh dear, so poor Amber Rudd had to be Theresa May's 'human shield' to allow the government to save face eh? The whole Windrush citizenship debacle is a reminder for many people of colour (not just black people like myself) that institutional and structural racism remains covertly prevalent in modern Britain.

It was clear Rudd was on the ropes when she initially chose to blame civil servants in her department, rather than shoulder any responsibility herself and was found to be (basically) lying about 'immigrant deportation targets'. May the author of the 'hostile environment' policy and Rudd the executioner. Maybe, Rudd was just in the wrong job at the wrong time and was left to take the flak for May's right-wing policies as Home Secretary. But is the problem with the personnel or the system? And is 'blame culture' holding back real progress?

The government are now quite happy to talk about the Windrush generation being in Britain legally and recognise their significant contributions to the country (fleetingly). In one breath, they now talk about the rights of those from the Caribbean (despite removing a key protection from the statute books in 2014 and ignoring their pleas for help thus far). In the next breath, they doggedly talk of a 'hard Brexit' and restoring this great island to its former glory – but what glory is this? The British Empire? Colonialism? Slavery? No, thanks. It's all sounds to me a bit like 'Trump patriotism' – "let's make England great again". Not if it involves mass exploitation, criminalisation, incarceration and racial inequality again thank you. How about we start with "let's make England more fair and equal" instead?

I'm fortunate that my parents were born in England, but also because I'm able to authenticate my own citizenship with a birth certificate, passport etc. However, I'm aware of people from my community who have been less fortunate and been left unemployed, isolated and traumatised.

All this talk of 'hostile environments' makes me wonder if the political elite care that Britain can already be a hostile environment for anyone who is from an ethnic minority group! Recent public examples of hostility include: the prelude to the EU referendum vote, which was epitomised by the infamous vans telling illegal immigrants to "go home" (provoking racial incidents in the street); the divisive rhetoric used by Leave campaigners (which is now the norm in mainstream politics); the significant rise in race-related hate-crimes and violent incidents; the rise of far-right extremist groups; the disproportionate representation of ethnic minority people in the mental health and criminal justice systems; the lack of support for the Grenfell Tower victims (who are mainly non-white); the torrent/severity of racial abuse Diane Abbott receives on social media etc. I'm pleased the BASW England Committee endorses a zero-tolerance position to all forms of hate crime.

It doesn't surprise me the government have known the impact of the 'hostile environment' policy on the Windrush generation since May 2013 (according to The Guardian). The suppressed voices of the Windrush generation silently became entangled with the plight of 'illegal immigrants' in a political context where racist ideologies are normalised and polarised. The dossier compiled by the Joint Council for the Welfare of Immigrants (JCWI) shed light on this situation and rightly held the Home Office to account. This expose is just the latest of many examples of poor treatment to black communities that have already experienced many well-documented injustices.

Even the terminology of 'hostile environments' (and "stateless citizens") seems inhumane to me. It creates automatic animosity towards a group of people who are all here for different reasons – some genuine – some not so – but do we really have to be hostile? Why can't we be 'compassionate', 'ethical' or 'fair'? I agree with the JCWI's call for an independent review of the workings of the Home Office and the framework of the 'hostile environment' policy.

Of course, in daily human interactions in social work (and life generally) we are subliminally influenced by government policies and ideas on 'hostile environments'; anti-terrorism; drugs; knife crime; gangs etc and how these are portrayed in the media. These divisive policies and the stereotypical coverage can often perpetuate negative outcomes for different ethic/cultural groups. This has a direct impact *personally* and *professionally* for ethnic minority social workers, managers, service-users and communities etc and affects how they are perceived in everyday settings. These influences can manifest themselves differently and lead us all to question who is: 'deserving', British/English 'enough', normal, good/bad etc – which ultimately encourages labelling and unethical decision-making. As social work practitioners from a cross-section of society, we should recognise our human tendency to prejudge certain people/groups and the subjectivity of this. I believe through self-awareness, cultural competence and reflective practice we can better understand the journeys of the people we work with and ascertain the layers of racism that might affect their personal/professional lives.

Racism has fallen down the pecking order in recent years and has perhaps been overtaken by the feminism (#Metoo) and sexuality (transgender) movements. In recent decades, we have created a 'diversity queue', where only one diversity issue can be examined at a time with few lessons learned. Whatever happened to the rhetoric of yesteryear such as: 'multiculturalism', 'anti-oppressive practice', 'positive discrimination' and 'respecting cultural diversity'? It may all sound a bit outdated and touch-feely, but I think we need to realign ourselves with these ideologies to promote humanism, unity and integration (including another EU referendum!). Otherwise, surely our civilisation will go backwards, and future generations will have to re-live the racial problems of past generations. The system is broken - we need to fix it. How many Amber Rudd's, Marie Morris', Nigel Farage's, Nick Griffin's et al do we need to go through, before we realise we have a political system which is institutionally and structurally racist and devalues the considerable contributions made by people from ethnic minorities? Let's step away from these lazy and divisive policies and move towards transparency and unity and recapture the essence of multiculturalism. The first step to making progress is recognising the underlying problem - racism has evolved.

[*This article was originally published by Professional Social Work magazine on May 2018*]

Social work's role in tackling knife crime

The cloud of Brexit continues to overshadow a range of critical domestic issues - now most prominently knife crime. There has been lots of commentary, debate and rhetoric but no swift action. Why? Because sadly meaningful compassion is lacking.

Organised gangs are increasingly using young people to carry out their criminal activities. They exploit the fact their young recruits are more likely to be cautioned or given community orders - instead of imprisoned.

I recently spoke on BBC radio about the 'divorce' of criminal justice from social work. Examples of this include the splintering of the Probation Services and youth offending yeams from children's services; the specialisation of youth justice education; the lack of youth justice content in social work training and the purely punitive impact of 'rehabilitation' programmes. There really needs to be an overhaul of criminal and youth justice.

This short-sighted approach is fundamentally flawed and damaging. Criminal justice - in its broadest sense, with adults and young people - and social work are intrinsically linked We need to rekindle the relationship between criminal justice, social work and community cohesion to make our streets safer.

The media portrays a two-dimensional view of knife crime and wrongly polarises it into 'offenders' and 'victims'. The reality is far more complex and multi-dimensional. Issues impacting on the current situation include lack of policing, the impact of austerity, decimated community resources, gang conflict, chaotic family lives, unemployment, substance misuse and school exclusion. But these are often glossed over.

Both victims and offenders are products of their environment and this needs to be more widely recognised. In some cases, both offenders and victims are known to children services, youth offending services or other local services. Let's give these workers the education, time and resources to tackle the problem effectively.

Many young people are increasingly rejected by the education system and placed in part-time alternative education provisions. But this is no substitute for proper full-time education and isolates them, heightening their vulnerability to various forms of exploitation.

Safe spaces where children and young people once congregated and socialised have disappeared making it easier for them to be exploited by sophisticated criminals. How can these socio-economic factors not require combined criminal justice and social work input?

Parts of the media perpetuate the negative racial stereotypes of young black men and do little to spotlight the real-life factors that contribute to youth violence and knife crime. The 'hostile environment' of Brexit hasn't helped, creating further racial tensions, dividing communities and marginalising disenfranchised black youths further.

We have to question why the lives of black young men appear to have less value. If the majority of knife crime victims were white, would the government response have been so slow to act? It's unhelpful for youth violence to be framed as a 'black problem' as this encourages compassion fatigue and blame.

In reality, knife crime is a societal problem, and we need a multi-layered strategy with sufficient funding to tackle it. More can be done to educate the public about its wider context and to highlight counter-narratives. It's so much deeper than "bored feral black youths killing each other for kicks". This is about exploitation, self-defence and limited life prospects.

We also need more positive black roles models to be given the limelight, such as the 56 Men project – which challenges the pervasive stereotyping of black men wearing hoodies (https://www.bbc.co.uk/news/uk-47298111) or the artist/historian Akala whose wide-ranging work on black culture is highly-acclaimed. Not all black men wield knives – some of us are victims and some of us are intellectuals!

It's important that as social workers we critically analyse the influence and impact of biased media coverage of youth violence. If we don't, our professional values and ethics will be gradually eroded, diminishing our practice. Social work is fundamentally about relationships. It's therefore helpful to identify resources that provide practical ways of working with young people involved or affected by youth violence. They exist, but practitioners must be proactive in accessing them.

Additional funding or targeted 'stop and search' alone will not eradicate knife crime. We need youth workers and reformed gang members to help us reconnect with young people and promote their citizenship.

We have generations of young people who wouldn't know how to behave in a youth club or comply with employment and training expectations. Scared young men will rehearse their fears, sometimes in clumsy and inarticulate ways. We must ensure we are educating and providing them with the basic skills to contribute to society.

Youth violence is now a national emergency. It must be treated with the same sense of seriousness and urgency as terrorism. Whilst social work cannot fix this problem alone, it can be part of the solution.

[*This article was originally published as 'Social work's role in tackling knife crime' by Professional Social Work magazine* (*online*) *in March* 2019].

Why Social Work Activism isn't Dead

My reasons for leaving frontline social work practice to join BASW in 2017 were plentiful. But mainly it was to influence social work policy, improve working conditions for practitioners, raise the profile of the profession and to empower social workers to achieve better outcomes for people who use services.

In a range of social care roles including supporting children and young people, families, adults and offenders, I've worked with numerous veteran practitioners who consistently emphasised how previous generations of social workers were 'activists'. They often bemoaned a lack of professional unity within the profession today.

They spoke of times from the 60s to the 80s when unions had much more influence and strike action would often be instigated swiftly if workers' rights were felt to be infringed. A retired BASW member told me: "We were probably too quick to strike back then, but that's just how it was. Now the pendulum has swung the other way due to weaker unions, 'managerialism', specialisation of services, high profile scandals, austerity, excessive paperwork, greater individual accountability..."

Another said: "My first involvement with BASW was as a member of a special interest group on adult family placements. As a collaborative group we met with civil servants and many of our proposals on standards later became regulations."

Another member added: "At the beginning of my career in the late 60s and early 70s it was accepted that being politically active on behalf of your client group and your community was a part of your role and purpose. It wasn't written into our job descriptions but, changing and improving community provision and stopping policy changes and closures that we would consider harmful to our client groups, it was just part of what we did. We went on strike and we demonstrated... I am sad that social workers today do not show more robustly their displeasure at the conditions under which they are working, the caseloads, the impositions of inspections, the closure of facilities, rationing of services and so on."

Other veteran social workers I spoke to reminisced about social work having a greater sense of community and professional identity back in the day. One told me this was "because most senior managers were social work trained and they encouraged activism". They went on to say: "The rise of managerialism over the last 25 years and the recruitment of managers from other professions has pushed social work activism down the pecking order. Also, the gulf between children and adults services and multi-disciplinary teams have diluted the profession and again suppressed social work activism and unity."

Unfortunately, the challenges of being a social worker in today's world (high caseloads, blame culture and basic survival!) understandably mean that activism, unity and promoting professional identity are not always priorities and can be suppressed in some debilitating workplace cultures. How can a social worker feel empowered to actively champion their profession when they feel overworked, overly-scrutinised, under-resourced and undervalued?

The good news is BASW's history demonstrates that social work activism and professional unity can make a difference in social work practice, policy and education. Recent examples include: influencing changes to legislation and proposed reforms; campaigning for better working conditions; working with partners to improve support for frontline workers wellbeing and playing a role in the development of Social Work England.

Many veteran practitioners (members and non-members) I have spoken with are proud of the impact BASW has had on policy, practice and education over the years and they are looking to the future generations of social workers to take the baton, show their passion through activism and move the profession forward at all levels.

Social workers from a variety of backgrounds and stages of their career have enabled BASW to be the voice for social workers and social work. We believe social work activism and professional unity begins at the student stage and is lifelong. Importantly, social work activism is needed now more than ever.

A good way to get started is to join one of BASW England's Policy, Practice & Education groups (PPEG). PPEGs are national groups that focus on: children and families, criminal justice, mental health, adults social work and students and newly qualified social workers.

The groups mainly consist of social workers, service users and academics with relevant knowledge and experience who come together to talk, share ideas, debate specific social work policy, practice and education issues and provide BASW with members' perspectives to influence and inform future work (see here for more information).

Alternatively, the BASW England 80/20 campaign is a much-needed attempt to reverse the current predicament of social workers spending up to 80 per cent of their time working on computers and/or completing paperwork and only 20 per cent of their time is spent in direct contact, building relationships with people who use services (see here for more information).

Another opportunity to be active is to become a BASW England Ambassador. The role involves championing the profession, advocating on behalf of BASW members, assisting at BASW events (including conferences and university visits), representing the profession in the media and supporting BASW campaigns.

The future of social work and its direction of travel depends enormously on ALL students, practitioners, managers, academics, retired members and service users. We need to make a stand NOW to shape our professional identity and ultimately protect the future of social work. For more information about BASW England's PPEGs, the 80/20 campaign or becoming a BASW England Ambassador please contact us at england@basw.co.uk.

[*This article was originally published in Professional Social Work magazine in January 2020*].

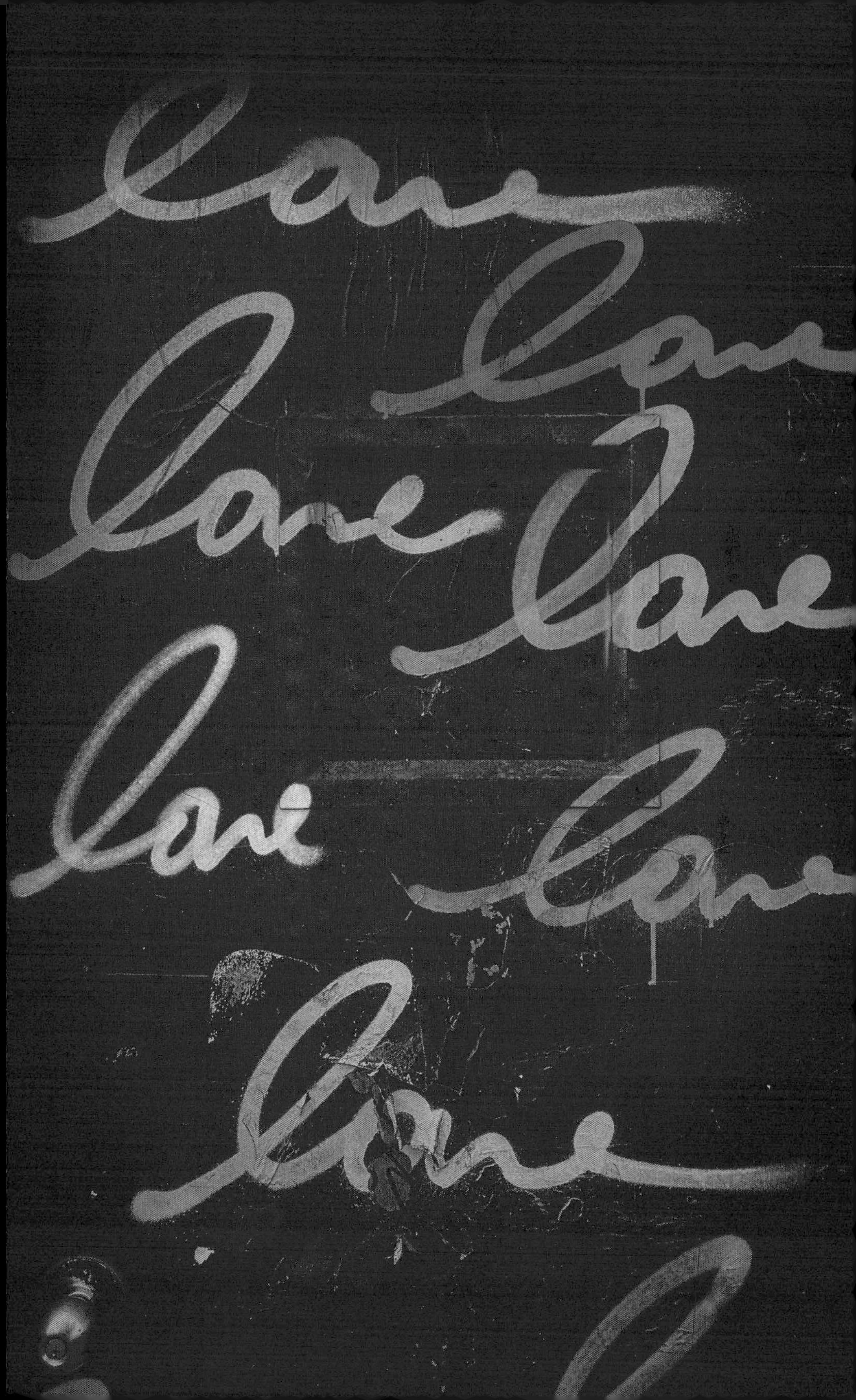

love
love
love
love
love
love
love

AUTHORS

About the Authors

- *Ahmina Akhtar*

Ahmina grew up in a racially segregated town in the north of England and felt the impact of racism from an early age. She therefore volunteered at a local youth club as a teenager and served as a regional youth councillor to promote equality, diversity, and inclusion. It was these early experiences, and her desire for greater social justice, which ultimately led to her becoming a social worker.

Ahmina qualified as a social worker in 2008. She completed an MA in Integrated Practice in 2017 and is also a certified trainer and coach. Ahmina is Regional Engagement Lead for Yorkshire and Humber at Social Work England, the specialist regulator for social workers in England. She is responsible for ensuring the consistent implementation of Social Work England's professional, education and training standards, and driving forward improvement across the region. She was previously the Senior Practitioner at the Independent Inquiry into Child Sexual Abuse, where she provided psychologically informed advice and consultation to staff in all strands of the Inquiry. Prior to this she worked in several educational, community, voluntary and health settings. She also serves on several boards where she is instrumental in driving strategic and cultural change.

Dedicated to my brother, who raised me and never let me lose hope.

Twitter: @AhminaAkhtar
Linkedin: ahmina-akhtar-4139b580

- Anneta Pinto-Young

I am a trained Social Worker and Workforce Development Consultant for newly qualified Social Workers and routes into social work. I qualified as a Social Worker Jamaica in 2007 and I was recruited to work in the UK in 2011.

I have provided research assistance around issues related to gender, water, hygiene and climate change and supported a research project around the participation of women on national boards in 2007. I have also coordinated a Youth Training & Empowerment Programme and was trained as a youth advocate for the Caribbean around sexual and reproductive health rights and represented the Caribbean at regional and international forums.

I am a trained Practice Educator, gained a merit in Systemic Family Therapy; trained in action facilitation by ILM; Practice Supervision Development Training; a Trained Trainer with over 10 years of experience delivering training and gained a Level 7 post graduate training in coaching in mentoring from Kingston University. I am currently the Dept. Chair for the Staff Race Advisory Group in Croydon.

LinkedIn: Anneta Pinto-Young

- Asmaat Khan

Dedicated to my father.

- Biant Singh

I am a social worker and Community Musician and I'm at my happiest when combining the two. I was born and bred in the inner city of Nottingham, where my family were directly exposed to complex issues of race, poverty and disability. From an early age, I grew up steeped in the traditions of Indian classical music.

I chose to train as a social worker, because I wanted an opportunity to support people to develop their independence and make their own choices and decisions. These principles were (and remain to this day) central to my belief system.

I am committed to community and passionate about service-user involvement.

- Brenda Herbert

Brenda works as counsellor with children who have experienced domestic abuse. She has worked both in the charity and social care setting. She is also currently studying part time for her PhD in Sociology at Goldsmiths, University of London.

Dedicated to: Antony, Madeleine & Ben

Twitter: @cloudchild9

- Bright Mawoko

I was born in Southern Africa, and my country of birth is Zimbabwe, previously known as Southern Rhodesia, Rhodesia and Zimbabwe Rhodesia during the colonial period. I'm a Social Worker and a parent. I'm a father of three children, a boy and twin girls. I draw from experiences of people I know as well as my life story when writing about the experiences of African immigrants. My first series of poems, The African Immigrant, and In Transit describes how a young African Immigrant moved to the Western world to seek freedom and a better life only to be faced with uncertainty and struggle to fit in the complex but unjust system. I have started writing a novel about most of these experiences. The novel is entitled Red Mist beyond the Blue horizon.

- *Chris Parker*

My name is Chris Parker and I am from the United States. I received my Master in Social Work from the University of Connecticut in 2011 and subsequently moved to the United Kingdom in 2014. I currently reside in London and work in Youth Offending with a focus on the intersectionality of racial inequality and the criminal justice system. I have always enjoyed educating as well as empowering others to go beyond their limits.

Being the first in my family to attend University, I recognize my privilege and responsibility to mentor and give back whenever possible. This has always kept me grounded and motivated in whatever endeavour I am involved in.

To my family and friends who have, and continue to, push and pull me away from harm and towards hope.

- Colleen Simon

Colleen has been a practicing social worker since 2003, she currently managers a dual diagnosis service, and has worked across substance use, mental health and criminal justice, within local authority/NHS and the voluntary sector. Colleen also practices as an AMHP, BIA and a Practice Educator, she lectures for Bournemouth University and delivers training for Edge training and consultancy. Colleen is passionate about promoting anti-racism, social equality and co-production.

To those who saw my strength & believed in me.

LinkedIn: Colleen Simon

- Cosmas Maruta

I am a dedicated children's social worker interested in looked after children, the care experienced and the research around their transitions and outcomes post care. I question the part I have adopted in the corporate parenting paradigm and my contribution to the outcomes of young people post involvement. I have an interest in the workings of trauma and resilience and their constant interactions, which I feel potentially impacts on practitioner congruence, positive regard and having an empathic frame of reference while simultaneously managing practitioner resilience. These conflictual workings of trauma and resilience draw me to my own practice and the world of fascinating young people for which I would like to make my life's work to research, support, guide and inform developing practice.

Dedicated to: Dr Stephen Cowden, Dr Gurnam Singh, Andy Walton Practice Educator & Nyasha Mutukwa Practice Educator

Twitter: @cosmasMaruta
Linkedin.com: cosmas-maruta-00216b1a5

- Diana Katoto

Diana Katoto is a social work student at the University of Birmingham. She has a passion for social justice and promoting human rights.

Twitter: dianakatoto
Linkedin: Diana Katoto

- Eddie Dube

I am originally from Zimbabwe and have been living in the United Kingdom since 2004. I have always had the passion to advocate for the disadvantaged and marginalized in the community and society, due to my upbringing values. My parents were schoolteachers. My mother used to pay school fees for children from poor backgrounds who could not afford fees.

My undergraduate dissertation was on the "Politics of Disability" which highlighted the marginalization and the ongoing disempowering of people with physical impairments and their long journey for emancipation. My post graduate dissertation was on the "Age Assessment of Young Asylum seekers" and how the methods and system can disadvantage, stereotype and prejudice young asylum seekers. I strongly believe that social work values should be strongly grounded on justice, equality, promotion of human rights and creating a society where there are equal opportunities and discrimination of any kind unacceptable.

Dedicated to my late Social Work lecturer, Colin Rones. All my practice educators and placement supervisors who were instrumental in my self-belief and confidence in speaking out against injustices and reminding me that Social Work is more than Care Management and assessments, advocacy is of paramount importance. My great South and West Somerset Adult Community Team for the great support and mentoring, the team spirit and the desire to make positive changes in people we support.

LinkedIn: Edwin Dube
Twitter: @EddieDu14777665

- Elicia May

Elicia was born (6 weeks prematurely) in Manchester. She was raised in a tower block in East London with her younger brother and wonderful mother.

She went to Uni at 18 and gained a degree in something random and went travelling. When she returned, she stumbled upon the weird and wonderful world of mental health social work and hasn't (had time to) look back since.

Social work has changed her life – she has never felt more frustrated, overwhelmed, challenged, fulfilled, hopeful or alive.

Likes: laughter, connection, napping
Dislikes: Mornings, olives, oppression

Dedicated to my wonderful community mental health team – COAST

Instragam: eliciamay_

- Ellah Kandi

Ellah is an astute social worker who is also an author, a chef, motivational speaker, founder of the El-Kind Charity for children with HIV/AIDS, and an ardent member of a gospel choir. She is a Pentecostal Chaplain at the De Montfort University who provides pastoral support to students. Ellah is a woman on a mission, full of resilience and no stranger to the struggles that arise in our journey through life. She has weathered the pangs of those storms that have blown her way and though there were moments of despair, Ellah overcame them and with much fortitude she has been able to educate others. These struggles have also helped to mould the dream of being a social worker. Her experiences have been the catalyst for her to succeed and empower those around her, both near and farther afield. She is determined to make her mark in social work as she adheres to the principles of the profession and is keen to employ these principles in her life overall.

Ellah cherishes her work within charitable causes. Whether as an individual or as a part of the choir, she attends to these causes with aplomb. She is an affable, loving and compassionate woman who, being full of an inward passion to make people's lives better has been active in creating a charity of her own. Ellah is a firm believer in putting theory into practice and therefore emphasises the need to be a person by whom others can be empowered.

Dedicated to Bishop Mark and Mrs Sharon Anderson & sons (Samaritan Family), Emmanu'-EL Apostolic Church, Elisha Kandi (Father), Cynthia Kandi (Sister), Pastor Samuel Gapara & Julie Roadnight (Manager & mentor).

Twitter: @ellah_kandi
Linkedin: Ellah Kandi

- Farrah Khan

I am a Pathaan woman having come to England as a child with my family when I was aged 4 in the early 70's. At the time my parents worked hard to give us the best in life as well as support family back home. We were taught to value opportunities and make the most of what we had. We were raised with a belief that no matter how little you have; you should share with those who have less and charity was at the heart of our family values. After working in the voluntary sector for many years, I decided social work is where my heart was at the age of 30 and I therefore pursued a career in social work having gained a Diploma in Social Work in 2002. I have worked various roles since being qualified and am now the Principal Social Worker in Leeds. I have faced the challenges, racism and discrimination faced by so many in my personal and professional life and want to use my position to influence change and raise the profile of women from diverse backgrounds in leadership.

Dedication: I want to acknowledge my father who showed embedded social work values in me without even knowing what social work was. We miss him dearly since he passed away in 2017 but he has left his legacy in the values he taught us.

Twitter: @farrahkhan152

- Gurnam Singh

Professor Gurnam Singh is currently Associate Professor of Educational Attainment at Coventry University and Associate Professor of Sociology (Hon) at the University of Warwick. He is also Visiting Professor of Social Work at the University of Chester and Visiting Fellow in Race and Education at the University of Arts, London. Prior to entering academia in 1993, Dr Singh worked as a professional social worker and community activist. Dr Singh has published widely on issues relating to social justice, social work and higher education. In 2013 he published a book '*Acts of knowing: Critical pedagogy in, against and beyond the university. Bloomsbury*' His latest book, published earlier this year (2020) by Palgrave Macmillian, is entitled *Anti-Racist Social Work Practice: International Perspectives.*

Twitter: @gurnamskhela

- *Irine Mano*

Irine is a qualified social worker, now working as a practice learning lecturer at Anglia Ruskin University since December 2017. With a Master of Science in Practice Education, Irine is passionate about working to support social work students navigate their placements successfully and provide training for practice educators. Her areas of interest are working with difference and diversity issues in social work, black women in leadership positions and social work practice education. Irine is exploring the experiences of Black social work students with additional support needs in social work education and practice learning for her professional doctorate research. In her previous role as Lecturer and Placement Lead at the University of Northampton, Irine also held the Padare Co-ordinator role. Padare was a support group for Black African students who experienced racism and or discrimination on placement. Irine led, co-ordinated and worked closely with the social work professional team and social work student team to develop strategies of support and monitor these. Irine's research interests emanate from her experiences as a Black African female practitioner and academic working in the United Kingdom.

To my system of support – my fiancée, my mum and all my siblings and in-laws. My friends who have all become family, your support is always appreciated.

Twitter: Irine Mano @tinyiry
LinkedIn: Irine Mano

- Dr. Jas Sangha

Jas has been a qualified Social Worker since 1996. He was born in England and classes himself as a second-generation British Indian. He began his career as a Social Worker in adult services, particularly working in disabilities, and he progressed to managing a multi-disciplinary team.

Jas joined Anglia Ruskin University as a Senior Lecturer and Course Leader in Social Work in 2012. Before that he was Programme Lead and Senior Lecturer at Oxford Brookes University. Jas has significant experience as a Lecturer and Practice Educator for Social Work Students at undergraduate and postgraduate level.

Jas recently completed his PhD where he researched the progression experiences of BAME social work students. Jas wanted to know what it felt like in modern society to be a BAME social work student and the strengths and challenges in trying to succeed in becoming a social worker. His research interests are in higher education, social work studies, race and racism.

Dedicated to my family and pets

Twitter: @JasSangha101

- Dr. Jean Dillon

I am of BAME, mixed heritage. I originally trained as a nurse, specialising in theatre nursing before training as a social worker. I have been a Social Work Lecturer for over 20 years, combining this with sessional work as Mental Health Act Manager for an NHS Foundation Trust and an independent hospital. I have an abiding commitment to raising awareness of the lived experiences and realities of people from BAME backgrounds. My areas of specialism are mental health, sociology, ethnicity, diversity and inclusion. My doctoral thesis explored educational inequalities among BAME students. This study and a previous small-scale study exploring BAME children under the age of 10's access to Children's Services, identified key barriers to access to education and welfare services, including stigma and discrimination and a mistrust of welfare professionals and services.

I sadly lost my 32-year-old son to suicide. From this devastating personal experience, and from my professional insights over many years, I argue that there is a pressing need to raise awareness of vulnerability factors among black men, for example, the impact of racism; for additional preventative measures and strategies based upon culturally sensitive/ appropriate risk assessment tools and interventions, and for more informal, non-stigmatising support services.

Dedicated in loving memory to my son, Brett Dillon

- Dr. Jennifer Simpson

Dr Jennifer Simpson is a Senior Lecturer in Social Work at Nottingham Trent University. Her responsibilities include teaching on a number of social work programmes and developing a programme of continuous professional development for qualified social work practitioners.

Jennifer's research interests include fostering and adoption, specifically how children and young people stay in touch with members of their birth family using mobile communication devices and the Internet. Jennifer is also interested in how technology is being used to deliver social work services. Additionally, Jennifer's interests extend to the experiences of students in Higher Education, specifically how those students from minority ethnic backgrounds can be supported and enabled.

Twitter: @Jenni54819843
LinkedIn: Jennifer Simpson - Senior Lecturer - Nottingham Trent University | LinkedIn

- Jeremiah Johnson

I am a young black man from South East London who enjoys reading, watching anime, playing football and discussing sociological issues. I got into social work because I wanted to give back to my community by supporting disadvantaged and marginalised groups.

Dedicated to my mum and dad for breathing life into me.

- *John Mapara*

John Mapara was born in Zimbabwe in 1972. He attended Hartzell High School near Mutare and Oriel Boys School in Harare. John holds a BSc (Hons) Social Work and a Master of Science in Social Work from the University of Zimbabwe and Midlands State University, respectively. John enjoys writing and some of his favourite authors are Raymond Carver, Anton Chekhov and Guy de Maupassant. He is married to Norah, with whom he has four children, Olga, Mufarowashe, Munesuishe and Shamiso.

- Lorraine Singlehurst

I grew up in Northampton with an English father and Trinidadian mother at a time when I was neither black nor white enough to fit anywhere. A worry that continues for my children.

After leaving school with no formal qualifications worth bragging about, I slowly worked my way through education despite having dyslexia. I have worked in health and social care for over 25 years qualifying as a social worker in 2012. I have gained experience in drug and alcohol services, mental health secure units, adoption, counselling, looked after children, leaving care and community mental health. I am BIA trained and currently completing AMHP stage 2 training. Social work and social justice run through my core. It is who I am meant to be. I am a happy mother of 3 who truly believes education, in all its forms, to be a liberating experience.

Much love to the Singlehurst/ Morgan tribe. We did good.

Dedicated to my family, they are everything and who ultimately keep me strong. Not forgetting Molly Gilbert, who reached out to me during the deafening silence of others and to Louise Gardener who listened to my personal uprising. Thank you.

- Lynrose Kirby

I will be celebrating 30 years as a social worker this year. I had the opportunity early on in my career to learn from value-driven, compassionate, and experienced social workers, not least Sarah Patrick who worked alongside me in developing the piece of work I describe in my contribution to this anthology.

Soon after qualifying I found my niche in the world of adoption and fostering and have trained, assessed and supported more foster carers and adopters than I can count! It is an area of social work where the ability to transform children's lives and provide a grounding for a successful adulthood is very apparent and I am committed to the highest standards of practice for myself, carers and other practitioners working with children who are looked after.

As the parent of children of mixed heritage, the issue of how we raise children of diverse backgrounds in modern Britain, balancing inclusion with the importance of developing and maintaining an identity to help them to cope with racism is both personal and professional.

I have also worked as a Team Manager, Panel Chair, Trainer, Consultant, Complaints Investigator, Social Work Placement Co-ordinator and Practice Educator.

- Mariah Wilde

Mariah Wilde is a social worker in an adults Mental Health Social Care Team in London. She qualified with her Master's in Social Work in 2020 with Distinction as part of the Think Ahead graduate scheme with a specialism in Systemic Practice with couples and families. Her academic background in Sociology and Contemporary Ethics teamed with her personal interest in justice and equality led her to a career in social work. Mariah is committed to continual learning, service user empowerment and ensuring that person-centred values remain the cornerstone of her practice.

Inspired by the unity and solidarity of communities following the death of George Floyd in 2020 and subsequent awareness of Black Lives Matter, Mariah began writing on her website www.riahwrites.com. On it, she shares reflections on social issues, wellness and creativity with a view to promoting community and self-care. She writes commissioned articles on these topics, and her writing has been featured in BASW's online publication as well as various online mental health platforms.

Dedicated to my parents, both wonderful social workers that introduced me to the values of compassion, equality and advocacy. Also dedicated to my social work mentor Edna Porter, who has been a supportive soundboard and shining example of black leadership in social work. Thanks to BASW, Wayne Reid and Siobhan Maclean for their collaboration to create this anthology sharing diverse voices in social work.

LinkedIn: https://www.linkedin.com/in/mariahwilde1/
Website: www.riahwrites.com
Twitter: @riah_writes

- Maureen Mguni

My name is Maureen Mguni, I am a Senior Social Worker in Mental Health, a Technical Instructor in Social Work Education and a Female Genital Mutilation/C (FGM/C) Expert Consultant. In addition to this, I am completing my Doctoral Research , exploring FGM/C in the South East (S.E.) (U.K.): An Analysis of Affectees' Lived Experiences and their Engagement with Social Work Practice. My interests include writing poetry and songs, singing, learning new languages, travelling and parenting. My research interests are mainly in the areas of Migration and Immigration, Race, Equality and Diversity, Gender Based Violence, HIV and Mental Health.

Dedicated to my daughter Muzi Siwawa, who is my inspiration and my reason for soaring to greater heights. My mum Charity Mukunga, for being a role model. My grandmother Monica Jabavu Sinyoka for teaching me how to be a fearless black woman. My PhD supervisor Nicola Khan for teaching me the value of hard work. The amazing humans I could not exist without Alvin, Shlomo, Nhlanhla and Nqobizitha.

Twitter: @maumguni
Twitter: @LangaSolutions
LinkedIn.com: Maureen-mguni-b-a-m-a-msc-991439167

- Narinder Sidhu

I am proud to be a Social Worker. I am currently employed by the NHS as a Mental Health Practitioner within the Child and Adolescent Mental Health Services (CAMHS). I am also a Guest Lecturer; I teach on the social work undergraduate and post-graduate programmes. I enjoy teaching on modules related to social work practice, social work law and policy, domestic abuse, female genital mutilation, honour-based violence and forced marriage. I have a keen interest and passion for equality, diversity and inclusion. Prior to these current roles, I was a Forensic Social Worker employed by the NHS in a low secure community setting working with inpatients in the criminal justice system. I enjoy nature, animals and music. I love travelling and having fun with my family and friends. I love new adventures and creating happy memories. I am passionate about making a positive impact to people's lives and society.

Big shout out to the NHS, BASW and their supporters.

LinkedIn: linkedin.com/in/nksidhu

- *Nushra Mansuri*

Nushra is a mixed-race woman who hails from the London Borough of Brent and is the daughter of what others termed 'immigrants' who settled in London. Nushra's dad was a Muslim originally from India (before partition) and her mum is from Germany (West Germany before reunification). Nushra's experiences growing up were both challenging and joyful as she navigated a pathway which represented dualities; dualities of rejection and acceptance, barriers and opportunities, despair and hope. These early experiences in her formative years undoubtedly led her to become a social worker and commit herself to the ideas and principles of social justice, equality and human rights for all. Nushra has always related to the experience of the 'other' in society and hopes that one day 'other' will be replaced by 'us' (all of us - there is just one 'us'). Nushra is currently an Assistant Professor in Social Work at Coventry University. Her background is children and families social work in a variety of settings as well as a long stint at BASW as a Professional Officer.

Dedicated to my parents.

Twitter: @NushraMansuri
Linked In: Nushra Mansuri

- *Omar Mohamed*

I am 20 years old, a sibling carer, and in my second year of the BA Social Work degree at the University of Birmingham. I have had many social workers involved in my life since birth to around the age of 16, and this lived experience was always negative. This continuously fuels my passion and need to be the difference in social work with children and families and emphasises the importance of social work being a profession recognised as needing to change. One area that was always a negative experience for me as a child, and still is being a social work student, is being Asian. I am dedicated to ensuring that this is different for children and families going forward, and that social work is a truly anti-racist profession committed to human rights, social justice, and equality. It is important for this to be the case for social work, and for the world to follow. My sister deserves to grow up in a world without hate, discrimination and racism.

Dedicated to my sister.

Twitter: @OmarMohamedSW

- *Patricia Clarke*

An MA/DipSW from the University of Nottingham.
Worked within the independent sector, a former special advisor to the CQC. I am currently a safeguarding lead within SLAM, an AMHP and have contributed to training staff within health and social care.

- Dr. Prospera Tedam

Dr Prospera Tedam is a Black African woman of Ghanaian heritage who has taught social work at the Open University, University of Northampton and Anglia Ruskin University. Prospera has written extensively around anti-oppressive and anti-racist social work practice and developed the MANDELA model used by practice educators and students in relationship building. Her recent publications include:

Tedam, P. (2021) Anti-oppressive Social Work Practice. London. Learning Matters

Tedam, P. (2021) 'We just don't matter': Articulating the experiences of Black African Social Work Students during the COVID-19 Pandemic in England in (ed) Turner, D ' Social Work and COVID-19 :Lessons for Education and Practice'. St Albans. Critical Publishing

Prospera is currently teaching Social Work at the United Arab Emirates University where she is extending her knowledge about social work within Islamic contexts.

- Rachel Pearce

I am a 36-year-old mother of one son. Also, a partner, a friend, an older sister, a step-sister, first born daughter, niece of many and aunt of 1. Qualified Social Worker for 4 years with a multitude of experience working with families in different guises.

I am a Brummy at heart with a country soul having been born in Birmingham on a leap year and brought up in Wiltshire from the age of 13.

I'm quite simple and enjoy binge watching box sets and eating out (when I can!) and singing in the car.

Dedicated to my colleagues, friends and family who have made life exciting and manageable with listening ears, bottles of prosecco or just because they did a visit for me!

- *Rebecca O.M. Olayinka*

I am a qualified social worker of 9 years, working within adult social care. My specialisms include older adults, learning disabilities, Adult Safeguarding and I am also a Best Interests Assessor.

I am from London; however, I have worked in the South West of England throughout my Social Work career. I have been writing poems all my life, since the age of 13.
In addition to my social work training, I am also an Associate Member of the CIPD.

I am an ambitious writer and I have written articles for The Everyday Magazine, an online Magazine; The Everyday (theeverydaymagazine.co.uk)

I have also had the opportunity to have accessed speaking events; on Ujima radio (local Bristol radio) and interviewed on YouTube by a feminist focused interviewer Kafayat Oklanlawon on the topic of Black Foster Children in Care. Interview link- https://youtu.be/EpLa3mPOz1U
I am also completing my own personal powerful memoir of being a care experienced Black Foster Child to inspire other Black Foster Children to live a life that's powerful and one which they love.

Acknowledgement Ethera Morgan.

Facebook: www.facebook.com/RebeccaOlayinka
Twitter: @RebeOlayinka
LinkedIn: Rebecca Olayinka

- *Robin Sen*

Robin is from a dual heritage English-Indian background and grew up in the north of England. He is currently a lecturer in social work at the University of Dundee having previously taught and researched at the University of Sheffield. He qualified and practiced as a social worker in Glasgow. His research interests include children and young people in the care system, family support and social work education.

Twitter: @robin_23_99

- S. Abraham

Dedicated to my mum, who taught me the value of perseverance. My heart, forever broken for losing you, eternally strong for having you.

- Shabnam Ahmed

I am social worker, practice educator and team manager. I remain dedicated to contributing to agenda's, which promote social justice, equality, and human rights and I feel strongly about best and inclusive practice. I express this through my practice, writing, training, You Tube channel- School of Shabs and initiatives that I associate myself with. This includes being a member of the Black and ethnic professional symposium with BASW. Leading on work related to race and equality within my own organisation, developing an on-line training on "Raising awareness of Modern Slavery" for my organisation.

I describe myself as a relational activist, believing in the power of relationships and the potential that relationships have to affect all aspects of one's life. I am passionate about connection, reflection and growth and this is what has led me to start my You Tube channel but also my Professional Doctorate in social work.

I dedicate this book to my late father Mr Farooq Ahmed, who was a writer and would stand tall and proud at my contribution to this anthology today. I also want to say a big thank you to all the adults and families who I have had the great privilege to walk alongside. They have unknowingly given me the greatest life lessons and I am humbled by their stories and to be touched by their lives.

Twitter: @schoolofshabs

- Sheree Von-Claire

I'm a 53-year-old black Christian woman, with two bi-racial adult children and a 3-year-old granddaughter. Exposure to racism's many guises comes both personally, as a British second-generation Jamaican, and vicariously through my children; for whom 50% of their DNA often appears discounted by tendencies to pigeonhole based on visible differences.

I taught years of GCSE Maths in an unqualified capacity at a challenging senior school, where many children were socially inept with emotional/behavioural difficulties. This inspired my entrance into Anglia Ruskin University at 40, as a newly divorced single parent to a teen son and pre-teen daughter. I gained a BA (Hons) in 2011 and have been a Supervising Social Worker since 2012. Through university, I worked as a Contact Supervisor, acquiring child and families' knowledge.

In 2015, I completed a post-graduation qualification in Therapeutic Fostering, which I utilize to create therapeutic and trauma informed placement settings. I'm particularly drawn towards supporting Carers looking after children of colour; especially when they've been placed cross-culturally. I wrote my dissertation on "Cultural Competency in Social Work: The Presence of its Absence". This area continues to require growth and promotion for our children to age out of care with positivity...

- Sherifa Adenmosun

I am a British Nigerian who has worked extensively within social care in the Children & Families arena since 2003. I am presently employed within a Local Government Quality Assurance Service as an Independent Reviewing Officer (IRO). I strive to ensure positive outcomes in all areas for children who are unable to live with their natural families many of whom have experienced trauma. As a Social Work practitioner, nothing gives me more joy than seeing the lives of children transformed for the better despite obstacles and an adverse start in life. I am an advocate for social justice and respect for persons within Children & Families; I find myself often asking "would this be good enough for my child?"

During the past 17 years, I have worked in a variety of Social Work settings with children and their families from all walks of life across the UK. My experience spans across YOT, Adoption, Early Help and Looked After Children.
In my spare time, you'll find me either baking, reading or spending time with my family and friends.

Shout out to all the children I have the pleasure of being their IRO.....

Dedicated to my husband and daughter, my inspiration and cheerleaders.

- Sumita Verma

I am Sumita Verma and am currently pursuing a Masters in social work. Over the last several years, I have been actively involved in social work activities. This is something that gives me enormous satisfaction and a sense of purpose. I have worked at organizations in the social sector as well as for corporations. However, working in social services is something that I really cherish, and I see myself engaged in it in the years to come.

The 'Black Lives Matter" movement is very close to my heart as I cannot see anyone being subjected to social injustice. I strongly feel the pain and discrimination that people belonging to ethnic minority have to go through, particularly those from the black community. At the same time, I am a firm believer that with empathy, compassion and concerted effort we can all build a future that is free from all forms of discrimination.

- Syra Shakir

Syra Shakir is a Senior Teaching Fellow and has worked as a senior academic since 2008. She is a qualified social worker with children and families and her background is professional, front-line practice with communities for over 18 years. She has also worked as an Independent Reviewing Officer for children in care, in youth work and in the probation service. Syra's passion is in supporting people to be the best they can be and challenging social injustices. Syra lives in Bradford, West Yorkshire.

Dedicated to My parents, sisters, Ray Lloyd and Jan Fook.

LinkedIn: Syra Shakir

- Vivian Okeze-Tirado

Vivian is a Senior Supervising Social Worker and a Practice Educator for West Sussex County Council. She sat as a Social Work member of Panel for West Sussex Adoption Panel between 2017 and 2019. Vivian facilitates Social Work Training to Social Workers and Foster carers around the Fostering Secure Base Model, Diversity & Black Lives Matter etc.

Vivian's previous discipline was in English Linguistics followed by a Masters' degree in Business Administration - Management. Having sufficiently explored her initial career, Vivian decided to move sideways to Social Work to pursue a more humanitarian career around improving outcomes for vulnerable children and families. Vivian obtained her second Masters' degree in Social Work from Brighton University in 2014.

Vivian is keen on Social Work research and practice development and has developed useful materials for Social Workers and Foster Carers to help enhance the experiences of children in care from all backgrounds. One of the resources include a one-page paper titled "What makes a good Foster Carer?" used as part of the Skills to Foster Training.

Vivian is the Author of the Diversity Acrostic Poem which is one of the resources produced to aid Culturally Sensitive Practice in Social Care. As a Social Worker of African origin, Vivian understands the importance of cultural competence in Social Work.

Linkedin: Vivian Okeze-Tirado

- Wayne Reid

I'm a qualified Social Worker and have over 20 years experiences in frontline practice in different roles.

I dedicate my contributions to my wife Melissa and our daughters Lexy-Bee and Lola-Pearl. They keep me grounded! Lexy-Bee's proofreading skills were helpful in this project and she was nicely rewarded.

Mad love to my parents for being reliable and stable and just letting me be my own man. Bear hugs to all my Reid family and longstanding friends for shaping my character and having my back.

I'm grateful to everyone who has helped me throughout my career so far (directly and indirectly), particularly: Andrew Thompson (the Obi-Wan Kenobi of Social Work), Karen Shearn, Ronny Tucker, Robert Cotterell, Nick Taylor, Jayne Ludlam, Jonathan Crossley-Holland, Rob Brennan, Surinder Kaur, Rosalyn Taylor and Clare Gibson.

I salute my boss, Maris Stratulis, for her sterling advice/support during the turbulent period in which this book was developed.

Thanks to everyone at BASW for championing social work and social workers.

Special thanks to Siobhan Maclean (and the project team) for a smooth collaboration and for giving me my Editorial debut on such a valuable and timeless publication.

Twitter: @wayne_reid79
@BASW_UK
#CrushingStereotypesDaily
LinkedIn: Wayne Reid

- Winnie Lwanda

I gained a Master of Arts in Social Work with Honours from the Glasgow School of Social Work in 2011. Post qualification, I began my professional career within the voluntary sector, before moving to a local authority in 2014. I have primarily worked within children and families, undertaking Child Protection and permanence work as part of a long-term social work team. More recently, I moved to a kinship team. My areas of interest include trauma, attachment and resilience.

Being a black woman is a key part of my identity and at times, I have struggled with this, especially growing up and living in areas where there are few people of colour. Racism has been an unavoidable element of my life, but something I have tried to deny in a bid to suppress the emotional impact. I have now found my voice and the confidence to speak out about my experiences. I am proud of my African heritage and proud to be a social worker.

Dedication and thank you to Alison.

- Zoe Thomas

Zoe is in the final stages of a social work PhD. She has been a registered social worker since 2007 and until 2016 has worked in local authority child protection teams.

More recently Zoe also provides independent social work practice, training and consultancy.

Dedicated to my little warrior.

Twitter: @ZoeThomas2016

REVIEWS
YOU
GOT
THIS

As we were compiling the anthology, we reached out to colleagues to begin a process of reviewing the book with peers. The following reviews were received before going to press and we thought it may be useful to include them here. Where comments are made on specific pieces it should be noted that we had only shared particular pieces rather than the whole anthology at that point.

Angie Bartoli
Principal Lecturer at Nottingham Trent University and Vice Chair for BASW England

Black male suicide, a ticking 'time bomb' is a personal and moving short piece told from the perspective of a mother who loses her son to suicide. With stark statistics which outline the prevalence of suicide amongst black men and some of the contributory factors, the piece concludes with a helpful range of creative recommendations which are noteworthy.

Wayne's story is a testament to how with the help of a supportive family, key individuals, dogged determination, and authentic curiosity, we can zig-zag our way successfully towards a career. I was particularly struck at how Wayne was able to reflect upon each experience, regardless of how challenging, confrontational, or uncomfortable it might have been at the time and take something positive away from each one. This is a candid and personal insight into a colleague's journey towards a career where he is making a mark in his own right with his own brand of charisma.

Are you sure you're in the right place? is a powerful read. Reviewing this piece as a white social work academic I am in equal measures, both ashamed and outraged. Far from being 'silenced' this story needs to be read, re-read and shared widely so that future stories can change. We can no longer just nod and listen empathetically, it's time for all white professionals and academic to act – now.

The Comment is a beautifully lyrical piece which demonstrates how one comment can leave a deep and indelible mark and is a stark reminder of the power of language and words.

The poems briming with emotions remind us of the devasting and long-lasting impact of racism.

Cliff Faulder
C.E.O of AboutFace Training.

Black male suicide, a ticking 'time bomb' by Dr Jean Dillon was very moving and unfortunately resonated deeply. Not only did I get a sense of how every day and common place the act of suicide has become in our society but also the pain of the writer.

Microaggressions by Ahmina Akhtar is a wonderfully accurate poem. It made me feel tired and annoyed just reading it. The opening salvo! I thoroughly enjoyed the poets wordplay.

The comment by Cosmas Maruta is a commentary on how black intellect has been discouraged and crushed not to mention punished as in times of slavery. The writer's ability to overcome the painful comments from the critical overseer that appears in the guise of a university professor is a triumphant moment for all wordsmiths and lovers of words. Inspiring.

Ambition Navigation by Wayne Reid encapsulates the Black British experience accurately and allows the reader to get in touch with the pressures and hurdle jumping that will be very all too familiar for many professionals of colour. Heart-warmingly Wayne also highlights the role that racial allies have played in his journey and leaves the reader with a sense of hope for the future. A fantastic feel good piece.

Are you sure you're in the right place? By Zoe Thomas "It's not just about a few bad apples". "The whole tree is rotten". This powerful piece is delivered with poise and simmering intent to shake the reader. From first sentence to last I found myself fluctuating between indignance and fury.

Christian Kerr
Social worker/Chair of BASW North East branch

In 'Black male suicide, a ticking 'time bomb': personal reflections and considerations for suicide awareness and prevention Dr Jean Dillon speaks from her experience of losing her son, Brett, highlighting how racial inequality, discrimination and race, culture and gender based stigma intersect to create social conditions in which black men are at particular risk from suicide. She concludes with five recommendations aimed at reducing that risk.

Ahmina Akhtar's 'Microaggressions' is a depiction in verse of the racism woven through the everyday discourse, from seemingly innocuous comments about regional accents to more overtly discriminatory statements such as "the problem with your folk". 'Microagressions' poetically highlights that, whether overt or covert, everyday racism has both immediate and cumulative impact, and serves to maintain the inherently racist status quo.

'The Comment' by Cosmas Maruta is a masterful, poetical exegesis on the power of language as both a destructive and a healing force. No review could do this piece justice, so self-aware, reflective and exquisitely rendered is it. I commend it for its message and the manner of its expression, which are artfully interwoven.

Wayne Reid's description of his post-school journey from aimless but enjoyable pop-cultural immersion and admin jobs to his burgeoning ambitions in social care and social work resonated greatly with me. Wayne did not have the benefit of white privilege as I did and so his piece speaks to challenges white people do not face. He ends positively and emphatically with some lesson from which we could all learn.

'Are You Sure You Are In The Right Place?' by Zoe Thomas is an excoriating depiction of the experience of racism as emanating from professionals and institutions, and in particular focuses on academia, in which "being white is considered as normal". Against this Zoe rails, in justifiably angry, undeniable terms, from her experience as "working-class black woman with multiple ethnic identities". Classism is one thing, but classism times racism times sexism is quite another and 'Are You Sure You Are In The Right Place?' is an urgent, necessary read.

This well-curated, varied collection is vital, powerful, urgent, funny, sad, in-your-face, ironic and, I have to say, enjoyably readable, if often necessarily challenging to people of privilege such as this reviewer. As it should be.

Dez Holmes
Director of Research in Practice

Each submission, though unique in its focus and narrative, offers a powerful common depiction of how racism, injustice and inequality manifests within social work. By combining evidence from research, data, personal stories, this anthology presents a compelling narrative and forces us to confront the inadequacy of our response to racism.

It is, for me, the expansive / wide-ranging lens of the anthology that amplifies its messages so effectively. From academia to practice, from the interpersonal to the structural, from poetry to policy analysis... racism is shown to be as endemic as it is destructive.

The heartache of losing a son, the anger of being unsupported by those with professional power, the sheer exhaustion and isolation of being subjected to repeated microaggressions – all of these emotions and more come through with painful clarity in these submissions. The use of personal story serves to 'make real' the abstract notion of structural oppression. Each submission acting as amplification to the last – reinforcing the common experiences of colleagues of colour, demanding that we hear these voices however painful it might be.

The submissions also offer hope – descriptions of valued mentors, allyship and 'lessons learned' are no less important than the tales of discrimination.

Duane Phillips
Student Social Worker Hub

Outlanders is an essential piece of reading for anyone wishing to understand the vast experiences, achievements and trauma faced by social workers of colour. The emotional journey of the materials read can only be described as a roller coaster ending with moments of relatability, pain and sheer pride for people that look like me. Painful stories that shed light on the realities affecting black men leave you thinking about the current state of institutional discrimination. Then the aftermath of hard-hitting facts, highlights the toll racism takes on not just black men, but the mothers that have to bury them. The Comment in particular then describes one of the most beautiful journeys encapsulated in plain, powered by the sheer will to succeed. Reflection on these pieces of art demonstrates how quite simply how one can have all the potential and a simple comment can destroy one's identity. The reflection of the impact of microaggressions on the writers is just powerful, significant and triggering. In a professional field heavily relied on critical analysis, poetry is a beautiful marriage, which encapsulates how common it is to be stripped of one's character in subtle, yet unforgiving ways. The agony of being a black woman in England is projected with a solid punch of the harsh reality whilst being part of social work academia. The writing formed reflections that justify the current decolonising of social work movement, with the insecurity and struggle that comes from feeling so rejected from who should be your equals. One particular piece of writing that is not only inspiring but should be sung loudly to young people to show that the alternative routes to learning can still lead to success and achievement. OUTLANDERS: Hidden Narratives from Social Workers of Colour is a must read for not only the social work community, but all to see that, in many respects, racism, prejudice and discrimination is alive and well in England.

Hannah Wilson
Co-Founder Diverse Educators

Each piece of writing in this collection explores the themes of identity, safe spaces, power, privilege, allyship and safe spaces whilst peeling back the layers of societal, systemic and structural inequities. The individual voices, come together to deliver a collective message.

This anthology is a must read for anyone who works in or with social care, but moreover it will shine a light on other professions within the public sector and the experience of those who are in service of our society to reflect on diversity both within and between different cultures.

Dr Jermaine M Ravalier
Reader in Work & Wellbeing (Bath Spa University)

As people with Black heritage in the UK, we are often asked to express examples of our pain, our personal experience – almost re-living it for the experience of others. While this is something that I refuse to do, if and when I am asked in future, I am simply going to refer the questioner to this anthology.

Each piece is written from the experience of an individual. Individuals who have differing backgrounds, differing educations, differing upbringings. But each emphasizes the difficulties (and blessings) associated with being Black in the social work community, in the UK community more widely.

Reading through each abstract has taught me something while reaffirming my own experiences. The pain of familial suicide and some of the reasons why it may happen; that I'm not the only academic of Caribbean/British heritage to experience microaggressions and outright prejudice while working in Higher Education; the importance of resilience and strength of character; the impact that seemingly innocuous words can have on the entire outlook of others; and the "diversity within cultures" which demonstrates the ridiculousness of 'BAME'.

These extracts clearly show that being the 'B' in 'BAME' can have so many difficulties, but also illustrates the importance of support from others. Support from friends and family outside of work, of Allies and adoptive families at work.

These extracts are not only about sharing the stories of the writers. The extracts expose the need for Allies in every situation faced.

While I am yet to read the rest of the extracts in this anthology, this book should be essential reading in any race and allyship training and discussion in this country.

John McGowan
General Secretary, Social Workers Union

In just one publication, this Anthology provides significantly in-depth knowledge and understanding linked to anti-racism and wider themes relevant to social work practice. No matter what stage you are at in your career and understanding, the key learning points will refresh and introduce learning opportunities in a mixed style that is easy to understand, and one that is extremely well written from the varied contributors and diverse formats. Racism can be an uncomfortable and difficult thing to talk about, but just because something does not directly impact on you does not mean you should turn away from it. In fact, that should be even more of a reason to speak up.

It is excellent to have available a publication that brings together key elements of the personalised impact of racism and importantly within this there is learning for us all to reflect on in one collection. Importantly, the subject is presented in a way that will be helpful to professional social workers across the whole continuum of professional life. Furthermore, other professions involved in working with people and developing professional practice will no doubt find its contents relevant and especially useful and insightful. I have no hesitation in recommending this publication for practice teachers, students, social workers, trade unionists and managers.

I will continue to use my position and privilege to amplify under-heard voices wherever I can and able to do so.

Mithran Samuel
Editor, Community Care

This powerful collection holds a mirror up to social work and lays bare the gap between its anti-oppressive, anti-discriminatory and anti-racist values and the realities experienced by social workers of colour and people from Black and ethnic minority communities who social workers serve. Anyone involved with the profession will benefit from reading it.

Neil Thompson
Independent writer, educator and adviser

I have been supporting and promoting anti-racism for decades as part of broader commitment to tackling discrimination and oppression and promoting social justice. However, as a white man, what I cannot offer is a black perspective. I therefore very much welcome this anthology that can play such an important role in making sure that black voices are heard and black perspectives represented.

It is my view that, whether from an ethnic minority or majority, we all have a part to play in promoting a fairer, safer and more humane society. However, established racialised power relations mean that it is generally harder for black voices to be heard and black needs to be given the attention they deserve.

I hope that this anthology initiative will not only be widely read, but will also serve as a stimulus to other initiatives that can move us forward in rectifying the imbalance. Black lives matter and so do black voices.

Peter Hay
Chair of the Social Worker of the Year Awards

This collection of personal narratives of social workers' lived experiences of the barriers of racism is an overdue prompt that social work has not done enough to be anti-racist, nor heard enough from the wisdom of its own. The narrative of this collection paints racism originating in actions, comments, inactions or microaggressions. Looking at the full picture, these layers cumulatively block out the talents of social workers from black, ethic and other minority backgrounds.

An author sets out how white colleagues must stop being shocked that racism 'still' expresses itself as it does. Instead, this collection invokes the profound shock of reflection that we have failed to change social work itself. In 21st century British social work, it's an uncomfortable truth that white social workers hold the power to change. Being anti-racist means occupying that discomfort to extend the radical transformative power of social work to all its practitioners. Some of these stories show social workers that occupy this space and the need to for more to follow their example.

Living with the discomfort of white privilege is nothing compared to tales of racism that led to bereavement or loss of identity. They tell of racism eroding confidence in lives entwined with the pain of living with pernicious hostilities. These are tales told with a directness that vaults over sympathy to demand action. They prompt personal reflections about times when I failed to recognise needs, made assumptions and when I failed to be the ally that was being sought. This book holds the challenge of these recollections alongside refreshing the commitment to change. It is our responsibility to take up the ideas that radiate from reading this timely anthology and for social work to listen as it commits to show what anti-racism looks like.

Sam Walby
Now Then Magazine

An eclectic and eye-opening view on social work and the many issues experienced – and dealt with – by social workers from global majority backgrounds.

Shahid Naqvi
Editor of Professional Social Work magazine

Anyone who is black in a majority white country will be familiar with the feeling of having to work that little bit harder to prove themselves. To show they are good enough.

Sometimes it's so subtle you wonder where it comes from – are you just being paranoid, over-sensitive, 'chippy'? Or perhaps you really aren't good enough, maybe you actually don't belong...

The accounts in this book bear testimony to this sense of disconnect as told by Black and Ethnic Minority social workers brave enough to talk about their lived experiences.

From the social work academic made to feel she didn't belong in her university department, to a practitioner's poetic description of the microaggressions that make him doubt himself - they are real and often raw.

Instances of casual racism have grown in society over the past two decades and sadly social work, despite its values and principles, appears not to have been immune to it.

The murder of George Floyd lifted a scab off an already festering wound and for many people of colour putting up and shutting up was no longer an option.

This book is part of that breaking of the wall of silence in social work and a journey that has seen anti-racist practice and thinking re-emerge within the profession.

It's also reminder that there is such a thing as white privilege and those who benefit from it have a responsibility to listen to and understand those who don't.

Vanessa Sibanda
Social Worker, Podcast Co-Host - @brunchandbantupod

I was deeply affected by Outlanders; the essays are unflinching, poignant and painfully relatable. Each essay is sprinkled with vulnerability, delving into the complexities of race, gender, class, the professional and the personal. The journey into Social Work education and practice is fulfilling yet for Black and Ethnic Minority individuals it is isolating due to the experiences of racism and microaggressions, that leave our colleagues shocked and in despair at its very existence in the 21st Century. Ahmina Akhtar and Zoe Thomas beautifully pen these indescribable feelings and experiences into paper.

In spite of the pain and memories that surfaced, it felt comforting to know that I am not alone in this. Many of us have once questioned ourselves if indeed our academic work was 'pretentious'; and if the racism and microaggressions we experience and feel in our deepest core are imaginary. Yet our psyche recognises and remembers the harmful effects of racism. It is violence upon the body, it takes its toll on you, and it is exhausting. It is a blow to the tissues of the mind and that of the body; disproportionately affecting black men.

The collection is essential, and a timely reminder of the need of anti-racist approaches in practice and education. We simply need to do more than just training on cultural competence in our pursuit of anti-racist and anti-oppressive social work. We simply need more than a one off-event about racism and diversity in October. Has George Floyd's murder and the recent uprisings left you feeling powerless, frantically wondering what to do about racism and microaggressions in practice? Ways to support your employees? In education? In your position as Service Lead? This collection would be a great start; it is a call for action!

LIVE FULLY
CREATE HAPPINESS
SPEAK KINDLY
HUG DAILY
SMILE OFTEN
HOPE MORE
LAUGH FREELY
SEEK TRUTH
INSPIRE CHANGE
LOVE DEEPLY

If you do not go after what you want, you'll never have it.

If you do not ask, the answer will always be no.

If you do not step forward, you will always be in the same place.

- Universal Quote

This anthology is a joint enterprise between BASW England & Kirwin Maclean Associates